Islamic Banking in Southeast Asia

The **Institute of Southeast Asian Studies** was established as an autonomous organization in May 1968. It is a regional research centre for scholars and other specialists concerned with modern Southeast Asia, particularly the multi-faceted problems of stability and security, economic development, and political and social change.

The Institute is governed by a twenty-two-member Board of Trustees comprising nominees from the Singapore Government, the National University of Singapore, the various Chambers of Commerce, and professional and civic organizations. A ten-man Executive Committee oversees day-to-day operations; it is chaired by the Director, the Institute's chief academic and administrative officer.

The **Social Issues in Southeast Asia (SISEA)** programme was established at the Institute in 1986. It addresses itself to the study of the nature and dynamics of ethnicity, religions, urbanism, and population change in Southeast Asia. These issues are examined with particular attention to the implications for, and relevance to, an understanding of problems of development and of societal conflict and co-operation. SISEA is guided by a Regional Advisory Board comprising senior scholars from the various Southeast Asian countries. At the Institute, SISEA comes under the overall charge of the Director while its day-to-day running is the responsibility of the Co-ordinator.

Islam and the Economic Development of Southeast Asia

Islamic Banking in Southeast Asia

Edited by
Mohamed Ariff
University of Malaya

Social Issues in Southeast Asia
INSTITUTE OF SOUTHEAST ASIAN STUDIES

Published by
Institute of Southeast Asian Studies
Heng Mui Keng Terrace
Pasir Panjang
Singapore 0511

The responsibility for facts and opinions expressed in this publication rests exclusively with the authors and their interpretations do not necessarily reflect the views or the policy of the Institute or its supporters.

Cataloguing in Publication Data

Islamic banking: Islam and the economic development of Southeast Asia/editor, Mohamed Ariff.

Papers presented at the Workshop on Islam and the Economic Development of Southeast Asia: Islamic Banking, held in Singapore from 24 to 26 June 1986.

1. Banks and banking — Islamic countries.
2. Economics — Religious aspects — Islam.
3. Asia, Southeastern — Economic conditions.

I. Mohamed Ariff, 1940 -
II. Workshop on Islam and the Economic Development of Southeast Asia: Islamic Banking (1986: Singapore)
III. Institute of Southeast Asian Studies.

HG3368 I821 1988

ISBN 9971-988-98-4 (soft cover)
ISBN 981-3035-03-X (hard cover)

Printed in Singapore by General Printing Services Pte. Ltd.

CONTENTS

LIST OF TABLES

FOREWORD

Ethnic and religious issues have, in the last few decades, confounded many social analysts by refusing to disappear. The "liberal expectancy" among social analysts used to be that modernization would blur ethnic distinctions, achievement would replace ascription and particularistic criteria, and wide-ranging communication and education systems would homogenize populations. The "radical expectancy" was that differences in religions, languages, and culture would be swallowed up, perhaps even across national boundaries by emergent class consciousness. Instead, religion and ethnicity continue to cut across and envelop almost every facet of Southeast Asian life. Indeed, if anything, such divisions in many societies have become sharper, ethnic and religious interest groups more insistent, and opposition more politicized and strident. Much of this activity seems to be increasingly played on the urban stage – and this at a time when the pace of urbanization in Southeast Asia is increasing rapidly, to the extent that by the turn of the century, cities such as Manila, Bangkok, and Jakarta could have populations of more than ten million each. In these settings, Southeast Asian ethnic, religious, and linguistic complexities are likely to be even more challenging than in the past.

It was therefore only natural that among other aspects of the Southeast Asian social and cultural scene, the Institute should identify the study of contemporary religion as one of its key areas of interest. Southeast Asia is after all not only home to all the major religions of the world -- Islam, Buddhism, Christianity, and Hinduism – but the geographical spread of these is such that the bonds that bind their adherents at one and the same time defy and accentuate political and territorial divides and boundaries. The case of Islam is especially striking in this respect, as its followers are present in significant numbers in almost every Southeast Asian country, and in several of these across constraining political borders. Acting on this, a group of Southeast Asian scholars met in 1980 and proposed a project to increase our understanding of Islam in its regional context.

Towards this end, two clusters were identified. The first of these was centred on the nature of Islam in the region, Islam and societal change, and Islam and education. The second concentration was to be on Islam and problems of economic development.

Each of these clusters in turn was to comprise three separate but related activities: (i) preparation of a basic reader containing significant contributions to the understanding of Islam in Southeast Asia; (ii) a research project on Islam and society in Southeast Asia; and (iii) another on Islam and higher education in Southeast Asia.

The basic reader was to comprise a systematic selection of seminal contributions articulating the nature of Islam in the region, including its origins and development. This collection, *Readings on Islam in Southeast Asia*, was published in late 1985.

The second and third of these activities saw the completion of a series of research papers. These were presented and discussed at two separate workshops. The papers were thereafter revised and edited for publication in two volumes: *Islam and Society in Southeast Asia* and *Muslim Society, Higher Education and Development in Southeast Asia*.

Building on the foregoing studies, work commenced on the second cluster of research, that is, "Islam and the Economic Development of Southeast Asia". The research here too is in three phases, spread over three years. They are: Islamic banking; Islam and resource mobilization through the voluntary sector; and Islam and the role of the private sector in economic development.

The papers completed during the first phase of research on Islamic banking in Southeast Asia were discussed at a workshop on 24-26 June 1986 in Singapore. They were subsequently revised and form the basis of the volume that follows.

The project on Islam stimulated considerable interest in not only other major religions in the region, but also issues relating to ethnicity and development, another of the Institute's long-standing and primary areas of research. Moreover, the experience gained in managing the project on Islam proved valuable in terms of co-ordinating comparative research involving numerous scholars from diverse backgrounds and disciplines – with the result that the Institute was encouraged not only to plan parallel projects on Buddhism and Christianity in Southeast Asia, but also to think in terms of developing a longer-term *programme* of research that would encompass all its projects on contemporary religions, together with those that might grow out of the Institute's interests in ethnicity, urbanism, and related areas.

To facilitate this, the Institute convened a meeting in 1985 of senior Southeast Asian social scientists to discuss issues of social change in Southeast Asia, in order to identify firm areas of research and a sharper focusing of such research and associated activities. The group were unanimous in their conclusion that it was "essential and desirable" to encourage research on social issues in Southeast Asia, in particular religion, ethnicity, urbanism, and population dynamics.

To allow for proper planning and incremental research, the group felt that work in these areas could be most effectively developed within the structure and support of a *programme*, rather than as *ad hoc* projects. Accordingly, it was proposed there be established a programme of research to be known as the "Social Issues in Southeast Asia (SISEA)" programme. This programme would address itself to the nature, persistence, and impact of religions, ethnicity, urbanism, and population change in terms of their intrinsic dynamism and potential for societal conflict, co-existence or co-operation in the context of development, stability, and nation-building.

SISEA would also allow for the consolidation of the various publications emanating from the Institute's work in ethnicity, religion, urbanism, and population change within a single and integrated series, "Social Issues in Southeast Asia", with *Islamic Banking in Southeast Asia* being its fourth number.

The preparation of *Islamic Banking in Southeast Asia* and the project on Islam as a whole have benefited greatly from the assistance of several institutions and individuals within and outside the region, and from the financial support provided by the Konrad Adenauer Foundation of the Federal Republic of Germany. The Institute would like to record its appreciation of all such help and support and to express the wish that the various numbers of "Social Issues in Southeast Asia" will circulate widely amongst all concerned with the social dynamics of the region.

In wishing the volumes in the "Social Issues in Southeast Asia" series all the best it is clearly understood that responsibility for facts and opinions expressed in them rests exclusively with the individual authors, editors, and compilers, and their interpretations do not necessarily reflect the views or policies of the Institute or its supporters.

K.S. Sandhu
Director
Institute of Southeast Asian Studies

ACKNOWLEDGEMENTS

The papers in this volume were first presented at a workshop which was held in Singapore on 24-26 June 1986. G. Ghaussy, M. Fahim Khan, Amina Tyabji, Chaiwat Satha-Anand, Abdillah Hashim, Halim Ismail, and Syed Othman Alhabshi participated as discussants for the various papers which were presented and I would like to thank them for their stimulating contributions to the discussions at the workshop.

The generous financial support of the Konrad Adenauer Foundation is also gratefully acknowledged. Due acknowledgements should also be given to Sharon Siddique, Co-ordinator of the Social Issues in Southeast Asia programme at ISEAS, for her help in organizing the workshop and for facilitating work on the papers which make up this volume. Thanks also go to Jane Ong, also of SISEA, and Susan Lopez-Nerney of the Institute's Publications Unit, for their professional assistance in the preparation of this volume. Last but not least, I would like to gratefully acknowledge the valuable help and assistance provided by Dr Ananda Rajah in putting this volume together.

Mohamed Ariff
University of Malaya

CONTRIBUTORS

M. Dawam Rahardjo is with LP3ES (Lembaga Penelitian, Pendidikan dan Penerangan Ekonomi dan Sosial [Institute for Social and Economic Research, Education, and Information]), Jakarta, Indonesia.

M.A. Mannan is with the Islamic Research and Training Institute (IRTI), Islamic Development Bank (IDB), Jeddah, Saudi Arabia.

Michael O. Mastura is President of the Philippine Amanah Bank, Manila, Philippines.

Mohamed Ariff is Professor of Analytical Eçonomics at the Faculty of Economics and Administration, University of Malaya, Kuala Lumpur, Malaysia.

Muhammad Nejatullah Sidiqqi is with the Islamic Economics Centre, Jeddah, Saudi Arabia.

Omar Farouk is a Lecturer at the Department of History, University of Malaya, Kuala Lumpur, Malaysia.

Surin Pitsuwan, formerly with the Faculty of Political Science, Thammasat University, Bangkok, is a Member of Parliament for Constituency 1, Nakhon Si Thammarat, Thailand.

Zakariya Man is lecturing in the Kulliyyah of Economics, International Islamic University, Petaling Jaya, Selangor, Malaysia.

1 INTRODUCTION

Mohamed Ariff

Islam is by no means new to Southeast Asia, as it dates back to the ninth century AD when Muslim traders began to participate in large numbers in the commerce of the region. Muslim settlements were already in existence in the region by the eleventh century and by the fifteenth century, Islam had taken firm root in the region, with the acceptance of the faith by people in power. Islam brought with it a new value system that encouraged learning and commerce. The coming of Islam thus marked the beginning of a new era of development for the region.

Contrary to Western thinking, Islam did not constitute a force which inhibited development, for the Islamic value system, by encouraging learning, research, and hard work, tended to promote economic progress. It was only under the impact of colonization that Muslim communities in the region downplayed all these positive values and opted to become inward-looking in the face of what was perceived to be a serious external threat. As a result, Islam in Southeast Asia became a religion of rituals and ceased to be the dynamic force that used to motivate Muslims in the region to reach greater heights. With the end of the era of colonization and the emergence of independent nation-states, however, Islam once again emerged as a force to be reckoned with.

Islamic revivalism has led to the rediscovery of Islamic values by the Muslims of the region who now tend to view Islam as a complete way of life rather than as a bundle of rituals in the narrow religious sense. The ideological component of Islam is now given, in several parts of Southeast Asia, as much importance as its theological content.

In Islam, prayer and worship cannot be separated from other worldly acts of man. Man, as a servant of his Creator, is urged always to be in a state of worship which requires man to observe, among other things, Islamic ethics and codes of conduct enshrined in the Holy Book of revelation (the Qur'an) and the Tradition of the Holy Prophet (the *Hadith*). It cannot be denied that the Western value system has by and large replaced the Islamic order in the worldly pursuits of modern Muslims. Nevertheless, the current wave of Islamic resurgence has led to a relentless search for Islamic solutions to inconsistencies posed by the adoption of Western values. This, does not mean that Islam is opposed to everything that is Western. Islam has never discouraged Muslims from adopting "alien" cultures, instruments, institutions, and the like, provided they are not incompatible with the fundamentals of the Islamic faith. To be sure, there is absolutely no room for any compromise on the basics. Thus, no one has any right to sanction what is categorically prohibited or to prohibit something that is clearly permitted by God Almighty.

In the economic domain, for example, Islam prohibits Muslims from taking or giving interest, regardless of the purpose for which loans are made and regardless of the rates at which interest is charged. Attempts to make a distinction between usury and interest, and between loans for consumption and that for production, and the arguments that *riba* (payments over and above that which is loaned) which is prohibited in Islam refers to usury practised by petty moneylenders and not to interest charged by modern banks and that no *riba* is involved when interest is imposed on productive loans, have long been refuted, discredited, and discarded. Except for a few dissenting opinions here and there, the general consensus clearly is that there is no difference between *riba* and interest, for it is unambiguous from the Qur'an and the *Hadith* that *riba* refers to any additional payment on whatever that is loaned. On the basis of accepted understandings of the *Hadith*, Muslim jurists unanimously hold that a tangible good must be returned in like kind (*mithl*): gold for gold, silver for silver, wheat for wheat, barley for barley, dates for dates, salt for salt, like for like, equal for equal, and hand-to-hand.

That interest is prohibited in Islam does not mean, however that capital is costless. All that Islam prohibits is the predetermined pricing of capital. Islam enjoins the owners of capital to have a share in the output which, of course, cannot be predetermined. To put it differently, owners of capital in the Islamic order have no right to demand a fixed rate of return, and one cannot legitimately ask for any additional payment without sharing the risks involved. Thus, if it is a simple loan without risk-sharing, any additional payment in excess of the loan is unambiguously *riba* and therefore *haram* (forbidden). However, the owners of capital (*rabbul-mal*) may "invest" by allowing others (*mudarib*) with ideas and expertise to use their funds for productive purposes and thereby share the profits with *mudarib*, with losses, if any, being borne by the owners of capital. This arrangement, called *mudaraba*, is quite compatible with Islam's stance on the role of capital as a factor of production. Alternatively, the owners of capital may form a partnership (*musharaka*) so that equity participation provides the basis for sharing of profits and losses.

It is clear, from the brief discussion above, that modern bank financing invariably involves *riba*. Islamic banking is seen as an alternative to conventional banking in that it can perform all commercial banking functions completely devoid of *riba*. Thus, for instance, the Islamic bank, acting as a *mudarib*, can accept deposits on a *mudaraba* basis and in turn invest the resources by entering into another *mudaraba* arrangement with its clients. Alternatively, the bank may resort to *musharaka* arrangements with its clients. In either case, there is no predetermined rate of return for the capital invested. In addition, Islamic banks can provide trade financing on a mark-up (*murabaha*) basis so that goods are purchased by the bank on behalf of its client with a profit margin. According to jurists, this arrangement is permissible if the bank is fully responsible for the merchandise until it is delivered to the client. The Islamic bank may also resort to leasing (*ijara*) whereby a good is purchased by the bank to be leased out at a price. It is also permissible for an Islamic bank to acquire properties on behalf of its client to be sold at a higher price on an instalment basis (*bai' muajjal*). Likewise, the bank can also finance production by buying the product in advance at a predetermined price (*bai' salam*).

Thus, the involvement of an Islamic bank in the economy is far more direct and active than that of a conventional bank. The former actually participates in production and commerce by taking an equity stake, whereas the latter's interest in commerce and production is limited to the interest it can get in addition to recovering the principal. It is quite obvious that Islamic banking is a risky business, but it is this risk-sharing that justifies profit-sharing and hence the return to capital in an Islamic system.

Islamic banking is a new phenomenon which is the product of the untiring search for interest-free alternatives to conventional banking. Islamic banking models were first introduced in the Middle East on a somewhat experimental basis. Successful operations by early comers encouraged the establishment of Islamic banks in several parts of the world. Iran and Pakistan have opted to Islamize the banking system as a whole, while in other countries Islamic banks have been set up in the midst of conventional banks. In Southeast Asia, Islamic banks exist only in Malaysia and the Philippines. Although the latter has had much longer experience in this regard, the bank concerned continues to operate a conventional banking "window" beside the Islamic one. It is in this sense that the Islamic bank in Malaysia outshines its counterpart in the Philippines. In other Southeast Asian countries, Islamic banks have yet to make their debut.

An attempt is made in this volume to evaluate the role and performance of Islamic banking in the region and to examine the problems and prospects of establishing Islamic banks in those Southeast Asian countries where Muslims constitute a minority group or where there are political and other constraints. Efforts are also made in this volume to study some of the informal financial arrangements that help Muslims do away with interest.

The present volume consists of nine chapters. The rest of this volume is structured as follows. Chapter 2, by Omar Farouk, provides an overview of the Muslims of Southeast Asia and serves as a backdrop for subsequent chapters. In Chapter 3, M.N. Siddiqi discusses the theoretical and practical dimensions of Islamic banking. The Malaysian experience in Islamic banking is highlighted by Zakariya Man in Chapter 4. Michael Mastura examines the Philippine experience in Chapter 5. The possibilities of introducing Islamic banking in Indonesia are scrutinized in Chapter 6 by M. Dawam Rahardjo. Chapter 7, by Surin Pitsuwan, examines such possibilities in the Thai context. In Chapter 8, the role of the Jeddah-based Islamic Development Bank – which is distinctly different from Islamic commercial banking – in the economic development of the Southeast Asian region is analysed by M.A. Mannan. Finally, in Chapter 9 an attempt is made by the editor of this volume to pull together the findings of the preceding chapters in order to draw some broad inferences.

The substantive chapters which form the core of this volume were first presented and discussed at a workshop, which was held in Singapore in July 1986, before they were revised for publication, with the notable exception of Chapter 7 by Surin Pitsuwan which is based on the transcript of his oral presentation made at the workshop.

2 THE MUSLIMS OF SOUTHEAST ASIA: AN OVERVIEW

Omar Farouk

Introduction

Islam is a major social and political force to be reckoned with in Southeast Asia. It is the state religion in Negara Brunei Darussalam;[1] the official religion of the Federation of Malaysia;[2] the religion professed by about 90 per cent of the population in the Republic of Indonesia, the world's fifth most populous nation; and the faith of large minorities in the Socialist Republic of the Union of Burma, the Republic of the Philippines, the Kingdom of Thailand, Kampuchea, and the Republic of Singapore. In terms of the number of adherents, there are close to 200 million people all over Southeast Asia who are Muslims. By virtue of this, Southeast Asia can claim the distinction of being the only geographical area in the world, outside the traditional Islamic belt stretching from northwest Africa to South Asia, with the largest concentration of Muslims.

Although Southeast Asian Muslims can be said to be living at the periphery of the heartland of Islam in the Middle East in terms of their geographical distribution, their psychological and spiritual attachment to Islam is deep and dynamic and distinguishes their devout very little from the most devout of Muslims elsewhere. Intellectually, the Southeast Asian Muslims have always been open and receptive to the ongoing process of Islamization that has characterized their societies for centuries. Conversely, and by the same token, they have become as vulnerable as Muslim communities elsewhere to the vicissitudes that have plagued Muslims from time to time. None the less, the search for the highest levels of piety and perfection in Islam continues to preoccupy the minds of a great number of Southeast Asian Muslims, limited only by their own individual capacities.

Southeast Asia, is however, no monolith. The picture of ethnic complexity in the region is amazing, even among the Muslims. It is true that Islam has contributed tremendously to homogenizing and unifying large segments of Southeast Asian populations. But even this is incomplete. Despite the general observable pattern of outward religious uniformity and common identity, the Muslims continue to be distinguishable from each other in a whole range of ways, linguistically, ethnically, and perhaps most important of all, by nationality. On the one hand, Muslims of Southeast Asia enjoy a religious fraternity in Islam which transcends national frontiers and allegiances. On the other hand, they are expected to submit themselves to the demands of citizenship and nationhood which often are in conflict with pre-existing forms of primordial and religious loyalties.

This chapter is meant to give a broad overview of the position of the Muslims in Southeast Asia. It begins with a historical description of the evolution of Muslim communities in the various traditional polities of the region. The contemporary scenario is then portrayed in which the problems confronting Muslims as citizens of their respective nation-states and as practitioners of Islam are also analysed.

The Historical Background

The Traditional Era

Interaction between Arabs and Indian traders and the people of the archipelagic region preceded Islam. By the fifth century AD, however, the Malay Archipelago had already become an important stopping place for traders *en route* to China and vice versa. With the emergence of the thalassocratic empire of Sri Vijaya in the seventh century and its ability to guarantee safety of passage in the Straits of Malacca, the importance of the region in respect of international trade and shipping was enhanced further. By the end of the ninth century, the participation of Muslim traders in the commerce of the region had become evident. By the eleventh century, there was already evidence of the existence of Muslim settlements in the archipelago.[3]

It was, however, not until after the rise to power of the Empire of Malacca that the Islamization of the archipelago was given a new impetus.[4] Malacca began to assume the leadership of states, which had converted to Islam like Aru, Pedir, and Lambri. New areas in Sumatra which came under the suzerainty of Malacca including Kampar, Indragiri, Siak, Jambi, Bengkalis, Riau, and Lingga were converted to Islam. In the Malay Peninsula, Pahang, Pattani, Kedah, Johor, and other states which acknowledged the suzerainty of Malacca also accepted Islam. From Malacca, the Islamization of the north coast of Java was undertaken. In 1478, the Kingdom of Majapahit was defeated by a coalition of Muslim states led by Demak.[5] Muslim missionaries from Demak then Islamized Banjarmasin in South Borneo. The Moluccas became Muslim in 1498. The island of Mindanao was Islamized a little earlier in 1460.[6] By the end of the fifteenth century Brunei had already become Muslim.[7] From Sulu and Mindanao, Islam spread to the northern islands of the Philippines and many Muslim sultanates were established. Even Manila came under Muslim rule which was only broken by the Spaniards in 1570.[8] The Sultanate of Brunei also undertook the Islamization of areas under its hegemony. The Macassarese, who had just been converted to Islam, in turn converted the Bugis and the people of the islands of Sumbawa and Lombok. The Bugis, after accepting Islam, introduced it to Flores. The whole of Java gradually became Islamized. Only Bali survived as a traditional Hindu-Buddhist kingdom in the archipelago.

The acceptance of Islam by people in power inevitably generated the process of the transformation of the culture and the polity they represented with varying degrees of effectiveness. The Hindu-Buddhist political tradition which used to be a feature of archipelagic polities was substituted by ideas and institutions inspired from Qur'anic and other legitimate Islamic sources. The Islamic concept of rulership replaced the Hindu concept of the *devaraja* or "god-king". Muslim honorifics and titles began to be used. Islamic law began to be implemented soon after the official adoption of Islam, although rather selectively. The *Undang Undang Melaka* (compiled c. 1450) contained clear Islamic legal provisions and stipulated that the governance of Malacca had to be in accordance with Qur'anic law.[9] The Trengganu Inscription, dated AD 1303, also clearly showed the implementation of Islamic law in that state.[10] In the Pattani region, Islamic law continued to be enforced until the end of the nineteenth century.[11] The *Undang Undang Pahang* had about forty-two articles out of a total of sixty-eight which were almost identical to the provisions of the Shafii School of Law.[12] In the case of Aceh, the implementation of Islamic law was more thorough than elsewhere in the region.

The political impact that Islam had on the region was greatly helped by the pre-eminent position which Muslim traders commanded in the archipelago. The control of trade and commerce in the region by the Muslims was almost total. External trade was in their hands. International shipping was virtually their monopoly. Major ports were under their influence. The Muslims had established an unassailable position of economic respectability. They had wealth and they were also people of learning. The conversions to Islam by the local rulers was a coup for the Muslims. Thereafter, the proselytization of the local people to Islam in the region followed very closely the trade routes. The role of the Sufis in promoting Islam in the archipelago was also great.

Islam transformed the culture of the Islamized people of the archipelago. Gradually, Islamic beliefs and their associated ethos emerged as the foundation of the common culture of the Islamized people in the region with slight local variations. The Islamization of the region brought about the egalitarianization of learning, which no longer became the preserve of the aristocracy. The Islamic tradition of learning demanded the involvement of all and sundry. Every Muslim was required to be able to recite the Qur'an and to comprehend the basic foundations of Islam rationally and through learning. The Arabic script was introduced and was almost universally used in the region from Aceh to Mindanao. Local languages began to be enriched with Arabic words and expressions. Malay, in particular, was adopted as the lingua franca of the region and the principal medium of religious instruction. It was also the pervasive role of Malay that significantly contributed to the consolidation of the linguistic unity of the region. A good number of works in Malay on literature, theology, law, and history began to be produced. Many areas in the region, from Pasai to Malacca, Aceh, and Pattani, emerged as centres of learning attracting scholars of repute from all over the region. An Islamic educational system was devised. In most cases, the mosque or the *surau* became institutionalized as a centre of learning. But separate institutions, known as *pesantren* in Java and *pondok* in the Malay Peninsula, soon came to be set up. Contacts with centres of learning in the Muslim world were established. The tradition of peripatetic teaching which probably preceded Islam in the region was continued. Pilgrimage to Mecca was observed and more importantly emotional, spiritual, psychological, and intellectual ties with the Muslim Middle East were maintained. In fact, even the immigration of the Arabs into the region was encouraged. Under the leadership of Arab scholars, and with the emphasis on learning which enjoyed official encouragement, the archipelago began to produce its own *ulama* (religious teachers) who would soon assume the leadership of Islam in the region. All these developments, brought about by Islam had, after a while, led to the evolution of a unique *Weltanschauung* for the Muslims of the archipelago. Whilst categorically upholding the primacy of Islam, this also allowed permissible elements of indigenous thoughts to prevail. And in respect of the question of identity, the internalization of Islam, or at least its outward aspects, by the people in the archipelago was so pronounced that Islam had emerged as an indivisible ingredient of their psyche and subjective identity. But, the political fragmentation that had characterized the archipelago, on the other hand, also nurtured a distinctive sense of separate political identities among the Islamized people of the region.

In the case of Thailand, Islam had made its presence felt in the first-ever unified Thai kingdom of Sukhothai in the thirteenth century largely through trading contacts established by Muslims. However, it was not until after the emergence of the Thai kingdom of Ayutthaya as the successor to Sukhothai in the fourteenth century that the Muslims began to establish a preponderant position and presence in the polity. Invariably, just as it was principally trade that ushered in the Islamization process and the political and economic development of the maritime states of the archipelago in the fifteenth, sixteenth, and seventeenth centuries, it was also the dominant factor of trade that inevitably brought Islam into closer contact with Ayutthaya.

Evidence of the dominant position of the Muslims in Ayutthaya can be seen from the fact that many of them at various times, had even served the King as his ministers and factors. The role of the Muslims as the King's ministers and merchants for successive rulers made them a very powerful group at the Ayutthayan court.[13] Against this background it was easy for them to gain royal favours. This, to some extent, explains why many accounts of the time attributed the power and influence of the Muslims elsewhere in the Thai kingdom, particularly on the trans-peninsular trading route, to the instrumental role of the Muslim ministers in promoting their cause from Ayutthaya. The Muslims had been able to not only totally control the trans-peninsula trade but managed to secure key administrative appointments all over the kingdom of Ayutthaya as well.[14] They also took up military duties in the service of successive Ayutthayan kings and were an important group manning the King's merchant navy.

In the case of Burma, the role of the Muslims was equally amazing. Though numerically small, the Muslims were entrenched in the fields of commerce, diplomacy, administration, politics, language, and culture. It has been established that Muslim seamen first reached Burma in the ninth century. As early as AD 860, for example, Chinese travellers had discovered Persian colonies on the borders of Yunnan. The Persian traveller, Ibn Khordabheh, the ninth century Arab traveller, Suleiman, and the Persian traveller, Ibn Al Faqih of the tenth century, in their writings, mentioned South Burma.[15] The tenth century Arab historian Al Magdisi speaks of the links that Burma had developed with India, the Malay archipelago, and Ceylon.[16] The Burmese Chronicles testify to the existence of Arabs, during the reign of King Anawratha (AD 1044-77), who served as royal horsemen.[17] Anawratha's successor, King Sawlu (AD 1077-88), was educated by a Muslim Arab and made the son of his teacher, Yaman Khan, the governor of the City of Ussa which is the Pegu of today.[18] A palace conspiracy led Yaman Khan to revolt. His attempt to overrun Pagan was crushed by Kyanzittha, Sawlu's brother, who introduced a Muslim settlement in the interior of Burma through his Indian Muslim captives. In the thirteenth century, when the Muslim-dominated armies of Kublai Khan under the command of Nasruddin, the son of the governor of Yunnan, ransacked Pagan, the Muslims yet again made their presence felt in Burma.[19]

Throughout the period when Muslim commercial hegemony in the Southeast Asia ranked supreme until about the seventeenth century, the coastal cities of Burma, through Muslim connections, were linked to the wider global trading network of the Muslims. Even when the commercial dominance of the Muslims began to wane before collapsing under external pressure as a result of the changing international political constellation arising from European rivalry and competition, the Muslims continued to maintain some kind of presence in these areas. It was not just in the sphere of trade that the Muslims of this area were active, they were also engaged in ship-repairing and shipbuilding. At one point of time in the seventeenth century, practically every major province from Mergui *en route* to Ayutthaya had Muslim governors and high-ranking administrators.[20] From the fifteenth to the middle of the eighteenth century, the Burmese army enlisted the services of Muslim riflemen and artillerymen in the bodyguard units. During the reign of King Pagan-Min (1846-53) a Muslim was made governor of Amarapura, the capital of the kingdom at that time, enjoying wide authority vested by the King.[21] In 1855, the governor of Pagan, too, was a Muslim.[22]

In the Arakan region, probably due to the factor of geographical propinquity with India, extensive diplomatic, political, commercial, cultural, and human contacts existed between the Arakanese kingdom and India. Muslim influence was so pronounced in the area that even the Buddhist kings of Arakan assumed Muslim titles and names.[23] Although the kingdom was Buddhist, Muslims were elevated to eminent positions. From the fifteenth century onwards, Arakanese history was orientated more and more towards Moghul India. From about the middle of the seventeenth century till 1785, when Arakan was re-annexed by Burma, the position of the Muslims in Arakan under the leadership of the Kamans was unchallenged.

Successive Burmese kings, particularly in the eighteenth century, resettled Muslim prisoners all over Burma. The collapse of the Sultanate of Yunnan under Sultan Sulaiman in 1873, at the hands of the Chinese imperial army, drove a new wave of Chinese Muslims into northern Burma in search of political refuge.[24] By the beginning of the eighteenth and nineteenth centuries, there were already considerable numbers of Muslims in practically every major city. The Muslims were involved in state affairs under Burmese patronage right through to the final days of the Burmese kingdom in Mandalay in 1885. In fact, they were known to be amongst the most vocal opponents of the British presence in Burma and were involved not just politically, economically, and diplomatically, but also militarily in attempting to ward off further British encroachments on Burma.

The kingdom of Cambodia, on the other hand, like the Buddhist polities of Burma and Ayutthaya, was inextricably linked to the political and commercial events that were unfolding in the region as a whole. The domination of trade by the Muslims in the region, coupled with the vigorous Islamization efforts that were being undertaken, helped facilitate the rise to prominence of Muslims in the kingdom of Cambodia. In the case of Cambodia, however, the role of the Muslims had perhaps an even greater significance particularly because, a few centuries earlier, Champa, which was then incorporated as part of the Cambodian kingdom, had become one of the earliest Muslim sultanates in the region. The Champa region had a majority Muslim population which was unambiguously Islamic in orientation; the region also maintained extensive relations with the archipelagic world of Southeast Asia, especially with the east coast states of the Malay Peninsula. The Muslim population of the kingdom of Cambodia, like that of other areas in the region, was cosmopolitan. Their zeal for spreading Islam was just as strong as that of other devout Muslims elsewhere. It was probably this factor that led to the successful conversion of the Cambodian ruler to Islam in the early part of the seventeenth century.[25] The conversion strengthened even further the position and the dominance of the Muslim community in Cambodia; but as with the experience of Ayutthaya, the fluid nature of international relations in the region — which began to undermine Muslim domination and supremacy — affected the position of the Muslims in Cambodia. They could not sustain their pre-eminent position, and Islam was not able to penetrate the ruling elites as it had been able to in the archipelagic states. A court conspiracy soon ended a very brief Muslim rule in Cambodia. The changing fortunes of the Muslims in the region as a whole as a consequence of a sustained European onslaught, ended the possibility of further Muslim domination.

The Colonial Period

The Portugese were the first to venture into the east with a missionary zeal. The problem for them, however, was not just how to subdue the indigenous people but rather how to maintain control over them. Thus, when Malacca was subdued in 1511, it was immediately linked to the emerging network of a Portugese sea-borne empire which was set up to rival and destroy Muslim economic and political dominance in Asia. However, for the next one hundred years or so, the Portugese had to cope with a continual war that was waged against them by local Muslim rulers, although they might not have been consistently religious in motivation. The Spaniards countenanced a similar situation in the Philippines. With the possible exception of the Muslim sultanate in Manila which fell to the Spaniards in 1570, the other Muslim sultanates in Mindanao and Sulu successfully resisted the southward penetration of the Spaniards. The Dutch, who came to the east, about a century later, were more subtle in their approach. Through a strategy based on treaties and alliances with local rulers, the Dutch were able to dislodge the traditionally powerful role of the Muslims, instigate intense interstate rivalry, and assert a critical role in the new economic and political order that was evolving in the region.

However, it was not until the nineteenth century that the full impact of Western colonial penetration was felt in Southeast Asia. Outwardly, the economic and political order of the region appeared to be only peripherally affected by the European presence. In reality, a whole new order was beginning to evolve. By the time the implications of Western colonial presence were realized, all the traditional states of Southeast Asia, with the exception of Thailand, had lost their political independence.

The attempt by colonial powers, particularly in the nineteenth century, to delineate artificial boundaries which divided their respective spheres of influence and areas of control in Southeast Asia, threatened to dislodge completely the traditional political framework for Southeast Asians. Thus, a line was drawn arbitrarily along the Straits of Malacca to divide the area into a British sphere of influence which covered the Malay Peninsula and a Dutch sphere of influence which covered Sumatra. The traditional links between these two areas were conveniently ignored. The same was true of the northern part of the Malay Peninsula which had a new political border which did not coincide by any means with traditional ethnic, linguistic, cultural, religious and, indeed, political boundaries. Southeast Asia had to be shared between France, Britain, the Netherlands, Spain, and Portugal; and this was decided by considerations of sheer power politics, with the Southeast Asians having little or no say at all.

Technically, in the case of Malaya, apart from Penang, Province Wellesley, Malacca, and Singapore, which were brought together and administered by the British as the Straits Settlements, the other nine Malay States continued to retain their sovereignty, at least in theory. However, in practice, even in the Malay States the British exerted a considerable amount of influence if not power through a system of Residents who acted in an "advisory" capacity. The economy of these states was brought under British direction and control. Massive immigration, particularly of Chinese and Indians, was encouraged. The ports of Singapore and Penang were developed as the principal economic outlets for the Malay Peninsula. A modern bureaucracy was introduced and, in the Straits Settlements, the British legal system enforced. As for the Malay States, because of their legal sovereign status, a good deal of British law came in through a process of selective adoption. In the Straits Settlements, however, in accordance with the British attitude of respect towards personal laws, Muslim law was at the same time upheld in this regard. A secular educational system was developed particularly in the Straits Settlements to meet the needs of the colonial government. However, a *laissez-faire* attitude was adopted towards education, thus enabling the growth and development of privately funded Chinese and Indian vernacular schools.

When Malay vernacular education was started by the British, they made no secret of their objective which was to help make the children of Malay fishermen become better fishermen, and the children of Malay farmers become better farmers.[26] The new economic and educational opportunities that were created largely benefited the immigrant communities particularly those in the Straits Settlements. The Malay aristocracy was only marginally able to take advantage of these new opportunities. The bulk of the Malay population in the Malay States was virtually insulated from the developments that were taking place. At the local level, however, the Malays continued to be exposed extensively to religious socialization. The traditional Islamic educational system, for example, continued to survive. The mosque, *surau*, *madrasah*, and *pondok* emerged as important centres of religious instruction. Further education in the field of religion was sought in the Middle East. The *ulama* continued to provide the social and religious leadership of the Malays at village level. Very few of the common Malays from the Malay States were given access to higher or modern education. Economically, the majority of the Malays, almost by design, remained in agriculture and fishing. The Malay entrepreneurial class had been suddenly displaced. Only the more cosmopolitan Muslims in the Straits Settlements survived in trade and commerce. A pattern of unequal development between the Malays and the immigrants emerged.

Sarawak, on the other hand, was ceded by the Sultan of Brunei to James Brooke in the 1840s.[27] It was not merely a cession of territorial rights but one which included the right to govern as personal sovereign. With the transfer of sovereignty to a non-indigene and a non-Muslim, the developments that occurred in this state naturally reflected the personal priorities that the new sovereign had. Accordingly, unlike the Malay States in British Malaya, Islam did not enjoy any special status in Sarawak.

Sabah, which was formerly known as North Borneo, came under the administration of the British North Borneo Company as a result of a series of treaties and agreements between the Sultan of Brunei and Sulu and the company. It was, like Sarawak, artificially carved out from the traditional political world to which it belonged. The absence of a powerful Muslim elite and the small number of Muslims in these states led to a decline in the official status of Islam in the area. On the other hand, emigration, particularly from China, was stimulated by the British to help bring about the economic exploitation of the new state. Proselytization among the natives was also undertaken by Christian missionaries brought in by the British company.

Similar to the other Malay States, the Sultanate of Brunei did not relinquish its sovereignty to the British. In 1888, an agreement was reached between the British and the Sultan of Brunei giving the sultanate the status of a British protectorate.[28] Internal administration remained in the hands of the Sultan; however, Brunei was also persuaded to accept a British adviser who would give counsel to the Sultan on all questions save those pertaining to the religion of Islam. The English legal system was also selectively adopted. A modern bureaucracy and a modern form of government began to evolve. The role of the Sultan as an absolute ruler was checked. In fact, the British Resident, whose job was to advise appeared to have taken over a great many of the duties that the Sultan used to perform. New institutions like a constitution, a police force, a bureaucracy manned by district officers, and so on, were created to assist in the modernization of the traditional polity. The defence of the country, internal security matters, and external relations became the responsibility of the British government in the United Kingdom. Chinese immigration was encouraged and the economic exploitation of the country was undertaken, especially with a view to serving British interests. The traditional hierarchy however survived. Religion continued to occupy a pivotal role in the lives of the people. Religious education continued to play an important role in resuscitating the Islamic identity of the Malays of Brunei. The Malay language was retained as the principal medium of religious instruction and communication among the Muslims of Brunei.

In the case of the Philippines, the history of the contacts between the Muslims of the south, or Moros as they were called, and the Spanish colonial masters was a history of perennial confrontation. The Muslim areas only gradually came to be integrated with the rest of the Philippines under the United States administration in the opening years of the present century. Following a military occupation of the region from 1899 to 1903, the Moro Province was established from 1903 to 1913 as a military and political unit.[29] From 1914 to 1920, the Department of Mindanao and Sulu was set up.[30] Subsequently, Muslim affairs were administered by the government of the Philippines. Despite efforts to integrate the area administratively and despite moves to introduce modern and secular education, the organization of Muslim society in the Philippines continued to be tradition-based. Religion remained a potent issue. In fact, Islamic religious education continued to play a crucial role in the socialization of the people. Contacts between the Muslims of the Philippines and their co-religionists across in Sabah, Brunei, and beyond were sustained. Interisland trade also played a role in keeping alive the ties between the Muslims of the Philippines and the Muslims in other parts of the archipelago.

In contrast to the other countries of Southeast Asia, it would appear that the Muslims in the southern Philippines were in many ways spared the impact of colonial penetration although, ironically, the Philippines was the country to have been colonized the longest in all of Southeast Asia. Even the American administration, which managed to bring about the formal political integration of the southern Philippines with the rest of the country, failed to bring about an acceptable level of social, cultural, and educational integration of the Muslims into the mainstream of Filipino society. The post-independence phenomenon of Christianization and Filipinization continued to cause grave anxieties among the Muslims of the Philippines over their future within the Filipino nation.

With regard to the Netherlands East Indies (that is, Indonesia), because of its sheer size and diversity, effective Dutch rule was only established in the island of Java. Even then, resistance and rebellion did take place. The Dutch had to solicit the collusion of local rulers to establish their authority. In Sumatra, rebellions were endemic and it was not until the late nineteenth century that Aceh was pacified. In all these cases, Islam featured as a factor that fuelled anti-Dutch sentiment, though it was by no means the only factor.

The Muslims of Indonesia, because of their diverse backgrounds, reacted in different ways to Dutch colonization. But, generally, in the more Islamized areas, and in the heartland of archipelagic Islam in Aceh and Minangkabau, the orientation towards religion, tradition, and the wider Muslim world continued to be strong. The well-established system of *pesantren*, or religious, education in Java and the *madrasah* (religious schools) in Aceh emerged as the bastion of Islamic thought and identity. The practice of the hadj (pilgrimage to Mecca) was observed zealously; and a permanent settlement of Muslims comprising Acehnese, Javanese, and others was even established in Mecca. Students from the region enrolled at tertiary religious institutions in the Middle East. Two-way communication was established between the Muslims of the archipelago and their co-religionists elsewhere. In the nineteenth century, an influx of Arab immigrants, who settled in the urban centres of the archipelago, added to the heterogeneity of the Muslim population of the archipelago. However, with Malay as a principal medium of religious instruction and the lingua franca of the region, elements of commonality could be traced among the Muslims, and the Malay language became a common denominator of the identity of the Muslims in the region.

In Burma, following colonization by the British, Muslim emigration from India was stimulated to meet the newly-created needs for labour and manpower within British Burma. The Indian Muslim immigrants, like their Hindu counterparts, came to British Burma as government clerks, labourers, servants, watchmen, shoemakers, soldiers, and merchants.[31] Practically no new government department that was created in Burma was set up without Indians. In fact, some departments were wholly Indian in terms of manpower. By the turn of the twentieth century, half of the population of Rangoon was Indian, among whom the Muslims constituted a substantial proportion.

The influx of massive immigration into Burma inevitably affected the relations between the Burmese and the Muslims. Assimilation into Burmese society was arrested. The sudden growth in numbers at a time when the indigenous Burmese leadership had been displaced, generated a resurgence of ethnic, cultural, and religious pride among the Muslims. Their relatively better economic position enabled them to undertake the development of organizations which served their narrow interests. Thus, associations and societies mushroomed among the Muslims. New mosques were built and Islamic education began to be promoted with enthusiasm. Burma, to the Muslim immigrants, was seen merely as an extension of British India. Urdu was made a principal language of religious instruction among the Muslims although Tamil and Bengali were also used by certain groups. Islamic religious literature, basically of Indian origin, was widely distributed among the Muslims.

The assimilated Burmese Muslims, understandably, went through a difficult period during British rule. On the one hand, new waves of Muslim immigrants helped strengthen their numbers. They too benefited from the revivalism of Islam that was brought by their immigrant brethren. At the same time, however, they were alarmed at the growing chauvinism that they saw in the immigrant Muslim community. Being part of the indigenous Burmese community, they had found it difficult to deny their Burmese identity.

In Siam, the fate of the Muslims was no better. Although Siam was never colonized politically, the impact of Western colonialism affected its internal structure critically. Its new political frontiers did not overlap with pre-existing ethnic, cultural, and religious boundaries. Siam had been forced to undertake the territorial consolidation of areas which were once only loosely attached to it. Tributary states were dismantled and their ruling élites displaced. The traditional Malay Muslim sultanate of Pattani lost its status as a consequence of this.

The whole exercise of internal restructuring within Siam occurred primarily in response to events following the signing of the Bowring Treaty in 1855 and a series of other unequal treaties with the West. These treaties led to an opening up of Siam to Western economic exploitation. Siam became forcibly linked economically to the international colonial economic network that was being established.

Just like the other states of Southeast Asia, a massive influx of labour from China began. In fact, labour also flowed into Siam from British Malaya and the Dutch East Indies. To a certain extent, especially in the case of the latter, this phenomenon helped to make the Muslim population of Bangkok, the capital city of Siam, even more diverse, not just in terms of the ethnic composition of the city, but also in relation to the areas of economic specialization of the population. Nevertheless, whilst the Muslims became involved in all sorts of jobs and positions at all levels, particularly in the capital city, they were never able to restore their once pre-eminent political position in Siam.

As for the Malays of the former Pattani kingdom, the erosion of their political power and the dislocation of the role of their traditional élites had a devastating effect. This was exacerbated when the economy came under the control of Chinese immigrants. Administratively and bureaucratically, they were subjected to greater control through more direct forms of Thai rule. The primacy of the Thai language began to be upheld officially. More Thais began to settle in their areas with the setting up of more modern departments and institutions. These developments, as they perceived it, constituted attempts to subjugate them completely. They inevitably turned towards religion for sanctuary. Islamic religious education was given a boost. The Malay language, which was the lingua franca of the area and the principal medium of religious instruction, was reinforced because it was seen as a primary resuscitator of their Malay identity which was then coming under serious threat from the Thai authorities.

Independence

Colonial rule had brought about a gradual erosion of the role of the indigenous population in politics and economy. The introduction of modern administration and a colonial legal system, which in most cases protected colonial interests, placed the indigenous people at a disadvantage. The secularization of administration which involved the separation of religion and even culture from politics undermined the primacy of the traditional political order which contained no such distinction. The integration of the economy of these colonized states into the larger colonial economy made the role of the indigenous people subservient to the dictates of the colonial order.

The majority of the indigenous people attempted to detach themselves from the major events that were unfolding and almost invariably retreated to religion. This helped to restore their pride and confidence as Muslims and reinforced their belief that although politically and economically they had lost their independence, spiritually they were still free; but then there were also negative effects. The content of religious education that they received tended to be static and ritualistic. The separation of religion and politics which brought about the curtailment of political activities in all probability led to this situation. The spiritual foundation, formed through religious instruction, was generally strong; but the over-emphasis on theology created a situation where an insulated orthodox Islamic education did not appear to be sufficiently equipped to cope with the complexities of a rapidly changing world. It is no wonder then that the nationalist leadership of the region which was inspired by the ideals of political independence came mainly from those educated in the colonial system of education. But, Islam remained an essential unifying element in the nationalist struggles of the Muslims, although the path to independence differed from country to country.

In the case of Indonesia, its independence was first granted by Japan in 1945 but that independence was challenged by the Dutch. It was only later in 1949 that the Netherlands agreed to recognize an independent Indonesia.[32] As part of the compromise, the Indonesians were to adopt the Dutch model of parliamentary democracy which created major problems for the government and led to several rebellions. President Soekarno had seen it fit to modify the political system to what was described as "guided democracy". The modification was thought necessary to bring about the co-operation of the nationalists, religious groups, and the communists. There were, however, continuing tensions between these conflicting groups which led to the abortive communist coup of 1965. Since then, the emphasis has been on de-politicization in the New Order being evolved which gives priority to economic development and stability over participatory politics.

In the Malay Peninsula, the Federation of Malaya, which comprised the nine sovereign Malay States, Penang, and Malacca, was formed as an independent nation-state in 1957. A new constitution which upheld a liberal democratic political system along the Westminster model was adopted. In 1963, together with the North Borneo States of Sabah and Sarawak, and Singapore, the Federation of Malaysia was formed. Due to serious policy differences, Singapore was separated from Malaysia in 1965 and became a fully independent republic with a British parliamentary form of government.

Brunei, which had turned down the offer to join Malaysia, fully regained its independence on 1 January 1984.[33] The traditional political system was resurrected in a modern form with the ruling family providing leadership of the kingdom which was renamed Negara Brunei Darussalam.

The sovereignty of the Republic of Philippines was restored on 4 July 1946, based on the 1935 constitution, after which a democratic system of government based on the American model was adopted.[34] The Union of Burma, on the other hand, achieved its independence from the British in 1948 and implemented a liberal democratic political system until March 1962 when a military coup abruptly ended it. Since then, Burma came under military rule which exercised power through the Burma Socialist Programme Party (BSPP), the only political party allowed to exist in post-1962 Burma. In 1974, a new constitution was adopted and Burma was renamed the Socialist Republic of the Union of Burma.[35]

Thailand had never been under direct colonial rule; but in 1932, a major structural development took place when an absolute monarchy was replaced with a constitutional monarchy. Thai politics in the constitutional era has been characterized by frequent breakdowns in participatory politics, caused by bureaucratic and military manipulation and intervention. Kampuchea underwent the most traumatic political experience of all nation-states in Southeast Asia in the modern era. Its independence was restored by the French in 1953 and it existed as the Kingdom of Kampuchea until 1970 when, after a coup, it was changed into the Khmer Republic. In 1975, after the collapse of the republic, the Khmer Rouge redesignated it Democratic Kampuchea. In 1979, following the defeat of the Khmer Rouge, the People's Republic of Kampuchea was set up but its legitimacy has not gone uncontested.[36]

The Contemporary Profile

The Republic of Indonesia

Today, with an estimated population of about 165 million people out of which about 90 per cent are Muslims, Indonesia is the largest Muslim country in the world. The Indonesian population, however, is not entirely homogeneous. There are over 300 ethnic groups and more than 250 distinct languages in Indonesia today. With a total land area of 1,904,569 square kilometres spread over 13,677 islands throughout the Indonesian archipelago, the heterogeneity that characterizes Indonesia is understandable. Java is the most populous island with more than half of Indonesia's total population.

Although Indonesia is predominantly Muslim, it declares itself a secular state espousing the ideals of *Pancasila* which symbolize its national ideology.[37] Apart from Islam, Hinduism, Buddhism, Catholicism, and Protestantism are accorded official recognition. Even the Muslims, apart from their ethnic, linguistic, and regional diversity, are divided further in numerous other ways. Broadly, in Java they can be classified as *abangan*, the more nominal Muslims, and *santri*, those steeped in Islam. There are further differentiations within these broad categories. For example, the *santri*s can be further divided into the reformists, the traditionalists, the mystics, and so on. The Muslim community may also be said to be divided along educational lines, for example, into those with a secular education and those with a religious education, and so forth. The more secular and Western-educated Muslims tend to display a more outward-looking orientation and to have Western life-styles. Often, they also have urban and rather more cosmopolitan backgrounds. The Muslims can also be divided into elite groups and those representing the masses. The majority of the Muslims, however, tend to come from rural areas and are of peasant background. The urban Muslim working classes often comprise petty traders and labourers.

The Indonesian legal system is secular. The application of Islamic law is accepted only to the extent that it is allowed by *adat* (customs).[38] Religious courts have a limited jurisdiction. Although Muslim family law is officially used for Muslims, in terms of implementation, some of the procedures appear secular in character. A religious council was established in 1962 and reorganized in 1975 to assume responsibility for issuing *fatwa* (decrees) on matters of religion to the government and the people.[39]

Politically, following independence, Indonesia has had to focus its attention on the search for a viable political system. The era of liberal democracy only served to heighten ethnic, religious, and ideological tensions among the Indonesians. Participatory politics had not only raised popular expectations to an unrealistic level but precipitated rifts between Muslims. Islam had been effectively used to rally support for Muslim political parties like Nahdatul Ulama and Masyumi, but at the same time the politicization of Islam drove a wedge between Muslim parties and other national political organizations. The eventual collapse of democracy itself was caused both by intense interparty politicking and outbreaks of regional rebellion fuelled by Islamic sentiments.[40]

Guided democracy was then envisaged by Soekarno as the only way to bring about a political compromise between the conflicting ideological forces of communism, nationalism, and Islam, thereby preserving national unity in Indonesia. But an abortive coup by the communists in 1965 abruptly ended Indonesia's experiment with guided democracy and with it the leadership of President Soekarno. The political system has since been restructured under military leadership with a view to removing the divisive and disruptive elements within it. The Partai Komunis Indonesia (PKI), or the Indonesian Communist Party, was demolished and its members eliminated. Under the *Orde Baru* or New Order, emphasis has been placed on economic development and political stability. Only *Pancasila* democracy is sanctioned. The position of the military-backed GOLKAR party has been strengthened. Political parties espousing Islam have been told to regroup under the banner of the Partai Perhimpunan Pembangunan (PPP) and to unquestioningly endorse

Pancasila. The extent to which these moves have been successful in preventing Islam from having a political platform is however still unclear.

The Federation of Malaysia

In Malaysia, the Muslims comprise no more than 55 per cent of the population of the country. Although not all Muslims are Malays, constitutionally, Malays must be Muslims.[41] For political purposes however, the indigenous people of Malaysia have been designated *bumiputera* (sons of the soil) while non-indigenous people of migrant stock have been designated non-*bumiputera*. It is a classification which does not coincide along religious lines as not all indigenous people are Muslims, especially those from Sabah and Sarawak, just as not all the Muslims qualify as *bumiputera*s. Generally, the non-*bumiputera*s, particularly the Chinese, are of urban backgrounds and are much more economically advanced. The majority of *bumiputera*s, on the other hand, come from rural areas and tend to be economically backward. Following the collapse of liberal democracy in 1969 as a result of racial riots caused by excessive communal politicking and the glaring economic disparities between the Malay and non-Malay communities, the political system has been restructured to incorporate new constitutional, legal, and political mechanisms to reduce direct communal political confrontation and to promote the politics of consensus. A more dynamic economic approach was developed with the formulation of the New Economic Policy (NEP) with its two-pronged objectives of eliminating poverty irrespective of race and restructuring Malaysian society in order to remove ethnic identification with economic vocation or specialization. The *bumiputera*s have become the immediate beneficiaries of the NEP, which has also at the same time created further business and economic opportunities for Malaysian society as a whole.

The ethnic factor, however, continues to be potent in Malaysian politics. Most political parties are still communally organized. Muslim interest is represented in a number of political parties, notably the United Malays National Organization (UMNO) which is in government, and Parti Islam (PAS), which is an opposition party. An interethnic forum exists in the ruling National Front, which is a coalition of twelve political parties representing the different communities in Malaysia. UMNO is the senior and strongest component of the National Front. The major non-Muslim opposition party is the Democratic Action Party (DAP) which purports to be multiracial and multireligious in objective but thrives basically on Chinese support.

The role of Islam in politics has become more pronounced in Malaysia particularly in the 1980s. It is now a crucial factor both in national as well as local politics. PAS has been more assertive in its demand for the creation of an Islamic state.[42] It commands considerable popular support in the Muslim-dominated states of Kelantan, Trengganu, Kedah, and Perlis. The UMNO-led National Front favours a policy of gradual and selective incorporation of Islamic values into government policies and upholds the existing Malaysian constitution as sacrosanct. The DAP has rejected both approaches and advocates an uncomprising commitment to the ideals of secularism given the realities of the multiethnic and multireligious situation in Malaysia.

The policy of the National Front on Islam appears to have been partly attributable to its desire to match the growing expectations of a much more religiously conscious Muslim society. The phenomenon of Islamic revivalism in Malaysia, particularly in the 1980s, has been pervasive. There are now visible and ubiquitous signs of greater conformity to the Islamic code of life in Malaysia. There has also been a revival of scholarly interest in Islam among the Muslims. Public discourses and debates in the mass media are now an accepted everyday event. New institutions in education, health, industry, commerce, and banking, which reflect more fully the Islamic vision, have been set up, often with government assistance. New Muslim associations and bodies committed to the pursuit of Islamic ideals have mushroomed. Among these organizations, the Angkatan Belia Islam Malaysia (ABIM) or Muslim Youth Movement of Malaysia, has been at the forefront of efforts to promote a positive image of Islam to Muslims as well as non-Muslims. The Darul Arqam, on the other hand, constitutes a non-political mass movement which aims to re-create the puritanical life-style of early Muslim communities of the time of Prophet Muhammad. *Tabligh* and *dakwah* (that is, missionary) activities are undertaken by motley groups with zeal. Interestingly, in spite of these developments, the Malaysian Muslims, either by design or otherwise, continue to possess a range of other overlapping and interlocking relationships with their non-Muslim counterparts in the country.

The Republic of Singapore

Singapore is a multiracial, multilingual, and multireligious city-state of about 2.5 million people.[43] The Chinese comprise about 77 per cent of the population. The Malays are a minority of about 15 per cent, while Indians account for 6 per cent, and others another 2 per cent. The total Muslim population exceeds 320,000 representing some 16 per cent of the population.[44] The Muslims in Singapore, like Muslims elsewhere in Southeast Asia, are a heterogeneous group, the majority of whom are Malays. But even the Malays come from diverse backgrounds. There are coastal Malays, Javanese, Bugis, Baweanese, and others; practically all of them are Muslims and can speak Malay. The number of Chinese Muslims in Singapore is very small.[45] The Pakistanis, Indians, and Arabs make up the rest of the population of the Muslim community in Singapore.

The Malay-Muslim community is generally more backward socio-economically compared with their non-Malay Muslim brethren and even more so in relation to other Singaporeans. Under a meritocratic educational system, the Malay-Muslims have lagged far behind educationally. In 1980, there were only 679 Malays in Singapore with university qualifications.[46] The emphasis on a bilingual school policy by the Singapore government and in particular the decision to make English a compulsory language in schools has had the effect of undermining the position of Malay primary schools in the republic which only had 316 students in 1983.[47]

Intermarriages between Malays and others are not uncommon in Singapore particularly with the Indians and Pakistanis. As a response to the rapid pace of urbanization and poor housing conditions, and as part of its development programme, over the past two decades, the government has instituted a public housing policy which includes the resettlement of the Malays from their traditional mono-ethnic village settlements to modern high-rise housing estates with ethnically mixed populations. The impact of such drastic human resettlement must be great and the Malays, in particular, appear to be still grappling with problems of adjustment and adaptation.

The attempt to forge a uniquely Singaporean national identity was perceived with caution by the Malays. For some Malays, it appeared that this would put them at a disadvantage. In the area of political representation, there is no electoral constituency in Singapore today where the Malays constitute a majority. Nevertheless, Malay representation exists in the Singapore government although this is not proportionately reflective of the size of the Malay community in the republic. Malay opposition political parties, such as the Persatuan Kebangsaan Melayu Singapura (PKMS) continue to exist but have not succeeded in their attempts at parliamentary representation in various elections.[48] There is also a range of non-political Muslim clubs and associations in Singapore.

In order to reassure the Muslims that the goverment upholds the principle of religious freedom and cares for their religious well-being, a council for Muslim religious affairs, the Majlis Ugama Islam Singapura (MUIS) was set up under the provisions of the Administration of Muslim Law Act of 1966.[49] MUIS has been charged with the responsibility for regulating the administration of Muslim Law in the state encompassing duties such as the collection of *zakat* and *fitrah* (religious tithes and dues), management of the pilgrimage to Mecca, organization of religious schools, and the award of scholarships to Muslim students. MUIS is also empowered to issue *fatwa*s.[50] The administration of the eighty mosques or so in Singapore is also entrusted to MUIS.[51] Since 1975, through its Mosque Building Fund, MUIS has been assisting in the construction of multifunctional mosques to facilitate religious as well as *dakwah* and other community activities.

There have also been other bodies set up by the government as well as the Muslim community to help bring about the uplifting of the socio-economic status of the Malays. The government has indicated that it recognizes that it is in the interest of all to have "Muslim Singaporeans better educated and better qualified and to increase their contribution to Singapore's development".[52]

The Republic of the Philippines

The Philippines is an archipelago of 7,107 islands. Its population of 47 million people speak eighty-seven different dialects reflecting as many tribal or ethnic communities.[53] Islam has had a long history in the Philippines beginning from the pre-colonial period and the Muslims of the southern region are notable for having successfully resisted Spanish colonial penetration for over three hundred years. It was only at the beginning of the twentieth century that Muslim areas in the south began to be administratively and systematically integrated into the wider polity. Even then, however, there was resistance.

The Muslims of the Philippines describe themselves as Moros. But this label is more political in nature, because in reality the Moros comprise several ethnolinguistic groups, for example, the Maranaos, the Maguindanaos, the Tausugs, the Samals, the Yakans, the Iranuns, the Jamamapuns, the Badjaos, the Kalibugans, the Kalagans, and the Sangils.[54] The Moros number about 4.5 million people or about 9 per cent of the national population.[55] They are still the predominant population in Sulu, Tawi-Tawi, Lanao del Sur, Maguindanao, and Basilan.

The majority of the Moros are farmers and fishermen. But there are also Muslims who are serving the government in various capacities as teachers, administrators, members of the Armed Forces, the judiciary, and even as elected mayors and governors. The Muslims who have gone through secular education tend to integrate fairly easily with the Filipino state. On the contrary, those who have shunned secular education and opted for traditional religious education are generally resistant to integration. Particularly for the local élite who have gone to the Middle East for their education, adaptation to the demands of Filipino citizenship has been more difficult. There also seems to be a gulf between the traditional élite and the masses among the Moros. Ethnic identification and consciousness, which is maintained by the geographical distribution of Muslim communities, seems very strong. Nevertheless, despite these variations and differences, there is a strong feeling of religious fraternity particularly in the face of what is perceived as a common dilemma.

It is not just religion that unites the Muslims. It is also the hardship and economic difficulties that Muslims of the south have had to face that have brought them together. The policy of resettling Christians in Mindanao over the past few decades since the end of the Second World War had upset the traditional demographic balance to the disadvantage of the Muslims. The massive inflow of capital and technology into Mindanao in various economic activities, which in some cases led to the displacement of Muslim communities from their traditional homelands did not, except rarely, benefit the Muslims. This served to reinforce the traditional prejudices they had against the non-Muslims. The political alienation that these developments brought about led to the formation of the Muslim Independence Movement (MIM) in the 1960s. This, and the subsequent formation of the Moro National Liberation Front (MNLF) and the Bansa Moro Army (BMA) to champion the cause of the Muslims in the Philippines should be seen in the context of the rising frustration among the Muslims in the south over their continued economic exploitation and political alienation.

The government, on the other hand, was keen to overcome the Muslim problem in the south because it recognized that they were facing serious economic difficulties with the grim prospect of further alienation. It was also realized that the Muslim problem in the south, though unique in many ways, could not be totally divorced from the wider problems facing the Philippines as a new nation-state. The political system that the Philippines adopted from the United States had problems of implementation. The communists had challenged the legitimacy of the state by rebelling; the gulf between the rich and the poor was widening; and politicians resorted to private armies to demonstrate their power. All, therefore, was not well. The declaration of martial law in 1972 by President Ferdinand Marcos was intended to arrest the deteriorating conditions of law and order. The New Society that President Marcos aspired to establish was also an attempt to remedy the ills that plagued the Philippines as a nation. The Muslims, of course, were affected; but at the governmental level concessions were given. The Muslim rebellion too was seen as costly and unnecessary. The Tripoli Agreement to end hostilities between the MNLF and the government was undertaken with this in mind. Many other positive measures were adopted by the government to demonstrate goodwill and concern. Among these were the establishment of the Philippine Pilgrimage Authority, the Agency for the Development and Welfare of the Muslims, and the implementation of Muslim family law for the Muslims.[56]

The recent political changes in the Philippines have aroused the anxiety of the Muslims. In the face of uncertainties, Muslim insurgents have consolidated their position even further. The Filipino democratic experiment is going through another crucial phase. A positive attitude on the part of Filipino Muslims would certainly help make the task of President Aquino a little less burdensome.

Negara Brunei Darussalam

The political situation in Negara Brunei Darussalam seems far more quiet due, perhaps, to its small size. Brunei has a population of only about 200,000 people with the Muslims being the majority group. They are almost wholly Malay, although there have also been a small number of Chinese converts. As the official religion, Islam is given state patronage. The domination of government by the royal family and the absence of democratic politics have enabled the goverment to prosecute religious and other public policies without much difficulty. Similarly, because Brunei has been cautious about outside influence, the traditional feudalistic society seems to survive.

The Socialist Republic of the Union of Burma

In terms of size, according to the 1983 population census (advance release), the Muslims constitute 3.9 per cent of the total population of Burma of 35.3 million people.[57] Geographically, the Muslims are dispersed all over Burma and constitute a predominantly urban group of people. They are to be found in practically all the major towns throughout Burma. The bigger cities such as Mandalay and Rangoon tend to have a heavier concentration of Muslims. There are even a number of towns, particularly in the Arakan region such as Buthidaung and Yathedaung, where the Muslims comprise the majority population. The area contiguous to Bangladesh also has an overwhelmingly large Muslim majority, unlike other parts of Burma. It is also in the Arakan region that there exists a large rural Muslim population.

As a general rule, there are four main distinctive categories of Muslims, namely the Indian Muslims or Kala Pathees, the Burmese Muslims or Zerbadees, the Malay Muslims or Pashus, and the Panthays or Chinese Muslims.[58] Numerically, only the Kala Pathees and the Zerbadees are of any consequence. Culturally, the Burmese Muslims appear more and more indistinguishable from their Burman Buddhist counterparts, save in the area of religious observances. Burmese Muslims have adopted Burmese names, although they may also have Muslim names which may be used in domestic contexts. Indian Muslims, however, prefer to retain Muslim names. Politically, too, the Burmese Muslims tend to have positive feelings and attitudes towards the state and identify themselves with it far more readily and willingly. The Indian Muslims in Burma, however, are still ambiguous about the role they could and should assume within Burma and therefore tend to appear as a group which has yet to develop strong roots in the Burmese polity. The economic specialization of the Burmese Muslims differs slightly from the Indian Muslims in that, whilst both categories are extensively engaged in business and commerce, the former tends to show a greater agricultural bias, a feature which is more consistent with the overall national pattern. The Indian Muslims in Burma have a more conspicuous commercial posture. It is for this reason, perhaps, that the pursuit of rigid socialist policies in the post-1962 period has adversely affected them more than any other Muslim groups. Their traditionally strong economic role was seriously undermined by the adoption of socialist economic policies which did not favour free enterprise, curtailed international trade, restricted imports, and tightened currency regulations.

Politically, it would appear that the Muslims in Burma enjoyed greater protection and freedom during the democratic era. They were not only well represented in government but existed as a significant political element in the electoral politics of Burma. The military coup of 1962 and the subsequent imposition of the new military-dominated political system, under the leadership of the Burma Socialist Programme Party (BSPP), the only legitimate political party, stifled the political position of the Muslims and constricted the avenues of their political participation. The divisions between the Muslims have also been effectively used to create a state of sustained disunity among the Muslims. Organizations like the Islamic Centre of Burma

(ICB) have adopted a much more sympathetic attitude towards the BSPP and the Burmese government,[59] whereas others, like Jamiatul Ulama, are at best ambivalent in their attitudes towards the present political leadership of Burma. In the case of the Arakan border with Bangladesh where Muslims predominate, the Rohingya National Liberation Front (RNLF) continues to wage an anti-government insurgency in pursuit of the goal of political secession from Burma. The Kawthoolay Muslim National Liberation Front (KMNLF) acting in collaboration with the Karen National Liberation Army, has also begun to harass the Burmese government with its propaganda as well as guerrilla warfare. On the other hand, Muslims are also represented in the BSPP and the government although on the basis of representing not the Muslims' interest but rather the interests of the Party and the wider Burmese society.[60]

Thailand

Islam is the second most important religion in Thailand after Buddhism in terms of the number of its adherents. According to official figures, Muslims constitute about 4 per cent of the total population of Thailand which now stands at over 50 million people.[61] Other accounts project an even higher percentage of Muslims in Thailand.[62] What is significant to note is that the Muslims are a significant minority group within the kingdom. Although there is a large concentration of the Muslims in the four southernmost provinces of Satun, Narathiwat, Pattani, and Yala where they constitute the majority group, they are also spread all over the kingdom in over thirty other provinces. There are over 2,000 registered mosques in Thailand, and the number in Metropolitan Bangkok alone is almost double that of the total number of mosques in the Republic of Singapore.

The Muslims are not a homogeneous group. Officially the term *Thai-Issalaam* or *Thai-Mussulim* is used to describe them. In some circles Muslims are referred to as *khaeg*, a label which is detested by them because of its derogatory connotations.[63]

Numerically, the Malay-Muslims constitute the largest single ethnic group within the Muslim community which also consists of non-Malay Muslims such as the Haw Muslims, the Javanese, the Sam Sams, the Baweanese, the Pathans, the Punjabis, the Tamils, the Bengalis, the Muslim-Siamese, and so on. Politically, the Malay-Muslims are a strong group, because they live in areas contiguous to Malaysia and continue to be drawn towards Malay culture. The other non-Malay Muslims have assimilated into Thai society linguistically and are hardly distinguishable from other Thais in many other ways except, of course, in the area of religious observances.

The Muslims in Thailand are basically of rural background. The majority of them are farmers and smallholders. In the southern region, a large number of Muslims are engaged in fishing. In Bangkok and other urban centres of Thailand, the majority of Muslims work as petty traders, hawkers, labourers, factory hands, and government employees. There is also, however, a small but growing category of Muslim professionals in industry, commerce, banking, medicine, and law. There are also Muslims in the police force and the military. On the whole, the economic profile of the Muslims differs little from that of their Thai-Buddhist counterparts.

Politically, the problem of Malay-Muslim secessionism continues to harass the kingdom. Malay-Muslim separatist insurgent movements led by a number of organizations like the Pattani United Liberation Organization (PULO), Barisan Nasional Pembebasan Pattani (BNPP) or the National Revolution Liberation Front, Barisan Revolusi Nasional (BRN) or the National Revolution Front, and other splinter groups, though ineffective, are far from over.[64] The desire for cultural autonomy by the Malay-Muslims is often viewed with apprehension by the Thai authorities who are suspicious of secessionist motives. The Malay-Muslims, on the other hand, view the reluctance to allow them to pursue their legitimate cultural aspirations as evidence of Thai designs to subjugate them culturally. Unsympathetic local officials, overzealous in carrying out their duties, have often made things even more difficult. But successive Thai governments, in their efforts to draw out positive responses from the Muslims, have given the Muslim community a range of religious concessions. This strategy has had the effect of motivating "assimilated" Muslims to undertake the political socialization of their Malay-Muslim brethren and to develop more positive attitudes towards Thailand. With the revival of democracy in Thailand in 1979, Malay-Muslim participation in the political system, as citizens of Thailand and not just Malay-Muslims or Muslims, has been slowly growing.[65]

The Muslims are given complete freedom in the practice of their religion. In fact, government assistance is provided to the Muslims to subsidize their religious activities. The Muslims are also permitted to conduct *dakwah* activities. They may also organize themselves and undertake the publication of Islamic religious literature, which is now on the increase. None the less, the Muslims themselves are not free from schisms. There are no less than four major groups that claim to represent the interests of the Muslims namely, the *Chularatmontri*[66] group which is state-supported, the modernist group which publishes the journal *Al-Jihad*, the orthodox group which publishes *Al-Rabbitah*, and the traditional Malay-Muslim group in the south which rejects the *Chularatmontri* leadership whilst refusing to be drawn into the *Al-Jihad-Al-Rabbitah* rivalry. Regardless of the schisms in Thai Muslim society, on the whole, there seems to be a growing concern and commitment to Islam by the Muslims of Thailand.

Conclusion

The great period of Islam in Southeast Asia appears to belong to the distant rather than the immediate past. This was the era when the Muslims were dominant in trade and commerce, controlled shipping, had political influence and power, were possessed with a missionary zeal to proselytize, were men of culture and learning, and belonged to an international order that controlled more than half of the world at that time. But, this era had been overshadowed by the developments of the last two hundred years or so which witnessed the gradual erosion and relegation of the civilization of Islam to the status and role of just another religious belief system, along with others. By the nineteenth century, the Western powers had succeeded in overpowering the Muslims politically. The economic supremacy of the Muslims, which was under challenge even earlier, was ended. Their technological know-how on shipping and trade was overtaken. The Muslim initiative was arrested. The international order, which strengthened the position of local rulers in the region, foundered. Islam itself had to face fierce competition from Christianity. Western colonialism brought in new ideas, new institutions, and a completely new international order; secular ideals were introduced; immigrants were brought in to the region from India and China; new political frontiers were created disregarding historical realities; Western legal systems were adopted; and modern bureaucracies set up.

The Muslims retreated to culture and religion, this time in a very narrow sense. Religious education was emphasized. Change was resisted and, by and large, they became immobilized. They continued to look towards the Middle East for inspiration and leadership, but the Middle East too was under severe attack from colonialism. New ideas on how Islam should grapple with modern conditions began to be generated and gave birth to Islamic revivalism which viewed the conventional and rigid approach to Islam as unhelpful.

The phenomenon of new nation-states, demanding new forms of loyalty, and heavily influenced by Western political culture, posed grave difficulties for the Muslims. To a great extent, they represented the old societies in Southeast Asia which actually survived in spite of colonialism. But the realities before them had changed so much, particularly at the national, regional, and global levels, that they found these incomprehensible. Compared to other religious communities in the region, the Muslims probably had far greater difficulties in readjusting to the demands brought about by the emergence of the nation-state. New political institutions which became integral to the nation-state, such as a constitution, a secular legal system, citizenship, political parties, elections, and so on, were unfamiliar to them. This was even more so for the Muslim masses who tried to insulate themselves from what was perceived as an undesirable colonial, Western, and Christian culture.

The chronic problem of armed Muslim insurgency in Southeast Asia in pursuit of the goals of secessionism is far from over. The post-Second World War experiment with nationhood is still going on. The shortcomings of liberal democracy are glaring. Following the phenomenon of global Islamic resurgence in the 1970s and the 1980s, there has been a demand among

Muslims to reassess the whole range of Western ideas, values, and concepts which appear to have created tensions, dissatisfactions, and even disillusionment among the people. There has been a demand for de-secularization and Islamization, whatever these may mean. But as it is, Islam, as represented by the Muslims themselves, has little or no attraction at all to the non-Muslims. In fact, even the Muslims are restless. This is largely because, in contrast to the all-encompassing civilizational role of its glorious past, Islam has now been merely reduced to a narrow religious faith. Hitherto, it was virtually theology alone that was emphasized. The single medium through which the message of Islam has been put through all these years, is not only ineffective but also outdated. All this notwithstanding, Islamic resurgence is clearly under way. With the tremendous resources available in Southeast Asia, in terms of manpower, raw materials, capital, markets, entrepreneurial skills, and a probably renewed and religiously-inspired vigour to look for alternatives, the future certainly looks promising not just for the Muslims or the people of Southeast Asia, but for humanity as a whole, especially if these resources are constructively and imaginatively mobilized and organized.

NOTES

1 The Constitution of Brunei explicitly makes this provision.

2 The Federal Constitution merely states that "Islam is the religion of the Federation". *The Federal Constitution*, Part 1, Art. 3(1). This, however, has been interpreted by the government to mean an official status. For further discussion on this, see L.A. Sheridan and H.E. Groves, *The Constitution of Malaysia* (Singapore: Malaysia Law Journal, 1979), pp. 35-37, and Datuk Justice Hashim bin Yeop A. Sani, *Our Constitution* (Kuala Lumpur: The Law Publishers, 1980), pp. 159-165.

3 S.Q. Fatimi, *Islam Comes to Malaysia* (Singapore: Malaysian Sociological Research Institute, 1963), pp. 66-69.

4 For a concise account of the role of Malacca in the spread of Islam, see D.G.E. Hall, *A History of Southeast Asia*, 4th ed. (London: Macmillan, 1981), pp. 221-235. See also M.A. Rauf, *A Brief History of Islam with Special Reference to Malaysia* (Kuala Lumpur: Oxford University Press, 1964), pp. 84.

5 Hall, op. cit., p. 230.

6 Cesar Adib Majul, *Muslims in the Philippines* (Quezon City: University of the Philippines, 1973), pp. 72-73.

7 Hall, op. cit., p. 198.

8 Majul, op. cit.

9 Lain Yock Fang, *Undang Undang Melaka* (The Hague: Martinus Nijhoff, 1976), p. 163.

10 M.G. Hooker, "The Trengganu Inscription in Malayan Legal History", *Journal of the Malaysian Branch of the Royal Asiatic Society* 49, no. 2 (1976): 127-131.

11 For a useful introduction on Islamic law in Pattani, see Mohd. Zawawi Salleh, "Pentadbiran Undang Undang Islam di Pattani" Kertas Projek (Kuala Lumpur: Fakulti Undang-Undang Universiti Malaya, 1978/79) (in Malay).

12 John E. Kempe and R.O. Windstedt, *A Malay Legal Digest*, compiled for Abd al-Ghafur Muhaiyuddin Shah Sultan of Pahang, *Journal of the Malayan Branch of the Royal Asiatic Society*, 21 (1948): 24-25.

13 Ibn Muhammad Ibrahim, *The Ship of Sulaiman*, trans. John O'Kane (London: Routledge and Kegan Paul, 1972), pp. 94-97. For an overview of the role of Muslims in this period, see Omar Farouk Shaeik Ahmad, "Muslims in the Kingdom of Ayutthaya", *JEBAT, Journal of the History Department Universiti Kebangsaan Malaysia*, Bil. 10. (1980/1): 206-214.

14 Andrew Forbes. "Tenasserim: The Thai Kingdom of Ayutthaya's Link with the Indian Ocean", *Indian Ocean Newsletter* 3, no. 1 (June 1982).

15 Moshe Yegar, *The Muslims of Burma: A Study of a Minority Group* (Wiesbaden: Otto Harrassowitz, 1972), p. 2.

16 Ibid.

17 Ibid.

18 Ibid.

19 Ibid., p. 3. See also G.E. Harvey, *Outline of Burmese History* (Calcutta: Orient Longman Ltd., 1954 rep.), p. 52 and G.H. Luce, "Geography of Burma under the Pagan Dynasty", *Journal of the Burma Research Society* 42, Part 1 (1959): 50.

20 Forbes, op. cit.

21 Yegar, op. cit., p. 10.

22 Ibid.

23 Harvey, op. cit., pp. 91-92.

24 Yegar, op. cit., p. 46; see also Moshe Yegar, "The 'Panthay' of Burma and Yunnan", *Journal of Southeast Asian History* 7 (March 1966): 73-85.

25 Hall, op. cit., p. 460.

26 *Annual Report 1920*, quoted in Ibrahim Saad, "Pemasyarakatan dan Pendidikan: Matlamat Persekolahan dari zaman penjajah ke zaman ekonomi baru", in *Pendidikan Arah Perpaduan: Sebuah Perspektif Sejarah*, edited by Awang Had Salleh (Kuala

Lumpur: Penerbit Fajar Bakti, 1980), p. 129.

27 Hall, op. cit., p. 572.

28 For a discussion on the implications of this, see Ranjit Singh, *Brunei, 1839-1983: The Problems of Political Survival* (Kuala Lumpur: Oxford University Press, 1985), pp. 7-11, 81-105.

29 *From Secession to Autonomy: Self-Government in Southern Philippines* (Manila: Ministry of Foreign Affairs, September 1980), p. 4.

30 Ibid.

31 Yegar, op. cit., p. 30.

32 Hall, op. cit., p. 895.

33 For a comprehensive history of the evolution of Brunei until the eve of independence, see Ranjit Singh, op. cit.

34 George McTurnan Kahin, ed., *Government and Politics of Southeast Asia* (Ithaca, New York: Cornell University Press, 1966), pp. 693-698.

35 For details on the constitution of 1974, see Albert D. Moscotti, *Burma's Constitution and Election of 1974*, Research Notes and Discussions No. 5 (Singapore: Institute of Southeast Asian Studies, 1977).

36 The United Nations and the ASEAN States and many other western countries do not recognize the sovereignty of the People's Republic of Kampuchea under Heng Samrin. They recognize the Coalition Government of Democratic Kampuchea in exile comprising the Khmer Rouge, Khmer People's National Liberation Front, and Prince Norodom Sihanouk and his loyalists.

37 *Pancasila* incorporates five basic principles which are (1) belief in the oneness of God or Divine Omnipotence; (2) humanitarianism; (3) national unity; (4) democracy or people's sovereignty; and (5) social justice. It is the state that further defines these principles and translates them into action. For more insights on the *Pancasila* in Indonesia and related issues, see Saifuddin Anshari, *The Jakarta Charter 1945* (Kuala Lumpur: Muslim Youth Movement of Malaysia, 1979), pp. 10-17.

38 Deliar Noer, *Administration of Islam in Indonesia*, Monograph Series No. 58 (Ithaca: New York, Cornell University, 1978), pp. 42-45.

39 Ibid., pp. 74-75.

40 For an interesting analysis on the problems of parliamentary democracy in Indonesia, see Herbert Feith, *The Decline of Constitutional Democracy in Indonesia* (Ithaca: New York, 1962).

41 *The Federal Constitution*, Art. 160(2).

42 It must be qualified though that the party has chosen to achieve this through constitutional means. See for example *Manifesto Pas Negeri Kelantan 1986* (Kelantan:

Perhubungan PAS Negeri Kelantan, 1986), p. 5, (in Malay).

43 *Singapore 1986* (Singapore, Information Division, Ministry of Communications and Information, 1986), p. 8.

44 Ibid., p. 11.

45 In 1985, there were 1,122 Chinese Muslims in Singapore (Ibid., p. 11).

46 *Muslims in Singapore: A Photographic Portrait* (Singapore: Muslim Religious Council of Singapore, 1985).

47 Ibid.

48 The others include Angkatan Islam and Persatuan Melayu Singapura. See *Singapore 1986*, op. cit., p. 210.

49 *Muslims in Singapore*, op. cit.

50 Ibid.

51 *Singapore 1986*, op. cit., p. 12.

52 *Muslims in Singapore*, op. cit.

53 *From Secession to Autonomy*, op. cit., p. 2.

54 Ibid., p. 4.

55 Michael O. Mastura, *Muslim Filipino Experience: A Collection of Essays* (Manila: Ministry of Muslim Affairs, 1984), p. 178.

56 *From Secession to Autonomy*, op. cit., pp. 20-23.

57 *1983 Population Census*. (Advance Release).

58 For a discussion on the terms Kala, Zerbadees, and Panthay, see Yegar, op. cit., p. 6, footnote 3 and pp. 33-35.

59 See for example, "Special Report for the Attention of the New Excom. of RISEAP 1983" (Islamic Centre of Burma, 1983). Typescript.

60 For example, U Vamthu Hashim has been a member of the State Council for some time now.

61 In 1983, there were 1,869,427 Muslims in Thailand. See *The Siam Directory 1986: The Book of Facts and Figures* (Bangkok: Tawanna Publicationns, 1986), pp. 2-37.

62 I have discussed this controversy elsewhere. See Omar Farouk, "The Muslims of Thailand", in *ISLAMIKA*, edited by Lutfi Ibrahim (Kuala Lumpur: Sarjana Enterprise, 1981), p. 98.

63 Ibid., pp. 116-117.

64 For a more detailed discussion of the problem of Malay-Muslim separatism, see Omar Farouk, "The Historical and Transnational Dimensions of Malay-Muslim Separatism in Southern Thailand", in *Armed Separatism in Southeast Asia*, edited by Lim Joo-Jock and Vani S. (Singapore: Institute of Southeast Asian Studies, 1984), pp. 234-257. See also Surin Pitsuwan, *Islam and Malay Nationalism* (Bangkok: Thai Khadi Research Institute, Thammasat University, 1985), pp. 226-244.

65 An impressive list of Malay-Muslim candidates representing all the political parties of Thailand took part in the 1979, 1983, and 1986 Thai general elections. The Malay-Muslim electorate also participated actively in these elections. In the July 1986 elections, the following Malay-Muslim candidates were elected to the Thai House of Representatives: Areepen Uttarasingh (Democrat), Seni Madakakul (Community Action), Den Tohmeena (Democrat), Sudin Phyuthanont (United Democratic), Wan Munamaduor Mata (Democrat), Adul Phuminarong (United Democratic), and Chirayus Naowakate (Progress).

66 *Chularatmontri* is the title of the office given to the Supreme Head of Islam (Shaikhul Islam) by the Thai government. The *Chularatmontri* is appointed by the Thai King and is head of a nation-wide Islamic religious bureaucracy which links up all the registered mosques in Thailand at all levels.

3 ISLAMIC BANKING: THEORY AND PRACTICE

Muhammad Nejatullah Siddiqi

Introduction

The Qur'an categorically prohibits interest and forbids any claim in excess of the sum lent, that is, the principal (Qu'ran, II: 278-279). This is irrespective of the purpose for which the loan is taken, so that interest is prohibited on loans for productive activities as well as on consumption loans.

The prohibition on interest automatically makes lending a charitable activity, leaving one's business to be financed either by one's own capital or capital acquired on the basis of profit-sharing. While interest is prohibited, trade is lawful and so is the resulting profit (Qur'an, II: 275; LXII: 10; IV: 29). One can seek profit singly, employing one's own capital, or jointly in partnership with others who also bring in their own capital. It is also perfectly legitimate to seek profit through *mudaraba* (profit-sharing), that is financing a working party on the condition that the latter will surrender a percentage of the realized profits to the financier. The risk of loss is borne by the owner of capital in all the three cases of self-finance, partnerships, and profit-sharing. Both partnerships and profit-sharing are explicitly approved by the Prophet.[1]

In a simple economy where agriculture and handicrafts are the main forms of economic activity, such activities are mostly owner-financed. As trade grows, direct finance appears on the scene, and business activity in a society which prohibits lending on interest is increasingly financed on the basis of partnerships and profit-sharing. Direct finance, where the owner of capital deals directly with the user of capital has, however, some serious drawbacks. It cannot cope with rapid trade flows in an expanding market. Fund owners seek someone in the neighbourhood whom they can entrust their funds with but the period for which the funds are sought or the risks involved in a particular venture may not suit a fund owner. This could lead to (unintended) hoarding and, ultimately, discourage savings. At this stage, middlemen would appear offering their services to manage these funds to the satisfaction of their owners, and the fund seekers would also find it more convenient to deal with the middlemen. Thus emerges a system of indirect finance in which the surplus units and deficit units do not deal with each other directly. Instead, there is an intermediary which obtains funds from the surplus units in order to supply them to the deficit units. Financial intermediation makes it possible to mobilize large funds by accommodating savers with different amounts of savings, different time horizons, and different levels of risk acceptance, and to cater to fund seekers with different needs with respect to the size of the funds required, the time horizon, and the risks involved, by adjusting the terms of the contract to suit the different categories. Financial intermediaries are able not only to spread risks, but also to develop the expertise needed for ascertaining the profitability of the projects for which the funds are sought. They are also in a better position than the fund owners to monitor the progress of the projects in which their funds are invested, advise the fund users, and ensure that the norms of sound management as well as the terms of the financial contract are being honoured. As a result of these advantages, indirect finance grows in size relative to direct finance as the economy diversifies itself and the market expands.

Self-finance and direct finance dominated the scene in seventh century Arabia. Interest-bearing loans as well as partnerships and *mudaraba* were in vogue. With the prohibition of interest, trade was financed by funds owned by the trader or acquired from fund owners on the basis of profit-sharing. Trade credit also continued, divested of any increment against delay in repayment. Agriculture, (if the landowner himself did not till the land) was conducted on the basis of sharing the crop between the landowner and the peasant. Share-cropping, as discussed by the jurists, is amenable to a variety of arrangements.[2] It can be reasonably presumed that the owner-cultivator or the one who cultivated a rented land could utilize *bai' salam* (prepaid orders) as a mode of financing agricultural activity. It could also be applied to non-agricultural goods, especially handicrafts and manufactures.[3] The *Hadith* relating to *bai' salam* implies that this mode of financing was in practice during the Prophet's time.[4]

As trade expanded and the economy became more diversified, Islamic jurists also approved indirect finance on the basis of profit-sharing, *al mudarib yudarib*. This is evidenced by their discussion on whether a party who had obtained capital from its owner on the basis of profit-sharing was entitled to enter into a profit-sharing arrangement with another party who would actually use the fund.[5] It is not clear if the practice of two-tier *mudaraba* reflected in these juristic discussions had evolved into pure financial intermediation, where one who obtained profit-sharing funds conducts the sole business of supplying these funds to other (working) parties on the basis of profit-sharing. What is important for us in this paper is, however, the fact that the permissibility of doing so was made the basis of a new model of banking by a large number of Muslim economists and jurists writing between 1945 and 1975.[6] This new model of banking rests essentially on a two-tier *mudaraba* contract, the first contract between the depositors and the bank and the second contract between the bank and the fund users.

This paper aims at providing some insight into the institution of Islamic banking as conceived by economists and jurists and as practised in several countries. The rest of this paper is structured as follows: there is, first, an exposition of the theory of commercial banking and the role of the central bank in an Islamic framework. This is followed by a brief discussion on non-bank financial intermediaries as well as possible modes of financing other than those based on profit-sharing. The practice of Islamic banking, covering not only country experiences where the whole financial system is being reorganized along Islamic lines but also experiments by individual Islamic financial institutions operating in the rest of the world, is then discussed. Separate notice is taken of the Islamic Development Bank, in this discussion. Finally, some of the problems facing Islamic banking and their possible solutions are examined.

Theory of Islamic Banking

Commercial Banking in Islam: A Simple Model

A bank is organized as a joint stock company with the shareholders supplying the initial capital. It is managed by the shareholders through their representatives on the board of directors. Its main business is to obtain funds from the public on the basis of *mudaraba* and to supply funds to businessmen on the same basis. Its gross income comprises the share in the actual profits of the fund users, in accordance with an agreed ratio of profit-sharing. This income, after deducting the expenses incurred in managing the funds, is distributed *pro rata* on share capital as well as deposits. The bank retains, in favour of its shareholders, a part of profits accruing to deposits in accordance with the predetermined profit-sharing ratio.

This is a very simplified picture which ignores variety in the type of deposits as well as variety in the nature of the activities of the bank. It also ignores reserves and taxes. It does enable us, however, to focus attention on the main difference between conventional banking and Islamic banking, that is, the replacement of interest by profit-sharing. It would be appropriate, therefore, to elaborate on this difference before additional factors are introduced in the model. We do so by asking what does the change from interest to profit-sharing mean for the three parties immediately involved: the fund users, the depositors, and the banks, and what would be the consequences for the system as a whole.

Debt finance carries an obligation to repay the sum borrowed plus a predetermined return, irrespective of the actual outcome of the project in which the funds are employed. The shift to profit-sharing relieves the fund user of this obligation, replacing it by an obligation to surrender an agreed percentage of realized profits to the bank, along with the funds acquired from it. Should there be no profits, the fund user repays only what he obtained. In the case of a loss, he returns the funds minus the losses incurred. In this case, as in the case where there are neither profits nor losses, the fund user's own entrepreneurial services go unrewarded, but he does not have to bear any losses accruing to capital obtained on a profit-sharing basis.

This change in the financial obligation of fund users towards the bank, from a fixed amount (that is, principal plus interest) to an amount varying with the actual results of the enterprise, has a deep impact on the behaviour of the fund users. They are still keen to make profits as their reward hinges on profits. But, they can now take more risks and embark upon promising innovative ventures, unfettered as they are by any fixed obligation. It should be noted, however, that they are able to do so only when they can convince the bank of the soundness of the proposed venture. Unlike debt finance, *mudaraba* finance would be available only after the financier has satisfied himself about the prospects of the project to be financed. Capital employed in business enterprise still carries a cost to the entrepreneur (the firm), but this cost is now a function of the actual returns to the enterprise.

The change in the financial obligation of the firm towards the bank, from a fixed amount to a variable amount, eliminates the asymmetry found in the conventional framework between the fixity of interest rates and the uncertainty in rates of profit. This removes a basic cause of instability in the economy. A profit-sharing contract between the financiers and the firms ensures that the payment commitments of the firm vary with the variations in the receipts of the firm.

As regards the bank itself, replacement of interest by profit-sharing in its contract with the depositors as well as with the fund users implies that there is always an equilibrium between its assets and liabilities as the latter is automatically adjusted to any change in the former. In the interest system, shocks to the bank's asset position caused by default or by bankruptcy of the debtors is not absorbed as the depositors' claims to their deposits and interest is not affected by a change in the asset position. The replacement of interest by profit-sharing would, therefore, prevent crises in the banking industry, thus contributing to stability in the system.

A change-over from interest to profit-sharing links the return on deposits to the actual returns in the production sector, via two-tier *mudaraba*. This would automatically protect their values from being eroded by inflation – whereas the rates of interest notoriously lag behind the rate of inflation, the average rate of profit in the economy does not. The possibility of receiving no returns at all is only a theoretical proposition as a policy of diversification of investment by the banks should be sufficient, in normal circumstances, to prevent such an eventuality. It is only during a global recession that depositors may be exposed to losses, something that no system, including the one based on interest, can prevent, except in so far as deposit insurance and reserves can mitigate the actual circumstances. It can also be convincingly argued that a shift from interest to profit-sharing minimizes the chances of a global recession.

A shift from interest to profit-sharing makes it necessary for the bank to scrutinize and assess the prospects of the projects for which bank funds are being sought. Instead of being a mere financier, the bank takes on the role of that of a financier-entrepreneur. The actual returns to the bank depend, in the profit-sharing framework, on the soundness of the project and the business acumen and managerial competence of the fund users, on whom would depend, among other factors, the actual profits of the project. The credit worthiness of the fund seeker, the decisive factor in the interest-based system, is irrelevant in the profit-sharing system. This would ensure that the allocation of investible funds is in accordance with the expected profitability of projects.

In a profit-sharing system of finance, the entrepeneurs, the banks, and the depositors, all stand to gain or lose together. Their prospects always move in the same direction. The bigger the profits in business enterprise, the higher the returns to the depositors and the shareholders of the banks. Any adverse change in the production sector causing profits to fall are equitably distributed among the three parties involved rather than sporadically causing bankruptcies and bank failures.

Islamic Commercial Banks: A Realistic Model

The deposits introduced in the simple model were in general investment accounts, to be pooled together and invested. There would also be specific investment accounts in which deposits are made for investments in particular projects. It is also possible to conceive special investment accounts in which deposits are made on the condition that they be invested in particular business activities, for example, trade financing on a *mudaraba* (mark-up) basis, or leasing, and so on. Then, there are current accounts in which deposits are made to be withdrawn at any time. These are checking accounts on which banks pay no profit but they are allowed to use these deposits profitably at their own risk. Demand deposits are in the nature of loans to banks whose repayment is guaranteed. In sum, bank funds now comprise share capital, demand deposits, and various types of investment deposits.

Bank activities, to begin with, now consist of, in the first instance, numerous conventional banking services, for example, safekeeping, transfer, agency functions, consultancy services, etc. These services are rendered for a fee or commission which is higher than their costs, yielding some net income to the bank. Secondly, banks also hold common stock, investment certificates, and any other financial instruments, available in a profit-sharing system, that can yield a return. Thirdly, banks enter into partnerships with businessmen providing part of the capital and participating in the management. In accordance with the rules governing partnership in Islamic law, banks will be liable to losses in proportion to the funds supplied by them to the total capital of the firm, but they can share the profits of the firm in any ratio agreed with the firm. Fourth, banks supply funds on a *mudaraba* basis as described in the simple model. A fifth activity would be to supply short-term interest-free loans. The availability to commercial banks of demand deposits on which no returns are to be paid justifies obliging them to supply interest-free loans to the public on a very limited scale. The system would need such loans in order to deal with situations in which needed funds cannot be arranged on any other basis. Part of these loans may be earmarked for the goverment, the banks being obliged to hold some government loan certificates,[7] and the rest for the customers, in the form of overdrafts.[8]

Compared to our simple model, banks may now be portrayed as playing a more pronounced entrepreneurial role. They are selling banking services, engaging in partnerships, and buying and selling financial instruments. But their actual involvement in productive activities, such as trade, industry, agriculture, etc., remains largely indirect. The model still retains the chief distinguishing feature of the simple *mudaraba*-based model in that the returns to the use of bank funds are uncertain.

These were the activities of Islamic banks as envisaged in the theoretical literature on Islamic banking published *before* the emergence of Islamic banks in the mid-1970s. With the establishment of Islamic financial institutions, the role of Islamic banks also branched into the actual conduct of businesses (for example, trading, construction, manufacture, farming, etc.). More important, they even began to adopt some modes of business with predetermined returns.

A review of Islamic banking practices is made in the next section, linking these activities to the theory of Islamic banking. This will enable us to update the "realistic" model described above by including the new activities in which the Islamic banks are presently engaged. There are basically three new activities to note: *murabaha*, *ijara*, and *bai' salam*.

Murabaha or cost-plus financing is also called *bai'-mu'ajjal* (that is, sale with deferred payment). The bank purchases the goods needed by a client and sells them to him with a mark-up (that is, cost plus an agreed profit margin), with payments being made in instalments over a specified period of time. It is business and not financial intermediation as the bank actually "buys" the goods and then sells them to the client. However, it is business only in name, as the bank buys only when it has a firm commitment[9] from the client to buy the goods at a price higher than the purchase price. The two acts of buying and selling may be done simultaneously so that, in effect, it amounts to the bank financing the clients' acquisition of goods against a predetermined "profit".

Ijara is a form of leasing. The bank acquires industrial equipment or a building and rents it to the user against a fixed charge paid periodically. Another variant of this contract is *ijara wa igtina'* (hire purchase) in which the client ultimately acquires ownership of the rented asset by paying its cost in instalments along with the rent or rental. The "rent" in this case decreases as the bank's share in the ownership of the asset decreases and that of the client increases. Though the bank is exposed to risks as long as it retains ownership of the asset, these risks are insurable and may be conveniently passed on to the client. As the rents are contractually fixed for the entire life of the asset, the whole operation earns a predetermined return on the bank funds involved.

As already noted above, *salam* is a sale contract in which the price is paid at the time of contracting whereas the delivery of the good sold takes place at a future date. Though generally applied to agricultural produce, it can also be applied to manufactures. Immediate payment of the full price is mandatory in the case of agricultural goods but it is not necessary in the case of handicrafts and manufactures.[10] It is permissible for the buyer to sell the goods purchased (which are to be delivered at a future date) to another party through a fresh *salam* contract.[11]

These contracts have been adapted by Islamic banks. It will be noted, however, that *murabaha*, *ijara*, and *salam* as discussed by the jurists were genuine trading activities and not financing operations.

The Financial Market

Commercial banks may not be the only financial institutions in an Islamic economy. Non-bank financial intermediaries may specialize in the creation and marketing of negotiable financial instruments. Some of the financial instruments envisaged in an interest-free Islamic economy are described below.

Investment Certificates. Funds may be mobilized from savers on the condition that a specified percentage of the profits resulting from their investment, which may accrue to the financial intermediary, will be paid to fund owners. The remaining part of the profit-share will be retained by the intermediary who will issue a certificate to the fund owner stating the amount, the period for which the funds are deposited, the ratio of profit-sharing and, where relevant, the business in which the investment is to be made. The fund owners will be exposed to any loss that occurs, limited to the amount of their deposits. These "investment certificates" could be traded.

Leasing Certificate. It is possible to devise financial instruments based on leasing. Assets such as buildings and industrial equipment may be acquired by a leasing agency and rented out against periodic payments. The leasing agency may finance its operations by selling leasing certificates, the owners of these certificates being entitled to a proportionate share in the yields of the assets leased net of administrative expenses. Different financial institutions may specialize in holding and marketing leasing certificates related to buildings, ships, aircraft, industrial equipment, agricultural machinery, warehouses, etc.[12]

Deposit Certificates. The government may also mobilize private savings for financing public sector enterprises by selling investment certificates. The central bank, in an interest-free Islamic economy, may sell investment certificates and invest the proceeds through the banking system.[13] These certificates may be issued in different denominations and with different maturities to suit the needs of various groups of savers.

It is envisaged that a secondary market will then develop in which the above mentioned financial papers could be sold and resold before maturity. This will widen the choice available to savers, facilitate the transfer of funds to entrepreneurs, and provide the monetary authorities with a monetary policy tool.

The Monetary Authority: Role of the Central Bank

Like any other society, an Islamic society needs a monetary authority to manage its money and supervise its financial market. Proper management of money has two main objectives. It should supply enough money to facilitate and promote exchange and satisfy the liquidity needs of the people. Its second objective is to ensure a reasonable degree of stability in the purchasing power of money in a growing economy. As economic growth cannot be taken for granted, monetary policy has to be geared consciously to promote economic development. One of the major impediments to development is inflation which saps public confidence in money and discourages savings by increasing the uncertainty about their real value in the future.

The central bank in an Islamic society will be the sole source of high-powered money. It will, therefore, be in a position to control the supply of money and credit whether we have a fractional reserve system, preferred by most because of the flexibility it affords,[14] or a 100 per cent reserve system.[15] The central bank will also enjoy the following powers:

a) Fixing reserve and liquidity ratios against various kinds of deposits;
b) Sale and purchase of deposit certificates and other negotiable financial papers;
c) Fixing the lending ratio (which refers to the percentage of the demand deposits which the commercial banks are obliged to lend free of interest);
d) Fixing the refinance ratio (which refers to the percentage of a commercial bank's lending which the central bank will finance free of interest);
e) Supplying funds to commercial banks on a profit-sharing basis;
f) Fixing certain profit-sharing ratios or prescribing a range within which they are allowed to vary;
g) Fixing the maximum and minimum percentage of profits the banks may realize from non-sharing modes of finance, for example,

murabaha, leasing, hire purchase and *salam*;

h) Regulating the service charges the banks may levy on interest-free loans;
i) Specifying the minimum percentage of expected profits which would qualify an investment project for selection by the banks;
j) Fixing the maximum and/or minimum amount of finance the banks may provide under the various financing techniques permissible;
k) Regulating the exchange rate of the currency;
l) Supervising foreign operations of domestic banks and domestic operations of foreign banks;
m) Obliging the commercial banks and other financial intermediaries to give priority to, or offer special terms to, certain sectors of the economy; and
n) Obliging the commercial banks to invest part of their demand deposits in the form of the central bank's deposit certificates or government loan certificates.

It should be noted, without going into details which are available elsewhere,[16] that the above list contains sufficient means of quantitative and qualitative control of the supply of money and credit. In addition to ensuring liquidity and maintaining stability, the Islamic central bank is obliged to ensure fair play and justice in the financial market through close supervision. One important aspect of this task is to ensure the proper maintenance of accounts by fund users as well as by the banks and other financial intermediaries. In a financial system based on profit-sharing, not only the returns to the funds supplied but also their repayment devolves on the actual profits of the enterprise in which these funds are invested. The interests of millions of depositors and buyers of investment certificates and financial instruments can be protected only through proper auditing of the accounts of firms, joint stock companies, banks, and other business and financial institutions. It is advisable that, in an Islamic economy, this function be performed by an autonomous agency working in close co-operation with the Monetary Authority.

Islamic Banking in Practice

Islamic Banks during the 1970s

Early theoretical works on Islamic banking envisaged a change in the entire system from interest to profit-sharing and equity participation. Little attention was paid to the possibility of individual financial institutions operating without interest within the existing system.[17] This issue was subsequently taken up by some scholars as well as businessmen,[18] and it was the establishment of individual financial institutions that heralded the modern practice of Islamic banking.

The reasons for the approach are quite understandable. The political conditions during the third quarter of the century in almost all Muslims countries were hardly favourable for a change in the entire system of banking and finance. As a matter of fact, the first modern experiment with Islamic banking was launched under cover[19] as local savings banks without projecting an Islamic image.[20] The most that could be expected from the rulers in these circumstances was "permission" to establish Islamic financial institutions through private initiatives. This is how a number of Islamic banks and financial institutions were established in the Middle East during the 1970s.[21]

There were also some beginnings in South and Southeast Asia. The Muslim Pilgrims' Savings Corporation (now known as the Pilgrims' Management and Fund Board) was launched in Malaysia in 1963 to help people save with a view to performing the hadj (pilgrimage to Mecca). These savings are invested in shares, real estate, and a number of subsidiary companies engaged in construction, transport, agriculture, etc. As at 30 June 1985, it had M$1,150 million in deposits belonging to 694,500 depositors.[22]

The idea of interest-free Islamic finance was also at work in Muslim minority countries as evidenced by the establishment of the Philippine Amanah Bank in 1973 and the proliferation of interest-free savings and loan societies in India during the 1970s. The first Islamic financial institution in a Western country, the Islamic Banking System (now known as the Islamic Finance House) in Luxembourg, was established in 1978.

Meanwhile the emergence of the Organization of Islamic Conference (OIC) in 1969 had created a viable basis for launching, in 1975, an international Islamic financial institution, the Islamic Development Bank (IDB), which would observe the rules of the *Shạria* (Islamic Law) while promoting economic development and social progress in Muslim countries and communities. An international Association of Islamic Banks was also established in 1977 to promote co-operation among Islamic banks and to co-ordinate their activities.

The Islamic banks accepted demand deposits with guaranteed repayment, on condition that they were allowed to use them profitably. They also accepted deposits in general investment accounts, the depositor being entitled to a share in the profits accruing to the bank. This share was specified as a percentage of total profits in most cases, but in some cases depositors were given a percentage return on their capital, announced at the end of the accounting period, increasing with the length of the periods for which the deposits were made.[23] There were also special investment accounts for long-term deposits.

Thus, the total bank funds consist of share capital supplied on the basis of *musharaka* (partnership) investment deposits mobilized on a *mudaraba* basis and demand deposits in the nature of loans (*qard*) without interest. There could also be trust funds managed for a fee, the bank acting as an agent. No Islamic bank operated any funds acquired with the promise to pay interest.

Islamic banks offered all the conventional banking services like safekeeping, transfer, etc., for a fee or a commission. They also opened letters of credit, generally on the basis of *murabaha*, but sometimes also on the basis of profit-sharing. In case of *murabaha*, the import documents are "purchased" by the bank and then "sold" to the importer with a mark-up on purchase price. This is how letters of credit are operated in Pakistan. In the case of letters of credit based on profit-sharing, the bank would share the profits with the importer.

All the Islamic banks have financed some projects on a *mudaraba* basis but *musharaka* has been more popular as it gives the banks a right to participate in the management of the fund-using enterprise. In view of the conditions prevailing in the developing countries in which most of the Islamic banks operate, financing under a partnership agreement has been found preferable to *mudaraba* in which management has to be entrusted to the fund-using party. *Murabaha* has become increasingly popular since the close of the 1970s. Some Islamic banks have also resorted to leasing.

Direct business – managing factories and farms, building houses to sell or rent, import, export, and trade in the domestic market, etc. – was mostly confined to the Dubai Islamic Bank, the Kuwait Finance House, and the Jordan Islamic Bank. While these activities overshadowed financial operations in these three institutions, they did not assume a dominant position in the activities of institutions elsewhere.

Islamic banks made steady progress during the seventies. Deposits increased in volume as well as in number.[24] More and more projects were financed and larger profits were distributed to shareholders as well as depositors, year after year.

Islamic Banks in the 1980s

At the end of 1979 there were twelve Islamic banks.[25] More Islamic banks were established during the next five years, so that their number (outside Pakistan and Iran) reached over fifty by 1985.[26] They follow more or less the same pattern as observed during the 1970s, but there is now a greater interaction among them because of the initiative taken by the Islamic Development Bank and the International Association of Islamic Banks. The emergence of Daral Mal al Islami (DMI), which has twenty-two subsidiaries and the Al Baraka Group to which nine institutions belong has introduced a new phase of integrated multinational institutions in the Islamic finance movement.

The DMI was established in 1981 as a holding company with an authorized capital of US$1 billion, divided in 10 million shares of equal value, for the purpose of conducting a diversity of financial business in accordance with the *Sharia*. The DMI functions only as a holding company, conducting business through operational subsidiaries which include banks, investment companies, and insurance (*takaful*) companies. As at 30 June 1985, its subscribed capital stood at US$316 million and it was administering funds exceeding US$1.3 billion.[27] The DMI distributed some modest profits to its shareholders for the first time in 1986 but the Islamic banks and investment companies affiliated to it have been regularly distributing profits comparable to other Islamic financial institutions. Part of the reason for not being able to distribute profits to DMI shareholders in the past was a net loss of US$48 million from investments in precious metals. The loss was, however, fully absorbed by the close of 1984, without any detriment to the planned expansion of the DMI.[28]

The DMI and its subsidiaries engage in four types of transactions: *murabaḥa*, *musharaka*, *mudaraba*, and leasing.[29] Some interest-free loans (without service charges) were also given with a view to promoting Islamic banking. According to its 1985 report, long-term investment on a *musharaka* basis accounted for 11 per cent of DMI income whereas *mudaraba* and other banking operations accounted for 62 per cent of its income. Another 24 per cent of the income came from short-term investments.[30]

Established in 1982, the Al Baraka group has nine affiliates. Besides *murabaha*, *musharaka*, *mudaraba*, and leasing, *bai' salam* is also mentioned as one of the activities planned. *Murabaha* has accounted for the bulk of the business so far,[31] but some effort is being made to use various profit-sharing modes of finance as well.

The Al Rajhi Company for Currency Exchange and Commerce, which has a very large network of branches in Saudi Arabia, has plans to operate as an Islamic investment company in the kingdom. It has already established the Al Rajhi Company for Islamic Investment as a consulting firm in London. Its main activity at present is money changing and some short-term investments but it is preparing itself for other investments once it establishes itself as an Islamic investment company.

Islamic Banking at the National Level

Islamic banking has been adopted at the national level in Pakistan and Iran. Sudan, which has the largest number of Islamic financial institutions of any country, also switched over to Islamic banking at the national level.

Pakistan. In Pakistan, the process began in September 1979 when the president of Pakistan asked the Council of Islamic Ideology to prepare a blueprint for an interest-free economic system. The Council submitted its *Report of Elimination of Interest from the Economy* in June 1980. Practical steps were taken during 1979-80 to reorganize non-bank financial institutions on an interest-free basis.[32] It is claimed that interest has been "eliminated", (gradually over a period starting 1981 and ending 1985) from the operations of commercial banks, the big five of which are nationalized. The only exceptions are foreign currency deposits which continue to be based on interest.[33] The State Bank of Pakistan, which is the country's central bank, has eliminated interest from all its domestic operations which are now based either on profit-sharing or on interest-free lending.[34] Also, "as from 1st July 1985 no banking company shall accept any interest bearing deposits" and "all savings accounts regardless of the date of opening shall be on the basis of participation in profit and loss of the banking company".[35]

Pakistani banks are now using four major forms of financing: lending, leasing, mark-ups, and profit-sharing. Each is briefly described below.

Lending takes the form either of *qardhasan* loans given on compassionate grounds with no interest or service charge (refundable if and when the borrower is able to pay) or of loans with a service charge not exceeding the proportionate cost of the operation. The State Bank of Pakistan is to determine the maximum service charge permissible to each bank from time to time. Finance of exports under the State Banks' Export Finance Scheme and the Scheme for Financing Locally Manufactured Machinery is also done on this basis. Interest-free loans without service charges, that is *qardhasan*, is provided to students for higher studies.[36]

Leasing is being used for financing fixed industrial investments. Equipment is rented to the project sponsor for a fixed payment over a specific period. "There are no limits on the rate of return which can be received by the bank or the financial institution."[37] Hire purchase is a form of lease in which "rental instalments are fixed in such a way that the actual amount invested by the bank and its share in rental income is recovered during the agreed period and within the normal useful life of the article financed".[38] This mode of finance is also used in the agricultural sector in the leasing of farm machinery, tube-wells, storage and other farm facilities, and dairy equipment. Consumer durables are also being financed on hire-purchase basis.[39]

Mark-ups are practised in the form of "purchase of goods by banks and their sale at appropriate mark up in price on deferred payment basis" and "purchase of moveable and immovable property by the banks from their clients with Buy-Back arrangement and otherwise".[40]

> In this mode of finance the customers owning property, goods or any other form of tangible security in order to put themselves in funds sell the property goods or tangible security to banks with a promise to buy back the same from the banks at a future date. The banks agree to resell the property, goods or tangible security to their customers on the basis of deferred payment either in lump sum or in instalments at a marked up price.[41]

It is interesting as well as instructive to note that the Pakistani system also allows "mark-down" on Documentary Inland Bills drawn against Letters of Credit and Export Bills in rupees. Mark-up is being used to finance commodity operations of the federal and provincial governments and their agencies, Import Bills drawn against Letters of Credit, fixed investments in industry, agricultural equipment, plough cattle, milch cattle and other livestock, orchards and nurseries, and forestry.[42] "Buy-back cum mark-up" is also allowed as a mode of financing housing.[43] Mark-up is also allowed in financing working capital for trade, industry, and agriculture,[44] using the buy-back arrangement described above.

In all cases where a mark-up or mark-down is allowed, the country's central bank is to fix a range for the annual rate of profit which can be realized in this manner.[45] In the absence of any specific formula, it should be presumed that this applies also to "development charges" allowed for financing land development and water course improvement[46] and may be described as a "share in the value added to the developed property".[47]

The Council of Islamic Ideology had recommended *bai' salam* as a mode of financing agriculture. It had also recommended enacting a law to ensure the observance of the *Sharia* rules relating to such transactions.[48] No such law has been enacted so far and *bai' salam* is not mentioned in the modes of finance approved by the Central Bank of Pakistan. It is reported, however, that "pre-finance of agricultural products is taking place on a relatively large scale in Sudan and recently in Pakistan and Bangladesh".[49]

Profit-sharing takes the forms of equity participation, Modaraba Certificates,[50] Participation Term Certificates (PTCs),[51] and supply of venture capital on profit- and loss-sharing (PLS) basis. The bank participates by providing finance to the venture. The party also provides finance and is also responsible for the management and operation of the *musharaka* venture. The bank can also evaluate, supervise, and monitor the performance of the venture. It has a right to demand adequate security from the party for the safety of the funds invested.[52] Rent-sharing is used to finance housing as well as storage of National Investment Trust Units and similar PLS-based transactions. Inter-bank call money is also based on profit-sharing.[53] Finance for meeting temporary liquidity difficulties is provided by the State Bank of Pakistan to banks and development finance institutions on the basis of profit and loss-sharing.

> The rate of profit to be derived by the State Bank from the finance will be equal to the rate of return which the bank obtaining the finance will pay on its savings accounts for the half year in question .... In case a bank incurs loss during the period, the profit received from it by the State Bank of Pakistan during the period will be refunded to it and the loss shared by all the financiers in proportion to the respective finances provided by them.[54]

The country's central bank has also fixed "the minimum annual rate of profit which a bank/development finance institution may keep in view while considering proposals for provision of finance, and the maximum annual rate of profit they may earn".[55] These rates may be changed from time to time. "Should losses occur, these shall be shared by all the financiers in proportion to the respective finances provided by them."[56]

As noted earlier, "all deposits accepted by a banking company shall be on the basis of participation in profit and loss of the banking company, except deposits received in current accounts on which no interest or profit shall be given by the banking company".[57] Banks and development finance institutions have to declare rates of profits on various types of PLS deposits on a half-yearly basis. The State Bank of Pakistan has laid down a detailed formula according to which these rates are to be worked out and presented to it for approval before they are declared.[58]

As of 30 June 1984, *murabaha* accounted for 86.7 per cent of the investment of PLS funds of the commercial banks in Pakistan, whereas equity participation, purchase of shares, Banker's equity, etc. accounted for 8 per cent, and *musharaka* accounted for 3.1 per cent.[59] This overwhelming predominance of predetermined returns has understandably left perceptive observers "with a frustrating feeling".[60] This is in addition to the fact that some of the transactions, like buy-back arrangements and mark-downs, as well as some of the financial instruments like the PTCs, have not been approved by the *Sharia* scholars in Pakistan.[61].

Iran. Iran enacted a new banking law in August 1983 resulting in the complete abolition of interest by March 1985. Commercial banks accept two kinds of deposits: interest-free loan deposits into current and savings accounts and term investment deposits. According to Article 3 of the new banking law, "Term investment deposit for the utilization of which the bank enjoys the power of attorney, shall be used in joint venture, Mozarebeh, hire purchase, instalment transaction, Mozaraah, Mosaqat, direct investment, forward dealings, and Joaalah transaction".[62] Article 4 stipulates that the "Banks are obliged to repay the principals of gharz-al-hasaneh[63] (saving and current) deposits and may undertake and/or insure the principals of the term investment deposits." As the jural bases are not elaborated, it is not possible to examine the last mentioned "undertaking" which is at variance from the practice of Islamic banking in the rest of the world. The rationale seems to be one provided for in *Shia* jurisprudence.[64]

The banks are allowed to undertake direct investment in production (Article 8). They may resort to construction of low-priced residential units for sale in instalment or hire purchase (Article 10). The law provides for *murabaha* and hire purchase in order to finance acquisition of industrial and agricultural equipment (Articles 11, 12, and 13A) as well as *bai' salam*: "to purchase, on a forward basis, the easier to sell products" of productive units for the provision of working capital needed by the productive units (Article 13B). Article 20 of the new banking law empowers the central bank of Iran to "to intervene in, and supervise, the monetary and banking activities" in the following ways:

a) Fixing a minimum and/or maximum ratio of profit for banks in their joint venture and Mozarebeh activities, these ratios may vary for different fields of activity.

b) Designation of various fields for investment and partnership within the framework of the approved economic policies, and the fixing of a minimum prospective rate of profit for the various investment and partnership projects; the minimum prospective rate of profit may vary with respect to different branches of activity.

c) Fixing a minimum and maximum margin of profit, as a proportion to the cost price of goods transacted for banks in installment and hire-purchase transactions.

d) Determination of types and the minimum and maximum amounts of commissions for banking services (provided that they do not exceed the expense of service rendered) and the fees charged for putting to use the deposits received by the banks).

e) Determination of the types, amounts, minimum and maximum bonuses subject of Article (6) and the establishment of guidelines for advertisement by banks in the cases referred to.[65]

f) Determination of the minimum and maximum ratio in joint venture, Mozarebeh, investment, hire-purchase, installment transactions, buying and selling on credit, forward deals, Mozaraah, Mosaqat, Joaalah, and Gharz-al-hasaneh for banks or any thereof with respect to various fields of activity; also fixing the maximum facility that can be granted to each customer.[66]

Sudan. In Sudan, the four largest (conventional) banks were owned by the state but the country also had six Islamic banks in the private sector by the end of 1983. Sudan opted for a total change when a presidential decree was issued in February 1984, directing all banks to stop dealing with interest. The central bank of Sudan, on 10 December 1984, directed all commercial banks to stop accepting time deposits or saving deposits on the basis of interest, with immediate effect, and to negotiate conversion of existing deposits into investment deposits or any other kind of deposits in accordance with well-known Islamic forms. All outstanding interest bearing advances were either to be settled through repayment or they had to be converted into one of the Islamic modes of finances. Foreign transactions were to continue on the basis of interest till an alternative way was available.

This sudden change forced the banks to adopt the nearest "Islamic" alternative available, that is, *murabaha*, which soon constituted 90 per cent of their financial operations.[67] It did result, however, in enhancing the popular acceptance of banking institutions, as reflected in the sudden increase in bank deposits and in the number of new branches.[68]

Islamic Development Bank. The IDB which started operations in 1976 has forty-three members and a subscribed capital of 1.85017 Islamic dinars (ID) billion.[69] Its major role over the nine years of its operation, for which data is available, has been in financing foreign trade of the member countries. Total foreign trade financing over these years was of the magnitude of ID2710.86 million. The IDB has provided development finance to member countries in the form of loans, equity, and leasing amounting to ID1,084.89 million including technical assistance during the last nine years. The IDB has been co-operating with the major financing institutions in the member countries in this respect. It has tried to strengthen co-operation among Islamic countries through specialized institutions and multilateral agreements.

IDB financing has mostly been on the basis of predetermined rates of return, even though it does not finance on the basis of interest. Foreign trade financing, based on *murabaha*, has accounted for 71.1 per cent of all IDB financing since its inception. Leasing accounted for 10.7 per cent, and loans on the basis of service charges covering administrative expenses accounted for another 10.3 per cent of all financing. *Mudaraba* has accounted for 0.19 per cent of all financing as the bank has entered into two such transactions only, one in 1978 (ID4.27 million) and the other in 1983 (ID3.06 million). *Musharaka* accounted for 6.8 per cent of total financing during 1976-84.

The bank's Articles of Agreement mention loans and equity participation as modes of financing (Articles 2-i, 2-ii, 2-iii; 16-20) and equity was accorded a prominent place in the bank's financing operations. However, as the IDB's *Ninth Annual Report* states, the equity projects "have been facing difficulties in one form or other". The report goes on to list some of these difficulties, namely a lack of infrastructural facilities, marketing difficulties, delays in implementation, and currency devaluations affecting the profitability of projects. As a result, IDB equity financing has been continuously declining over the last three years.

Unlike equity, *murabaha* is not mentioned in the Articles of Agreement at all, although in practice it overshadows all other modes of financing, and despite the fact that its importance has been growing over time. Lately, the IDB has taken some interest in "Muquarada Bonds"[70] and it is also trying to develop "Investment Certificates" which can be traded in the market.

Problems

The track record of Islamic banking has been impressive. Geographically, it has spread far and wide. It has been adopted at the national level by some countries. As an inter-Islamic institution, the Islamic Development Bank had a record of continuous growth. In terms of activities and transactions, too, there have been innovations and extensions. Islamic banks have shown profits, and there has been no instance of failure so far. Yet, this successful record is not free of problems.

Islamic financial institutions have demonstrated effectively that it is possible to conduct financial activities without interest. They have succeeded in eliminating interest completely in liabilities as they do not operate interest-bearing funds. Where assets are concerned, they have had to rely heavily on *murabaha* and some other modes of financing, all of which share a common characteristic: the return to capital is predetermined. The issue, therefore, warrants close scrutiny.

Profit-Sharing, Interest, and Murabaha

It would be appropriate to recall that all the main advantages of Islamic banking compared to interest-based banking devolve on the replacement of a fixed charge on capital by profit-sharing. The arguments for the superiority of a system based on sharing over a system based on interest can be summarized as follows:

1. A fixed charge on capital is unjust since the results of a productive enterprise in which capital is invested are uncertain. It will be just, if capital shares the actual profits of the enterprise.
2. Interest results in a less efficient allocation of resources than profit-sharing. Profit-sharing makes investible funds go to the projects with the highest (expected) profitability, whereas, in the interest-based system, funds go to the most creditworthy borrowers whose projects may not necessarily be the most profitable.
3. A system based on profit-sharing will be more stable than a system based on a fixed charge for capital as the cost of capital in a sharing system automatically adjusts itself to variations in productivity under changing business conditions. Besides preventing business failures, this flexibility ensures symmetry between a firm's cash inflows and its payment commitments, enabling the financial system to work smoothly. Furthermore, a shock to the assets position is automatically absorbed on the liabilities side when both of them are based on profit-sharing. In addition, money creation in a profit-sharing system would be based on investment, thus preventing an over-supply of money which is always possible in a system of money creation based on lending.[7]
4. A switch-over from interest to profit-sharing is more conducive to economic growth, as this would increase the supply of risk capital for investment, and as the cost of capital in a sharing system is always below the productivity of capital – which the interest-based system fails to ensure.

Of course, above all, an alternative to interest-based banking was sought because of the prohibition of interest in Islam. The point under discussion relates, however, to the alternative to interest advocated by Muslim economists. This alternative is based on sharing and the economic rationale for this alternative is built around that concept. If, in practice, we adopt an alternative which is free of interest but is not based on sharing, the above rationale would no longer apply. We cannot claim, for an interest-free alternative not based on sharing, the superiority which could not be claimed on the basis of profit-sharing. What is worse, if the alternative in practice is built around predetermined rates of return to investible funds, it would be exposed to the same criticism which was directed at interest as a fixed charge on capital. It so happens that the returns to finance provided in the modes of finance based on *murabaha*, *bai' salam*, leasing and lending with a service charge, are all predetermined as in the case of interest. Some of these modes of finance are said to contain some element of risk, but that all these risks are insurable and are actually insured against. The uncertainty or risk to which the business being so financed is exposed is fully passed over to the other party. A financial system built solely around these modes of financing can hardly claim superiority over an interest-based system on grounds of equity, efficiency, stability, and growth.

Let us now turn to the viability of a financial system based on profit-sharing and examine the factors causing its unpopularity in practice. It would be appropriate to note that the case for its viability rests essentially on two arguments both of which are relevant at the macro-economic level. These arguments are quite valid and convincing for the economy as a whole, although they may not necessarily apply, at the micro-economic level, to individual financiers and enterprises.

Firstly, it is axiomatic that capital employed in enterprise is productive so that there will be a net profit at the micro-economic level, since the nature of the world does not change merely because interest is replaced by profit-sharing. We can safely assume that, on the whole, if all financing is based on profit-sharing, there will be a net positive return to the capital supplied to enterprise. For the suppliers of capital as a whole, therefore, there is no problem in earning a positive return. Assuming that Islamic banks diversify their investments, the same argument can be applied to the entire range of finance provided by any one bank. It is very unlikely that the net return to all the advances made by a bank on the basis of profit-sharing will be negative.

The second argument relates to the possibility of cheating by fund users who may not report their time profits to the bank, thereby depriving it of its due share in the actual profit or even of part of the capital which the bank had supplied. It has been argued, however, that cheating would not pay as such a fund user cannot expect to obtain funds in the next round and would soon be forced out of business. While some entrepreneurs may cheat some suppliers of capital sometimes, the practice cannot become so general as to threaten the continuation of a system of profit-sharing, as the system will be continuously weeding out the delinquents. Financiers will not supply funds to fund-seekers who failed to report good profits in the past. They will always prefer fundseekers who had been able to give them a good return on the capital supplied.

Since the practice of Islamic banking started in the form of individual banks operating in an environment of an interest-based financial system, it is quite obvious that the second argument could not apply to them. As a fund seeker refused by an Islamic bank could always go back to the myriad avenues of interest-based funds, there could be no penalty on cheating. For, it will be possible for a one-time defaulter to get away with it and still stay in business by borrowing from the interest-based banks.

As regards the first argument, its applicability to the individual Islamic banks is also weakened by the predominant presence of interest-based banks. Entrepreneurs with very promising projects would prefer interest-based loans that would leave them larger (expected) profits as compared to what sharing would yield. Those who are not so sure about the profitability of their ventures would prefer profit-sharing as it would, at the least, relieve them of the obligation of paying a fixed return on the funds obtained. This may leave the average profitability of Islamic banks lower, in a mixed environment, than it would be in a purely profit-sharing system.

It will be noted that we have made no reference to the moral qualities of the individuals. It has been argued that a profit-sharing system for an economy is viable on economic grounds alone. Its viability will be enhanced as the moral fibre of the individuals improve. The more honest the individuals are the lower the costs implicit in the process of weeding out the defaulters,

Any reluctance in adopting profit-sharing as the basis of an interest-free Islamic financial system at the national level, therefore, seems to be without any rational basis. This is especially so, as it would be possible for a society adopting the sharing system to arrange, at the national level, for proper bookkeeping and audit of accounts, which would further reduce the incidence of cheating.

Firms applying for *mudaraba* funds may be obliged to submit properly audited accounts for ascertaining the financial position. Once funds are supplied their movements may be monitored by obliging fund users to follow certain standard procedures in recording payments and receipts. Final settlement with fund users may also be subjected to third party audit of accounts.

It is also possible, when profit-sharing is adopted as the basis of banking at the national level, to deal with cheating at the national level instead of leaving this matter to the banks themselves. Fund users could be blacklisted and denied funds from the banking system as a whole. They may also be denied permission to solicit public funds in any other manner, for example, raising share capital.

As regards the individual Islamic banks, the fact that they have succeeded in practising profit-sharing to some extent must be ascribed partly to the good moral quality of their customers and partly to the economic advantages of this arrangement. The difficulty they face in enlarging the scope of this practice is quite understandable. The problem of moral hazard can be handled effectively, both at the institutional and the moral level, when the entire system is switched over to profit-sharing. But it may assume serious proportions for individual Islamic banks operating in a "hostile" environment.

Three things must be done before Islamic banks, including the Islamic Development Bank, can enlarge the scope of their profit-sharing operations:

1. The financing institutions should have adequate machinery to evaluate projects with respect to their (expected) profitability *and* to monitor their progress.
2. Advances made on the basis of profit-sharing should be secured against deliberate mismanagement and cheating.
3. A system of guaranteeing the principal involved and/or insuring investment on a profit-sharing basis fully or partly against losses need to be developed through institutional arrangements.

The first measure, that is, monitoring of projects, is increasingly being adopted in practice and the available evidence indicates that successful profit-sharing largely depends on this. What is needed is for institutions like the IDB to have personnel to watch if the fund users are adopting sound business practices and abiding by their contractual obligations. Islamic banks need expertise in project evaluation and project supervision which institutions like the Islamic Research and Training Institute of the IDB can help develop.

The second measure calls for spelling out the circumstances in which the working partner in a *mudaraba* contract becomes liable according to Islamic law. Also, a recourse to obtaining securities against advances based on profit-sharing seems inevitable in the present transitional phase of Islamic banking.

Lastly, it may be possible to organize insurance for the benefit of individual Islamic banks so that they can be protected from the financial consequences of moral lapses. The idea is presently being explored by some scholars[72] and further research is needed to make it worthy of a trial. But it is easier for those countries which have switched over to Islamic banking at the national level to provide such insurance under the auspices of the state.

A Western scholar who has examined the issue has observed that:

> Among the factors militating against profit and loss partnerships are uncertainty of the banks' future earnings in the absolute terms, the danger of accumulation of bad risks, the problem of identifying and judging market opportunities from among the proposed entrepreneurial projects, problems of evaluation and profit assessment, supervision of the partner's management of the enterprise, etc.[73]

Out of the five factors listed, the first is not very specific to Islamic banks whereas the second can be taken care of if the third and fifth problems are solved. The fourth problem, that is, the evaluation and assessment of profits, is gradually being solved as Islamic banks adopt more sophisticated accounting techniques and oblige their clients to do the same. Moreover, its solution in the framework of a national system of Islamic banking is easier than it is for individual Islamic banks. As suggested in the theoretical writings on the subject,[74] the function is best performed by an autonomous audit and accounts agency set up at the national level.

Thus, the real practical problems are project evaluation and supervision of the management of the project by the partners or working parties. There is already some evidence that the latter can and does help improve the situation. Thus, we hear from the General Manager of the Faisal Islamic Bank of Sudan:

> A classic example is our experience with financing oil seed mills. The result on investment was about 5 per cent before introducing the follow up system. Afterwards the return rose to more than 18 per cent whereas the system cost the project an extra 1.5 per cent only.[75]

It would, therefore, be advisable for Islamic banks to invest some resources in improving their capability to evaluate projects and monitor their progress. As noted earlier, the IDB training programme can make a significant contribution towards developing the requisite skills. But the most important contribution has to come from Sudan, Iran, and Pakistan, countries which have committed themselves to restructuring their entire system in banking and finance on Islamic lines. The creation of the skills needed for the project evaluation and follow-up supervision should be regarded as a national responsibility. Expertise should be developed and personnel trained at special institutes set up for the purpose and then made available to the banks and financial institutions at subsidized costs, so that one of the basic prerequisites for the success of a profit-sharing system is adequately met. This would go a long way in assuring individual Islamic financial institutions in the rest of the world that the difficulties faced by them in operationalizing profit-sharing are institutional and transitional, not fundamental.

It will definitely require some courage and ingenuity on the part of the individual financial institutions to practise profit-sharing. Should they decide to choose between *halal* (religiously approved) modes of financing purely on the criteria of safety and convenience, profit-sharing is doomed to take a back seat. But, then, one wonders if these institutions will not be undermining their very *raison d'etre*, thereby eroding their credibility among the Muslim masses. If the establishment of individual Islamic financial institutions, including the IDB, is seen as part of a drive to change the whole financial system along Islamic lines, it may be worthwhile investing some resources to demonstrate the virtues of profit-sharing.

Of the various non-sharing modes of finance currently being practised by Islamic banking, *murabaha* has proven to be the most popular form. Even though technically a correct and permissible transaction,[76] in effect it operates very much like interest-based lending, leaving friend and foe alike wondering if this is "Islamic" banking about which there has been so much fuss. Theorists as well as practitioners of Islamic banking are rightly disturbed at this phenomenon.

> There is a genuine concern among Islamic scholars that if interest is largely substituted by devices like "mark up" it would represent a change just in name rather than in substance, and the new system would not be rid of the iniquitious nature of the interest-based system. It is also emphasised that, apart from equity considerations, the prohibition of interest in Islam is meant to stimulate overall productive activity, generate maximum employment and encourage innovation which is the mainspring of growth. These blessings can only be reaped if the interest system is completely uprooted in the real sense of the term and replaced by a fundamentally different system like profit/loss sharing.[77]

Also, as noted by the senior practitioner of Islamic banking, *murabaha*

> ... is not suitable except for trading operations. As a result the capital deposited in Islamic banks invigorates only trading activities whereas the assumption was that it would be distributed over all kinds of activities and between different sectors of the economy: agriculture, industry, services and the other sectors. The *murabaha* form of transaction is by its very nature a sale deed, and a sale contract is trading. So the ultimate result of the employment of these huge funds in *murabaha* deals is to narrow down the activities of Islamic banks in comparison to what they were expected to do in the light of the Islamic economic vision.[78]

In this context, Islamic banks may find it worth considering to

> ... limit the use of this transaction to a certain percentage of their assets in order to push them into more productive and somehow more risky economic activities, rather than merely getting a profit margin on their *murabaha* financing.[79]

As provided for in Iranian law and suggested by us above, it would be advisable for the central banks in the countries which have abolished interest to intervene with a view to gradually reducing the present high incidence of *murabaha* in the operation of commercial banks. Needless to emphasize, they will have to minimize the use of "mark-up" in their own operations first.

While the predominance of *murabaha* is the main problem of contemporary Islamic banking, so much so that it can be characterized as a crisis of identity of the Islamic financial movement, there are also some lesser problems which have to be sorted out. Some of these are discussed below.

Penalizing Delays in Payment by a Fine

One of the problems facing Islamic financial institutions is how to handle delays in payment, and those of default by a client. Lending with a service charge, sale with a mark-up and deferred payment (*murabaha*) and leasing, all involve dated payments. What does an Islamic bank do if payment is delayed? What does it do if the delay seems indefinite? It cannot charge interest for the payment delayed. In theory, it can realize the dues by selling the collateral, if any. But, in practice, not all advances are secured. This applies especially to *murabaha* financing. These consequences are disastrous. Delays in payment have severely affected the performance of the IDB, as reported by its president:

> The bank could have committed five times as much financing into its foreign trade programme, $3,132 million, if there had been no problem of delays and arrears in repayment by some countries.[80]

It has been suggested that a financial penalty should be imposed on the defaulter which should be adequate to compensate the financier against the "loss" suffered due to the delay.[81] The idea has already been adopted officially in Pakistan. It is interesting to note, however, that the conditions laid down by the scholars who have suggested it, for such a penalty to be valid, have been totally ignored in the Pakistani regulations. This should serve as a timely warning that once the principle of a fine against delay in payment is accepted, *with a view to compensating the financier*, it would degenerate into something similar to interest as the principle amounts to putting a price on time.

It should be possible, however, to penalize the defaulter with the sole purpose of deterrence. If and when this penalty takes the form of a fine, the proceeds of the fine should not go to the financier but to the public treasury. The deterrent, as well as the practice of demanding collateral against all advances, should protect the interests of the financiers to a great extent. It is advisable, however, to offer refinance by the central bank to all financiers affected by "inordinate" delay in payment on the part of their clients. Should payment be delayed beyond a specified period, to be defined by the central bank for each activity, the central bank would lend, free of interest, the sum involved to the affected financial institution. These sums would be paid back to the central bank on recovery from the defaulting client, against whom all possible steps must be taken to expedite recovery.

Letters of Guarantee

Issuing letters of guarantee (LG) is a normal operation for conventional banks, but it poses a problem for Islamic banks. Even though some of them are doing so against a fee for the service,[82] the subject remains controversial in view of jural opinions which hold that guarantees should be a free service. Islamic scholars would allow a fee to cover the administrative costs only, provided the fee does not vary with the sum of money involved in the guarantee. But charging a percentage on the sum involved is not approved by most of them.

A letter of guarantee issued by a well-known banker provides the needed trust in a customer's capacity to fulfil his obligations if the customer is bidding for a contract or buying a shipment from a foreign seller who does not know his financial position. Should the customer fail to honour his commitment, the guarantor has to fulfil all necessary obligations. This, in turn, would involve him in proceeding against the customer to realize payment. The guarantor's claim to recompensation arises partly from the administrative costs involved and partly from the risk it runs by exposing his own resources to a possible need of payment. It appears, therefore, that if only a service charge is allowed to cover administrative costs, the recompensation will not be complete, and the system will therefore not work.

While scholars continue to debate the issue, practice is taking new forms: "Some Islamic banks ... require a partial cover of 20-30 per cent on which they give no return to the client and while giving LG to him free of charge, they in fact benefit from this free deposit as long as the LG is valid."[83] Reference must also be made to innovation of Islamic banks where the LG is considered as a kind of finance remunerated by a percentage of the profits of the transaction for which the LG was issued.[84]

Placement of Short-term Funds

Some financial institutions may face a temporary shortage of liquidity which has to be met by obtaining funds for a day or two. Similarly, some institutions have excess liquidity which they would like to use profitably, even though temporarily. Abolition of interest obliges the system to find an alternative basis for transaction between the deficit units and surplus units. But the time periods involved are too short to be amenable to genuine profit-sharing. It has, therefore, been suggested that the transactions be based on a share in the "normal" profits of the fund users calculated pro rata for the period involved.[85] This is in line with the relevant recommendation of the Council of Islamic Ideology (Pakistan), which reads:

> Commercial banks usually keep deposits with each other and, when needed, also avail of financial assistance mutually. At present these transactions are interest bearing. After the elimination of interest such transactions may be carried out under PLS arrangements on the basis of daily product of accounts.[86]

Prospects

Jural traditions in Islam are rich enough to take care of the lesser problems of Islamic banking noted above. The real test lies in resisting the pull towards the convenient modes of finance which tend to take the system back to a regime of predetermined guaranteed rates of return with all its inequity, inefficiency, and instability. As noted above, it is to the countries embarking upon a total change to an Islamic economic system that one must look for the means to meet this challenge successfully. Meanwhile, the individual Islamic financial institutions, which heralded the movement in the first instance, can make a significant contribution towards this goal by striving as best as they can to remain faithful to the original vision.

The many difficult problems encountered by the nations of the world, because of the regime of interest in particular and the capitalist economic system in general, have led mankind to consider alternatives and to experiment with new solutions. A "share economy" is being advocated as a solution to stagflation albeit with reference to the employment of labour only.[87] Why then should the economists be averse to applying the same to the employment of capital? The global debt crisis is also a pointer to the need for an alternative basis for the international flow of capital. As long as man refuses to care for fellow human beings and asserts an absolute claim to what he possesses, exercises such as the North-South dialogue or the search for a New International Economic Order are not likely to yield promising results. Could the Islamic view of life beyond its earthly phase and its emphasis on co-operation and sharing with fellow humans in submission to the real Owner, the Creator of all, catch man's imagination once more? Questions such as this may not seem directly related to the prospects of Islamic banking, but the prospects of Islamic banking in the modern world will largely depend on the way Muslims respond to such questions both intellectually and practically.

APPENDIX

Islamic Financial Institutions (outside Pakistan and Iran)*

Australia	Islamic Investment Company, Melbourne.
Bahamas	Dar al Mal al Islami, Nassau. Islamic Investment Company, Ltd., Nassau. Masar Faisal Islamic Bank & Trust, Bahamas Ltd., Nassau.
Bahrain	Albaraka Islamic Investment Bank, Manama. Bahrain Islamic Bank, Manama. Bahrain Islamic Investment Company, Manama. Islamic Investment Company of the Gulf. Masraf Faisal al Islami, Bahrain.
Bangladesh	Islamic Bank of Bangladesh Ltd., Dhaka.
Denmark	Islamic Bank International of Denmark, Copenhagen.

Egypt	Albaraka Nile Valley Company, Cairo. Arab Investment Bank (Islamic Banking Operations), Cairo. Bank Misr (Islamic Branches), Cairo. Faisal Islamic Bank of Egypt, Cairo. General Investment Company, Cairo. Islamic International Bank for Investment and Development, Cairo. Islamic Investment and Development Company, Cairo. Nasir Social Bank, Cairo.
Guinea	Islamic Investment Company of Guinea, Conakry. Masraf Faisal al Islami of Guinea, Conakry.
India	Baitun Nasr Urban Cooperative Society, Bombay.
Jordan	Islamic Investment House Company Ltd., Amman. Jordan Finance House, Amman. Jordan Islamic Bank for Finance and Investment, Amman.
Kibris (Turkish Cyprus)	Faisal Islamic Bank of Kibris, Lefkosa.
Kuwait	Al Tukhaim International Exchange Company, Safat. Kuwait Finance House, Safat.
Liberia	African Arabian Islamic Bank, Monkovia.
Liechtenstein	Arinco Arab Investment Company, Vaduz. Islamic Banking System Finance S.A., Vaduz.
Luxembourg	Islamic Finance House Universal Holdings S.A.
Malaysia	Bank Islam Malaysia Berhad, Kuala Lumpur. Pilgrims' Management and Fund Board, Kuala Lumpur.
Niger	Faisal Islamic Bank of Niger, Niamy.
Philippines	The Philippine Amanah Bank, Zamboanga City.
Qatar	Islamic Exchange and Investment Company, Doha Qatar Islamic Bank.
Saudi Arabia	Albaraka Investment and Development Company, Jeddah. Islamic Development Bank, Jeddah,
Senegal	Faisal Islamic Bank of Senegal, Dakar. Islamic Investment Company of Senegal, Dakar.
South Africa	JAAME Ltd., Durban.

Sudan	Bank al Baraka al Sudani, Khartoum. Faisal Islamic Bank of Sudan, Khartoum. Islamic Bank of Western Sudan, Khartoum. Islamic Cooperative Development Bank, Khartoum. Islamic Investment Company of Sudan, Khartoum. Sudan Islamic Bank, Khartoum. Tadamun Islamic Bank, Khartoum.
St. Heleir	The Islamic Investment Company, Jersey. Masraf Faisal al Islami, Jersey.
Switzerland	Dar al Mal al Islami, Geneva. Islamic Investment Company, Ltd., Geneva. Sharia Investment Services, PIG, Geneva.
Thailand	Arabian Thai Investment Company, Ltd., Bangkok.
Tunisia	Bank al Tamwil al Saudi al Tunisi.
Turkey	Albarakah Turkish Finance House, Istanbul. Faisal Finance Institution, Istanbul.
United Arab Emirates	Dubai Islamic Bank, Dubai. Islamic Investment Company, Ltd. Sharjah.
United Kingdom	Albarakah International Ltd., London. Albaraka Investment Co. Ltd., London. Al Rajhi Company for Islamic Investment Ltd., London. Islamic Finance House Public Ltd. Co., London.

* The list includes Islamic banks as well as Islamic investment companies but it does not include Islamic insurance companies.

NOTES

* The author gratefully acknowledges the helpful comments he received from Monzer Kahf, Munawar Iqbal, and Ausaf Ahmad during the preparation of this paper.

1 See M.N. Siddiqi, *Partnership and Profit-sharing in Islamic Law* (Leicester: The Islamic Foundation, 1985), pp. 11-19.

2 See H.M. Masood, *Land Tenure System in Islamic Framework* (Islamabad: International Institute of Islamic Economics (IIE), 1985), pp. 26-31.

3 See Kasib Abdul Karim Bardan, *Aqbal Istisna Fi'l Fiqh al Islamiah Dirasah Mugarinah* (Alexandria: Dar al Da'wah, 1978).

4 "Ibn Abbas, May Allah be pleased with him, reports that when the Prophet, peace be upon him, came (to Madina) people were advancing (money) against dates (to be delivered after) two years or three years, so he said: "One who advances (money) against something (to be delivered later) should (make the advance) against a known quantity in measure or weight for a known time (of delivery)" (Bukhari: *Kitab al Salam, Bab al Salam fi Wazan Ma'lum*).

5 See, for example, Abraham L. Udovitch, *Partnership and Profit in Medieval Islam* (Princeton, N.J.: Princeton University Press, 1970), pp. 204-205.

6 M.N. Siddiqi, *Muslim Economic Thinking* (Leicester: The Islamic Foundation, 1981), pp. 29-37.

7 M.N. Siddiqi, *Banking Without Interest* (Leicester: The Islamic Foundation, 1983), pp. 151.

8 Ibid., p. 159.

9 See Yusuf Al Qardawi, *Bai al Murabaha li'l 'Amir bi'l Shira' Kama Tujrih al Masarif al Islamiyah* (Kuwait: Dar al Qalam, 1984), pp. 15-17, and Jordan Islamic Bank, *al Fatawa al Shari'yah* (Amman, Jordan Islamic Bank, 1984), p. 29. Some Islamic banks do allow the customer, after having made a commitment to buy certain goods from the bank, to change his mind. The actual incidence of exercising this option has been, however, minimal.

10 Wahaba al Zuhaili, *Al Fiqh al Islami wa Adillatuh* (Damascus: Dar al Fikr, 1984), vol. 4, p. 635.

11 Kuwait Finance House, *Al Fatawa al Shariyah fi'l Masa'il al Iqtisadiyah* (Kuwait: Kuwait Finance House, 1981), p. 43.

12 Ma'bid Ali al Jarhi, "A Monetary and Financial Structure for an Interest-Free Economy: Institutions, Mechanisms and Policy", in *Money and Banking in Islam*, edited by Ziauddin Ahmad et al. (Islamabad: Institute of Policy Studies (IPS), 1983), p. 81.

13 Ibid.

14 M.U. Chapra, *Towards a Just Monetary System* (Leicester: The Islamic Foundation, 1985), pp. 198-199.

15 See Ziauddin Ahmad et al., op. cit., pp. 74-75.

16 M.N. Siddiqi, *Central Banking in Islamic Framework* (Amman: Royal Academy for Islamic Civilization Research, 1986).

17 See M.N. Siddiqi, *Muslim Economic Thinking*, op. cit., pp. 29-37.

18 See M.N. Siddiqi, *Banking Without Interest*, op. cit., pp. 184-188.

19 Ahmad Al-Najjar, *Manhaj al Sahwat Al Islamiyah* (Jeddah: 1976), p. 83.

20 Starting in 1963 in the town of Mit Ghamr, eighty kilometres from Cairo, this experiment lasted till 1967 by which time there were nine banks in operation including those in Cairo. With more than 250,000 depositors and a total of 1.8 million Egyptian pounds in deposits, these banks neither paid nor charged interest. They made profits for their depositors

sometimes by financing business on profit-sharing basis, but mostly by engaging in trade and industry directly or in partnership with others. Though the character of this institution changed when its pioneering spirit was reined in, its popularity with the masses contributed to the establishment of the Nasir Social Bank in 1971. It was barred from charging or paying interest but its charter did not refer to Islam or the *Sharia*.

21 The Dubai Islamic Bank (1975), The Kuwait Finance House (1977), The Faisal Islamic Bank of Sudan (1977) and Egypt (1977), The Islamic Investment Company of the Gulf (1977), The Bahrain Islamic Bank (1979), and the Iran Islamic Bank (1979).

22 Bangunan Tabung Haji, *Al Tariq ila al Ka'bah* (Kuala Lumpur: Bangunan Tabung Haji, 1985), p. 18.

23 Bank Dubai al Islami, *Al Taqrir al Sanawi al Khamis* (Dubai: Bank Dubai al Islami, 1980), p. 4.

24 Volker Ninehaus, "Islamic Economics, Finance and Banking — Theory and Practice". Paper presented at the Conference on Islamic Banking and Finance, organized by Business Research International, London, 30 October-1 November 1985, Annex 3a.

25 This includes the Malaysian Pilgrims' Management and Fund Board.

26 See the Appendix for a list of Islamic banks and financial institutions in operation throughout the world.

27 Dar al Mal al Islami (DMI), *Al Taqrir al Sanawi* (Nassau: Dar al Mal Islami, 1985), p. 7.

28 DMI, *Al Taqrir al Sanawi* (Nassau: Dar al Mal Islami, 1984), p. 19.

29 DMI, *Al Taqrir al Sanawi* (1985), op. cit., p. 25.

30 Ibid. p. 13.

31 See the 1984 *Annual Reports* of the various Al Baraka institutions.

32 These are: The House Building Finance Corporation, The Investment Corporation of Pakistan, The National Investment (Unit) Trust, The Bankers Equity Limited, and the Small Business Finance Corporation. Interest was replaced by rent-sharing in the case of the first and by service charge in the case of the last mentioned institution. In the three remaining institutions it was replaced by profit-sharing See also United Bank Limited, *Islamisation of Banking in Pakistan* (Karachi: United Bank Limited, 1984), pp. 11-12.

33 State Bank of Pakistan, *Elimination of the Interest from the Banking System in Pakistan* (Karachi: State Bank of Pakistan, 1985), p. 2.

34 Ibid., pp. 12-13.

35 State Bank of Pakistan, Circular No. 29 dated 12 June 1985.

36 United Bank Limited, op. cit., pp. 32-34.

37 Ibid., p. 31.

38 Ibid., pp. 30-33.

39 State Bank of Pakistan, Circular No. 29, pp. 4-6.

40 Ibid., p. 3.

41 United Bank Limited, *Islamic Banking — Procedural Instructions* (Karachi: United Bank Limited, 1984), p. 14.

42 State Bank of Pakistan, Circular No. 29, p. 24.

43 Ibid., p. 6.

44 Ibid., pp. 4-5.

45 Ibid., p. 24.

46 Ibid., pp. 5-6.

47 United Bank Limited, *Islamic Banking — Procedural Instructions*, op. cit., p. 15.

48 Council of Islamic Ideology, "Report on the Elimination of Interest from the Economy", in *Money and Banking in Islam*, edited by Zianuddin Ahmad et al. (Islamabad: IPS, 1983), pp. 141-142.

49 Younus al Tarmimi, "The Experience of Islamic Banks in the Middle East" (Paper presented at the Conference on Islamic Banking and Finance, organized by Business Research International, London, 31 October-1 November 1985), p. 16.

50 Mudaraba Certificates are sold to the public and the proceeds are invested in business. The specific terms governing profit- and loss-sharing are left to be determined by market forces but a religious board set up by the government ensures conformity with the *Sharia*. Mudaraba Certificates are transferable.

51 Participation Term Certificates are negotiable instruments designed to replace debentures for financing long- and medium-term projects. A trustee is appointed for appraising the project and inspecting records, etc. in order to protect the interest of PTC holders. The share of PTCs in profit is deducted prior to the claim of the shareholders. In the case of losses, first recourse is made to the free reserves including any credit balance in the profit and loss account. The balance of the loss is shared among the providers of funds in proportion to the funds provided by each. PTCs are secured by a legal mortgage on the fixed assets of the company. Corporations or commercial banks have to get permission from appropriate authorities before they can issue PTCs. But the ratio of sharing profits and other terms such as repayment are left to the issuer. (See United Bank Limited, *Islamisation of Banking in Pakistan*, op. cit., pp. 18.)

52 Ibid., p. 28.

53 Ibid., p. 29.

54 State Bank of Pakistan, op. cit., p. 12.

55 Ibid., p. 26.

56 Ibid., p. 27.

57 Ibid., p. 2.

58 Ibid., pp. 14-23.

59 Ziauddin Ahmad, op cit., p. 45.

60 Waqar Masood Khan, *Towards an Interest Free Islamic Economic System* (Leicester: The Islamic Foundation, 1985), p. 17.

61 See Government of Pakistan, *Pakistan Economic Survey (1984-1985)*, (Islamabad: Government of Pakistan, Economic Advisors Wing, Finance Division, 1985), pp. 10-11, and Manzoor Ali, "Islamisation of Banking: An Appraisal of Techniques" (Paper presented at Workshop on Interest-Free Banking in Pakistan, Islamabad, 8-11 July 1985), pp. 33-34.

62 Bank Markazi Jamhouri Islami Iran, *The Law For Usury Free Banking* (Tehran: Bank Markazi Jamhouri Islamic Iran, 1983) (approved on 30 August 1983). *Mozarebeh* refers to *mudaraba* arrangements applied to orchards and gardens, and *joaalah* to a fee for services rendered. The law defines it as "The undertaking by one party (the Jael, Bank or employer) to pay a specified amount of money (The Joal) to another party in return for rendering a specified service in accordance with the terms of the contract. The party rendering the service shall be called "Amel" (agent or contractor)."

63 *Qardhasan*, that is, interest-free loans.

64 Muhammad Baqir al Sadr, *al Bank al la Rabawi fi'l Islam* (Beirut: Daral Kitab al Lubani, 1973), pp. 184-204.

65 Article 6 reads:

In order to attract and mobilize deposits the banks may, through promotional methods, give the following rewards to the depositors:
(A) Non-fixed bonuses in cash or in kind to gharz-al-hasaneh deposits.
(B) Exempting the depositors from, or granting discounts thereto, in payment of commissions and/or fee.
(C) According priority to depositors in the use of banking facilities as specified in chapter III.

66 Bank Markazi Jamhouri Islami Iran, op. cit., pp. 6-7.

67 Abdul Wahab, Hasan, "Tajribat al Sudan fi'l Tahawwul m'in al Nizam al Masrafi al Rabawi li'l Nizam al Masrafi al Islami", mimeographed (Paper presented at Nadwah al Iqtisad al Islami wa'l Takamul al Tanmawi fi'l watan al Arabi, a seminar in Tunis, November 1985), p. 3.

68 Ibid.

69 One Islamic Dinar (ID) is equal to one Special Drawing Right (SDR) of the IMF. This section on the IDB is, unless otherwise specified, based on the *Ninth Annual Report* of the IDB, issued in 1985.

70 *Muquarada* is a symbol of *mudaraba*, that is, profit-sharing.

71 M.N. Siddiqi, *Issues in Islamic Banking* (Leicester: The Islamic Foundation, 1983), pp. 55-57.

72 See Monzer Khaf, "Sanadat al Qirrad wa Daman al Fariq al Thalith wa Tatbiqatihima fi Tamwil al Tanmiyah fi'l Buldan al Islamiyah". Unpublished paper, January 1986, pp. 24-26.

73 Volker Ninehaus, op. cit., p. 236.

74 M.U. Chapra, op. cit., pp. 180-181.

75 Mudawi al Bagkiry, "Placing Medium and Long Term Finance by Islamic Financial Institutions" (Paper presented at the Conference on Islamic Banking and Finance, organized by Business Research International, London 31 October-1 November 1985).

76 This is a view held by an overwhelming majority of scholars. See Yusuf al Qardawi, *Bai al Murabaha li'l Amir bil Shira' Kama Tujrih al Mas arif al Islamiyah* (Kuwait: Dar al Qalam, 1984). For a dissenting view, see Rafiq al Misri, "Bai' al Murabaha li'l Amir bil Shira Kama Tujrih al Masarif al Islamiyah", *Al Ummah* (Kuwait) no. 61, September 1985, pp. 24-27, and (by the same author) "Kashf al Ghita' 'an Bai' al Murabaha li'l Amir bil Shira'", *Al Muslim al Mu'asir* (Kuwait), no. 32, August-October 1982, pp. 179-189.

77 Ziauddin Ahmad, *The Present State of Islamic Finance Movement* (Islamabad: IPS, 1985), pp. 19-20.

78 Gamaluddin Atiyah, "Al Bunuk al Islamiyah bain al Nazariyah wa'l Tatbiq", *Al Ummah* (Kuwait), Ramadan 1405 [June 1985], p. 67.

79 Gamaludin Atiyah, "Financial Instruments Used by Islamic Banks" (Paper presented at the Conference on Islamic Banking and Finance organized by Business Research International, London, 31 October-1 November 1985), p. 19.

80 Thomas C. Goltz, "Milestone on the Common Market Road?" *Arabia* 4, no. 42 (1985) p. 48.

81 Mustafa Ahmad al Zarqa, "Hal Yuqbal Shar'an al Hukum, 'ala al Madin al Mumatil bi'l ta'wid ala al Das", *Journal of Research in Islamic Economics* 2, no. 2 (Winter 1985): 89-97.

82 Bank Islam Malaysia Berhad, *Organization and Operations*, p. 20, clause 9.4(d).

83 Gamaluddin Atiyah, "Financial Instruments Used by Islamic Banking", op. cit., p. 8.

84 Ibid.

85 Ibid.

86 Council of Islamic Ideology, op. cit., p. 149.

87 Martin L. Weitzman, *The Share Economy — Conquering Stagflation* (Cambridge, Masachussetts: Harvard University Press, 1984).

4 ISLAMIC BANKING: THE MALAYSIAN EXPERIENCE*

Zakariya Man

Introduction

At the theoretical level, the concept of Islamic banking on the basis of profit-sharing was initially developed under the explicit assumption of a general prohibition of interest[1] – which was widely accepted as one form of *riba* and strictly prohibited in Islam.[2] Practically, however, all existing Islamic banks were established and operated in capitalistic economies where the system of interest persists.[3]

The establishment of an Islamic bank under such an environment is not without juristification. Islamic banking is widely recognized by Muslim scholars as one of the approaches to be adopted in the process of Islamizing an economy. This approach is based on the premise that under the existing political, social, and technical constraints, Islamization should be so phased as to avoid any abrupt changes which might cause unpredictable disarray in the economy. According to this approach, Islamization of the banking sector is to be implemented by first establishing a model Islamic bank side by side with the existing interest-based banks. It is hoped that, through time, the superiority of the Islamic banking model will cause the practice of interest-based banking to be phased out without any adverse effect on the economy.[4] Experiences so far have shown that Islamic banks can co-exist with conventional banks, and there are signs that they can continue to grow and progress.

A similar approach has been adopted in the implementation of Islamic banking in Malaysia. It was in a capitalistic environment that the Bank Islam Malaysia Berhad (BIMB) was established in July 1983. The promulgation of a new Islamic Banking Act 1983 was effectively legislated with only certain minor changes being made to the existing Banking Act 1973 and the government enacting an additional provision so as to allow the establishment of the BIMB. Thus, even after the promulgation of the Islamic Banking Act 1983, the interest system has continued to play a key role in the financial sector of the economy. Consequently, it is of interest to examine how the BIMB has fared. In view of the high expectations of the Muslims in Malaysia about the prospects of Islamic banking, the operations of the BIMB had to be carefully devised and implemented. A failure would imply not just the failure of the BIMB per se, but to Muslims, it would be a failure of the Islamic system in general, which would hardly be acceptable to them. After more than two years of operation, however, the BIMB has proved its viability within the Malaysian capitalistic environment. The BIMB has so far set up eleven branches in almost all the major towns in the peninsula and has started to make profit after eighteen months of operation which is only half the time period normally required by most conventional banks to break even.

This paper is basically a preliminary attempt to examine and evaluate the performance of the BIMB, after it has been in operation for more than two years. The paper is divided into three major sections. The first section provides a description of the theoretical aspects of the BIMB and discusses its rationale, legal framework, organizational structure, and proposed functions. The second section is mainly concerned with the examination and evaluation of the experiences of the BIMB. The last section will highlight some of the unresolved practical problems faced by the BIMB and suggest possible solutions.

Principles and Framework of the BIMB

Historical Perspectives

The need for Islamic banking has been felt ever since the Muslims had established relations with the modern interest-based banking system. The evaluation of modern banking by Muslim scholars basically centred around the evils of interest which is strictly prohibited in Islam. Then, the discussion developed into an effort by many Muslims scholars to propose an alternative banking system which would be just and free from interest.

Preliminary discussions of the Islamic banking concept dated as far back as 1945.[5] Ten years later, in 1955, an extensive model of an Islamic bank was proposed.[6] However, it was only in the late 1960s that a more comprehensive model of interest-free banking appeared, thanks to the meticulous efforts of many scholars like Abdullah al Araby, Baqir al Sadr, M.N. Siddiqi, and Ahmad El Nagar.[7]

The first experiment on Islamic banking was launched in 1963 in Mit Ghamr, one of the provinces in the Arab Republic of Egypt. The experiment was led by Ahmad El Nagar and it continued until 1967.[8] Though this experiment in Islamic banking was undertaken on a very limited scale, it provided a basis for similar efforts elsewhere.

Following the first experiment, there was a call for the establishment of an Islamic bank at the international level. The Egyptian and Pakistani delegations to the second Islamic Conference of Foreign Ministers (1971) submitted two separate proposals for establishing such an Islamic Bank and an Association of Islamic Banks. This was followed by the Egyptian studies in 1972 that led to the adoption of the charter of the Islamic Development Bank in 1974. Since then several Islamic banks have come into existence. Among the first few were Dubai Islamic Bank (1975), Faisal Islamic Bank of Sudan (1977), Kuwait Finance House (1977), and some other individual Islamic banks in various countries, with the total number exceeding forty.

In the case of Malaysia, the first major move towards establishing an interest-free institution was the setting up of the Pilgrims' Management and Fund Board (PMBF). The Board was set up by statute in August 1969 through a merger of the Malayan Muslim Pilgrims Savings Corporation and the Pilgrims Affairs Department of the government to promote and co-ordinate all aspects of activities connected with the Muslims going on pilgrimage. The Board manages a fund derived from the accumulation of savings of intending pilgrims and organizes the pilgrimage for them. The savings of its members are utilized to defray the expenses of the pilgrimage, during which the Board looks after the transportation and the general welfare of the pilgrims. Since its inception, the PMFB has grown in size with its total resources rising at an average annual rate of 28.6 per cent, from M$12.9 million in 1969 to M$338.7 million at the end of 1982. The total number of depositors registered with PMFB has increased at an average annual rate of 20.4 per cent from 47,970 at the end of 1969 to 535,900 at the end of 1982. By the end of 1982, total savings deposits amounted to M$227 million or 67 per cent of its total resources.[9]

Following the successful implementation of the PMFB, there was a continuous pressure on the government to help establish an Islamic bank. A more formal demand for the establishment of such a bank was first made in 1980 when the Bumiputra Economic Congress 1980 passed a resolution urging the government to allow the PMFB to establish an Islamic bank in Malaysia to mobilize the savings of the Muslims and to invest them in a productive manner. During the same year, in various seminars at the state levels, similar resolutions were passed urging the government to establish Islamic banks with the PMFB playing a major role.

Again at the "National Seminar on the Concept of Development in Islam" organized by the Universiti Kebangsaan Malaysia in March 1981, another resolution was passed urging the government to take an immediate initiative to enact a special provision of the laws as a first step towards establishing Islamic banks and financial institutions consistent with Islamic principles. Here again, the Seminar agreed that the PMFB should be given the task of initiating the implementation of the project.

Starting in 1980 committees were formed to study the various aspects of

Islamic banking and its implementation in Malaysia. These efforts were taken independently by such organizations as the Muslim Welfare Organization of Malaysia (PERKIM), PMFB, and the Development Bank of Malaysia Berhad. The government accepted the proposal put forward by the PMFB so that independent efforts to establish Islamic banks could be co-ordinated at a national level. In addition, the government also agreed to form a National Steering Committee of Islamic Banks on 30 July 1981. The twenty-member Steering Committee headed by the Raja Tan Sri Mohar, the special Advisor to the Prime Minister, was given the following tasks:

1. To study and identify various critical aspects of Islamic banking such as the basis of establishment, areas of operation, and business relationship with the customers and other financial institutions.
2. To examine the suitability of Islamic banking in the Malaysian context from various points of view including religious, legal, racial, social, and developmental angles; and
3. To present to the government a proposal to establish Bank Islam Malaysia in a complete report encompassing the following aspects: (a) fundamental concepts of Islamic bank; (b) legal framework; (c) structure of the company; (d) areas of operation; and (e) organizational structure.

The National Steering Committee set up three technical committees, namely the Religious Committee, Legal Committee, and Banking Operation Committee.

In order to facilitate their studies, the technical committees were supplied with reference materials, information, and the "Model Islamic Bank" document prepared by the International Association of Islamic Banks. The committees also studied the operation of Faisal Islamic Bank of Sudan and Faisal Islamic Bank of Egypt. References were also made to the report entitled "Memorandum on the Establishment of Islamic Bank for Malaysia" prepared by the Research Committee of PERKIM, chaired by Tan Sri Abdul Aziz Zain, vice-president of PERKIM, and the report on "Establishment of an Islamic Bank in Malaysia" prepared by Bank Negara Malaysia. In addition, the committees also referred to the various available texts on Islamic economics, banking, and insurance.

It is clear from the above sketch that the Muslims in Malaysia had to wait for more than twenty years for the government to make any serious effort towards implementing the idea of Islamic banking in the country. This was partly due to the fact that the idea of Islamic banking was not readily acceptable to conventional banks and the Central Bank. It was only after 1980, in the face of continuous pressure from local Muslims and in the wake of a world-wide Islamic resurgence, that the government responded positively by establishing the National Steering Committee of Islamic Banks that led to the promulgation of the Islamic Banking Act 1983 which paved the way for Islamic banking in the country.

Basic Principles of the BIMB

The report of the National Steering Committee on Islamic Bank Malaysia outlines three major principles that will govern the operation of the BIMB. They are as follows:

1. Prohibition of *riba* and the sharing of profit and losses.
   Profit- and loss-sharing is the basis of all economic activities involving money, wealth, and labour in Islam. This concept of profit-sharing should replace interest as an important mechanism in the present banking system.
2. Management of Islamic banks based on Islamic transactions (*Mu'amalah*).
   The success of Islamic banks is largely dependent on the understanding and the implementation of the Islamic principle of transactions on the part of the management. Thus, Islamic banks must ensure that their activities will not be in conflict with the *Sharia* (Islamic law).
3. Avoidance of the activities contradictory to the interest of the Muslim *ummah*.
   Any activity which is not in conformity with the interest of the *ummah* is tantamount to misuse and abuse of the wealth entrusted by God.

Legal Framework and Control

Incorporation. The National Steering Committee submitted its report on 5 July 1982, and the report was accepted by the government. The recommendations of the committee include the following:

1. An Islamic bank which operates according to the principles of the *Sharia* should be established.
2. The bank should be incorporated as a limited company under the Companies Act 1965.
3. An act styled the Islamic Banking Act 1983 should be legislated and some consequential amendments should be made to other existing related Acts.
4. Bank Negara Malaysia should administer the Islamic Banking Act 1983.
5. The bank should set up a Religious Supervisory Council to ensure that the operations of the bank comply with the *Sharia* principles.

The BIMB was finally incorporated as a limited company under the Companies Act 1965 on 1 March 1983. To comply with its philosophy and principles, the Memorandum of Association of the BIMB prefaces that "all business of the company will be transacted in accordance with Islamic principles, rules and practices". In addition, the memorandum also lists all the objectives of the company. The main objective of the company is to carry on the business of an Islamic bank in all its branches and departments. Islamic banking business here refers to banking business the aims and operations of which do not involve any un-Islamic element.

Shareholders. The BIMB has an authorized capital of M$500 million, divided into 500 million ordinary shares of M$1 each. The initial paid-up capital of the bank is M$80 million, which is M$20 million less than the amount recommended by the National Steering Committee. The paid-up capital, currently held by the Malaysian government and various other parties, is structured as follows:

	M$million
Government of Malaysia	30
Pilgrims' Management and Fund Board	10
Muslim Welfare Organization of Malaysia	5
State Religious Council	20
State Religious Agencies	3
Federal Agencies	12
Total	80

Islamic Banking Act 1983

The Banking Act 1973 requires the rate of interest to be an important mechanism for banking operations and prohibits banks from trading.[10] In contrast, the Qur'an explicitly states that "Allah has permitted trade and prohibited usury [interest]". This divergence between Banking Act 1973 and Qur'anic injunction implies that the initial legal environment in Malaysia did not permit the establishment of an Islamic bank that would operate without the element of interest.

In view of the above conflict, the National Steering Committee recommended an Islamic Banking Act be legislated to facilitate the establishment of an Islamic bank. Thus, following the acceptance of the Report of the Committee, the Islamic Banking Act was legislated towards the end of 1982. The Act, gazetted in 1983, is now known as the Islamic Banking Act 1983.

The Act amounted to making a few changes in the Banking Act 1973 by adding some additional provisions and making appropriate amendments to permit Islamic banking operations. The powers of supervision and regulation over the BIMB were vested in the Central Bank, as in the case of all other licensed banks. The Islamic Banking Act 1983 also made it mandatory for the Islamic bank to set up a Religious Supervisory Council.[11] This requirement is further clarified in the bank's Articles of Associations relating to the nature and roles of the said Council. The provision states that the Council, comprising a minimum of three and maximum seven members of the Muslim Religious Scholars, shall be established to advise the bank of its banking business in order to ensure that they do not involve any element contrary to Islam. [12]

Government Investment Act

According to the *Sharia* rules, an Islamic bank is not allowed to trade in Treasury Bills or other papers such as government bonds and securities which are interest-based. From the operation point of view, however, it is important for the bank to trade in these papers in order to meet its legal liquidity requirements.

Consequently, to make the operation of the Islamic bank possible, the Government Investment Act 1982 was passed and gazetted on 10 March 1983 enabling the government to issue non-interest bearing investment certificates. The Act specifies that the Minister of Finance shall declare the rate of dividend to be paid on the investment certificate, but without stating how the rate of dividend is to be determined.

Accepting the fact that fixed return in the form of interest is forbidden, the return on investment certificates must be made in the form of a variable rate of return. For this purpose, an appropriate method to determine the rate of dividend is one based on the *qardhasan* principle, whereby the purchase of investment certificates by the public would be considered as a benevolent loan to the government, and as such, the providers of the funds would not expect any return on their loan. They would, however, expect the principal amount to be returned in full at maturity. Although the government is not obliged to provide any return to the holders of the investment certificates, it is expected that the government would provide some form of return to them, but the rate would be at the absolute discretion of the government. The Government Investment Certificate Dividend Committee determines the rate of return, taking into account a number of factors, including the economic and financial conditions of the country.

Corporate Organization

Corporative Objective. In view of the primary objective for which it is set up, the BIMB has formulated its corporate objective as follows:

> The corporate objective of the Bank is to provide banking facilities and services in accordance with Islamic principles, rules and practices to all Muslims and the population of this country. The Bank's effort to provide these banking facilities and services is to be undertaken within the framework of its viability and capability to continuously grow and expand.[13]

Organizational Structure. The organizational structure of the bank is as depicted in Appendix A. The structure consists of three divisions with line functions of operations (trade finance, treasury, and corporate investments) and three other divisions with staff functions (establishment, accounts, and legal and secretarial). Each division is divided into departments and further subdivided into units as deemed necessary.

Branch Network. It was envisaged that the BIMB would be the country's only Islamic commercial bank for a number of years to come. To ensure that a majority of the people, particularly Muslims, can benefit, it is contingent upon the bank to make its services available to them as widely and as speedily as possible. This can be done by expanding the domestic branch network of the bank.

Thus, during its first year of operation (July 1983-June 1984) the bank was granted permission to open four branches. The bank now has eleven branches in all major towns in almost all states in Peninsular Malaysia. It was expected that, within the first three years of its existence, the bank would seek to establish at least one branch in each of the fourteen states in Malaysia. The BIMB plans to establish five to six branches throughout the country every year.

Banking Operation

Customer's Deposit. The bank receives deposits from its ordinary customers through the following three accounts:

1. Current Account

   The Current Account is operated in the same way as it is operated in the conventional banks. The BIMB accepts deposits from its customers for safe custody on the *Sharia* principle of *al-wadiah* (safekeeping). With the permission of the customers, the bank uses these funds to generate profit which would entirely belong to the bank. In return, the bank provides the customer with cheque books and other usual current account services. The minimum for a Current Account deposit is M$500.
2. Saving Account

   This is an account where the bank receives deposits from its customers who are seeking safe custody of their funds with some degree of convenience in their use, again on the *Al-Wadiah* basis. The customers may withdraw part or the whole of their balances at any time they desire; the bank guarantees the refund of such balances. The bank asks permission from the customers so that it can use the funds to generate profits. However, in contrast with current account, the bank may, at its absolute discretion, reward the customers by returning a part of the profits generated from the use of their funds from time to time.

3. Investment Account

   There are two types of Investment Accounts both of which are operated on the *mudaraba* (profit-sharing) principle:

   a. General Investment Account

      Deposits received under this account are invested by the bank on behalf of the depositors. The bank accepts such deposits on the following basis:

1 month	15 months
3 months	18 months
6 months	24 months
9 months	36 months
12 months	48 months

      The *mudaraba* principle requires the bank to act as the "entrepreneur" and the customers as the "providers of capital", and both parties to agree on how to distribute the profits, if any, generated by the bank from the investment of the funds. At present, the bank offers a profit-sharing ratio of 70:30 (70 per cent to the customers and 30 per cent to the bank from the gross profits made). This ratio may be changed from time to time so as to maintain an equitable distribution of profits between the two parties. In the event of a loss, the depositors will bear all the losses. The management of the investment of the funds is entirely under the supervision of the bank. The minimum amount for this investment account is M$500.

   b. Special Investment Account

      The bank also selectively accepts deposits from the government and corporate customers in the form of Special Investment Accounts which are also operated on the *mudaraba* principle; but the modes of investment of the funds and the ratios of distribution of profits may be individually negotiated.

Project Financing. Two methods used by the BIMB to finance acceptable projects are governed by the principles of *mudaraba* and *musharaka* (equity participation).

Financing the Acquisition of Assets

1. *Murabahah* (Cost-plus or Mark-up)
   Under this mode of financing the bank first purchases the asset, movable or immovable, and subsequently sells the relevant asset to the customer at the agreed price which consists of the actual cost of the asset to the bank plus the bank's margin of profit.
2. *Bai'Bithaman Ajil* (Deferred Sale)
   Under this mode of financing, the bank first determines the requirements of the customer in relation to the duration and manner of repayment. The bank then purchases the asset and subsequently sells the relevant assets to the customer at the agreed price which comprises (a) the actual cost of the asset to the bank; and (b) the bank's margin of profit which varies according to the value and type of the project, especially in the case of housing.
3. *Ijara* (Leasing)
   Financing under the prnciple of *ijara* requires the bank first to purchase the asset required by the customer and subsequently to lease the asset to the customer for a fixed period on a lease rental basis.
4. *Bai'Al-Takjiri* (Leasing Ending with Ownership)
   This mode of financing requires the bank to finance its customers who initially wish to acquire the right to use the service of a required asset and subsequently own it. The procedure involved is the same as the above principle of *ijara*, except that both parties agree that the customer will eventually purchase from the bank the asset concerned at an agreed price with all the lease rentals previously paid constituting part of the price.
5. *Qard ul-Hassan* (Benevolent Loan)
   The bank may use an appropriate proportion of the funds at its disposal in the form of loans to deserving customers under the principle of *qard ul-hassan*. The borrower is obliged to repay only the principal amount of the loan, according to its terms and conditions. The *Sharia*, however, encourages the borrower to pay anything over and above the principal amount at his own discretion without any demand from the bank.

Trade Finance. The bank may provide specific facilities and/or financing, mostly on short-term basis, for the purpose of facilitating trade or providing working capital for its customers. Such facilities/financing may be granted in connection with the purchase/import and sale/export of goods and machinery, and the acquisition and holding of stocks and inventories, spares and replacements, raw materials, and semi-finished goods.

The facilities/financing currently provided include Letter of Credit, Letter of Guarantee, and working capital.

1. Letter of Credit under the Principle of *Al-Wakala*

   Under the principle of *wakala*, the customer first informs the banks of his Letter of Credit requirements and requests the bank to provide the facility. The bank may require the customer to place a deposit equal to the full amount of the value of the goods to be purchased or imported. The bank accepts the deposit under the principle of *Al-Wadia*.

   The bank then establishes the Letter of Credit and pays the proceeds to the negotiating bank utilizing the customer's deposit, and subsequently releases the documents to the customer. For its services the bank will charge the customer fees and commissions.
2. Letter of Credit under the Principle of *Al-Musharaka*

   This mode of financing requires the customer to inform the bank of his Letter of Credit requirements and negotiate the terms of *musharaka* financing. The customer places with the bank a deposit for his share of the cost of the goods to be purchased/imported which the bank accepts under the principle of *Al-Wadia*.

   The bank then issues the Letter of Credit and pays the proceeds to the negotiating bank utilizing the customer's deposit as well as its own share of financing, and subsequently releases the documents to the customer. The customer takes possession of the goods and disposes of them in the manner stimulated in the agreement. Profits derived from the venture will be shared as per agreement.
3. Letter of Credit under the Principle of *Al-Murabaha*

   This mode of financing requires the customer to inform the bank of his Letter of Credit requirements and to request the bank to purchase/import the goods, indicating thereby that he would be willing to buy the goods from the bank on their arrival on the principle of *murabaha*. The bank issues the Letter of Credit and pays the proceeds to the negotiating bank utilizing its own funds. The bank sells the goods to the customer at a price comprising the cost of the goods and a profit margin under the principle of *murabaha* for settlement by cash or on a deferred payment (*bai'bithaman ajil*) basis.
4. Letter of Guarantee

   The bank may provide the facility of Letter of Guarantee to its customers for certain purposes. This may be provided in respect of the performance of a task, the settlement of a loan, etc.

   To provide this facility the bank may require the customer to place a certain amount of deposit which the bank receives under the principle of *Al-Wadia*. The bank charges the customer a fee for the services it provides.

5. Working Capital under the Principle of *Al-Murabaha*

   This mode of financing requires the customer to approach the bank to provide financing for his working capital requirements to purchase stocks and inventories, spares and replacements, semi-finished goods, and raw materials.

   The bank first purchases or appoints the customer as its agent to purchase the required goods on its behalf and the bank pays from its own funds. The bank subsequently sells the goods to the customer at an agreed price on a cost-plus basis. The customer is allowed to settle this sale price on a deferred term of 30 days, 60 days, 90 days, or any other duration as the case may be.

Other Services. The bank also provides other usual banking services at a fee under various rules of the *Sharia*. Among others, the common modes are as follows:

1. remittances and transfers;
2. sale and purchase of foreign currency;
3. investment/portfolio management;
4. trustee and nominee company services.

An Examination and Evaluation of the BIMB's Performance

Incorporation and Commencement of Business

The BIMB was incorporated on 1 March 1983 and it started operating on 1 July 1983. The first four months prior to the bank's operations were spent in recruiting the pioneer staff and in familiarizing them with the *Sharia* rules and principles on banking and finance. The first quarter of its first financial year was devoted mainly to dissemination of information and familiarization of the public and potential customers with the various Islamic modes of operations. The bank really began its business operations in the second quarter of the financial year.

The BIMB was incorporated with an authorized capital of M$500 million and a paid-up capital of M$79.9 million subscribed by the shareholders in three calls with the last call completed in December 1983. Based on the size of the shareholders' funds of the bank as at 31 December 1984 which amounted to M$80.364 million, the BIMB can be placed among the seven largest locally incorporated commercial banks in Malaysia. This comparison is clearly shown in Table 4.1. A comparison of the BIMB with other Islamic banks in other countries, based on the amount of paid-up capital, shows that it ranks fifth among the fourteen Islamic banks (Table 4.2). Based on these comparisons, obviously the BIMB has a sound base to conduct its operations and to gain the people's confidence. The confidence of the people towards the bank also stems from the fact that the government and other major religious agencies and Muslim institutions in the country have contributed to the bank shareholders' funds. It is significant to note that the BIMB is the first Islamic bank to be established with direct government involvement, while other earlier Islamic commercial banks in other Muslim countries were established mainly by private individuals.

Customer's Deposits

During the financial year ending 30 June 1984, the bank accepted deposits from customers in the form of Current Account deposits, Saving Account deposits, and Investment Account deposits for periods ranging from six months to five years and over. During the second financial year, the range of periods for Investment Account deposits was extended to include periods of one and three months. From these various accounts the bank had customers' deposits amounting to M$241.1 million as institutional customers under the Special Investment Account. By 30 June 1985, the total customers' deposits had increased to M$410.2 million, including M$49.4 million short-term deposits from the institutional customers. Thus, the level of deposit had increased by about 70 per cent within a year.

The detailed breakdown of the size of customers' deposits and the number of depositors according to various accounts excluding the deposits of the institutional customers is presented in Table 4.3. As at December 1985, the number of depositors in the Saving Account stood at 72,309 with deposits amounting to M$61.09 million. This yields an average of M$845 per depositor. The number of depositors in the Investment Account is small, but the size of the deposit is large. As at 31 December 1985, there were 10,520 depositors and M$346.37 million deposits in the Investment Account which represented 73 per cent of the aggregate deposits of M$473.01 million.

Between 1 January 1984 and 31 December 1985, the size of Current Account deposits increased by 31 per cent, Saving Account deposits by 535 per cent, Investment Account deposits by 910 per cent, and the overall total by 420 per cent. This can be considered a remarkable progress in terms of mobilizing the deposits within a short span of time, although the large percentages are due mainly to the small base values.

As already explained before, both Current and Saving Accounts deposits of the bank are accepted under the principle of safe custodianship (*wadiah*) and the bank is not obliged to distribute any profit to the depositors. However, in the case of only Saving Account, the bank has been, at its absolute discretion, distributing profits to the depositors. The rate of profit paid to depositors has ranged from 4.96 per annum in June 1984 to 5.46 per cent in June 1985.

TABLE 4.1
Commercial Banks (Locally Incorporated): Assets, Deposits, Shareholders' Funds, and Net Pre-tax Profits as at 31 December 1984
(M$'000)

Name of Institution	Assets 1		Deposits		Shareholders' Funds		Net Pre-tax/After Tax + (Profit/Loss)	
	Size	Ranking	Size	Ranking	Size	Ranking	Size	Ranking
Malaya Banking Berhad****	22,067,881	1	14,066,847	2	1,132,053	1	121,343+	1
Bank Bumiputra Malaysia Berhad	21,102,385	2	14,657,965	1	1,074,469	2	(78,474)	23
United Malayan Banking Corporation Berhad*	7,494,271	3	4,517,494	4	200,911	4	30,599	3
Public Bank Berhad	5,811,853	4	4,785,041	3	319,047	3	21,089	7
Development and Commercial Bank Berhad	4,154,034	5	2,999,118	5	174,496	5	32,681	2
United Asian Bank Berhad*	3,543,871	6	2,161,914	6	132,655	6	9,401	9
Perwira Habib Bank Malaysia Berhad	2,346,128	7	1,844,733	7	76,443	8	(18,863)	22
Malayan United Bank Berhad	1,540,000	8	1,262,000	8	75,000	9	25,800	5
Kwong Yik Bank Berhad	1,341,262	9	1,090,175	9	72,744	11	23,260	6
Hock Hua Bank Berhad	1,313,330	10	973,370	10	74,380	10	27,130	4
The Pacific Bank Berhad	1,073,118	11	608,604	15	46,010	14	12,754	8
Southern Bank Berhad	1,050,906	12	799,162	11	68,976	12	8,987	10

TABLE 4.1 (cont'd)

Name of Institution	Assets 1		Deposits		Shareholders' Funds		Net Pre-tax/After Tax + (Profit/Loss)	
	Size	Ranking	Size	Ranking	Size	Ranking	Size	Ranking
Bank Utama (Malaysia) Berhad	1,026,600	13	725,334	13	38,163	17	6,051+	14
Sabah Bank Berhad*	844,688	14	657,873	14	39,590	15	1,005	20
The Oriental Bank*	838,795	15	731,953	12	38,127	18	2,955	17
Bank of Commerce Berhad***	762,055	16	478,064	16	25,348	21	1,653	19
Malaysia French Bank Berhad	731,467	17	307,380	18	46,559	13	7,867	12
Bee Hin Lee Bank Berhad	684,315	18	472,634	17	38,608	16	6,404	13
Bank Islam Malaysia Berhad*	563,429	19	279,609	19	80,364	7	2,234	18
Hock Hua Bank (Sabah) Berhad	307,107	20	215,348	20	26,213	20	8,358	11
Wah Tat Bank Berhad	215,307	21	163,812	21	13,480	22	4,080	15
Kong Ming Bank Berhad*	180,217	22	154,797	22	11,929	23	3,096	16
Bank Buruh (Malaysia) Berhad****	167,759	23	68,868	23	28,213	19	438	21

* Position as at 31 December 1983.
** Position as at 30 June 1984.
*** Position as at 31 August 1984.
**** Position as at 30 June 1985.
\+ Including Contra Accounts

SOURCE: Arab-Malaysia Merchant Bank Berhad, *The Kuala Lumpur Bankers Directory*, 1986.

TABLE 4.2

Islamic Banks Throughout the World: Assets, Deposits, Capital, and Depositors' Remuneration as of Their Last Financial Year of 1984

Name of Institution	Date of Incorporation & Operation	Exchange Rate NC/US$	Authorized Capital		Paid-up Capital		Assets		Deposits		Depositors' Remuneration
			Size US$	Ranking	Size US$	Ranking	Size US$	Ranking	Size US$	Ranking	%
Dubai Islamic Bank, Dubai	3/1975 10/1975	3.671	13.6	10	13.6	8	311.1	5	283.3	4	—
Faisal Islamic Bank of (Sudan), Khartoum	8/1977 5/1978	1.300	76.9	5	44.9	3	344.1	4	212.4	5	5.0
Kuwait Finance House, Safat	3/1977 8/1978	0.304	61.7	6	61.5	1	2782.1	1	2338.8	1	—
Faisal Islamic Bank of Egypt, Cairo	10/1977 7/1979		100.0	4	40.0	4	1861.9	2	1531.1	2	9.0
Jordan Islamic Bank for Finance & Dev., Amman	11/1978 9/1979	0.405	9.9	12	9.0	10	252.1	6	204.7	6	2.85 - 5.13
Bahrain Islamic Bank, Manama	3/1979 11/1979	0.376	61.2	7	15.3	6	104.7	9	78.0	8	6.0
Islamic International Bank Investment & Dev., Cairo	11/1980 10/1981		12.0	11	11.4	9	680.6	3	502.9	3	n.d.

TABLE 4.2 (cont'd)

Name of Institution	Date of Incorporation & Operation	Exchange Rate NC/US$	Authorized Capital		Paid-up Capital		Assets		Deposits		Depositors' Remuneration
			Size US$	Ranking	Size US$	Ranking	Size US$	Ranking	Size US$	Ranking	%
Islamic Investment House, Amman	9/1981	0.405	9.9	13	9.4	11	32.0	12	16.3	13	5.55 - 8.325
Al-Baraka International, Ltd., London 1983	1983	0.804	124.3	3	6.2	12	28.8	14	22.0	12	n.d.
Islamic Bank International of Denmark, Copenhagen	11/1982 4/1983	11.26	3.5	14	3.5	13	30.2	13	9.5	14	8.2
Bank Islam Malaysia Bhd., Kuala Lumpur	3/1983 7/1983	2.425	206.2	1	32.9	5	134.2	7	99.5	7	4.96 - 6.95
Islamic Bank of Qatar, Doha 7/1983	3/1983	3.640	54.9	8	13.7	7	101.6	10	77.3	9	4.325 - 7.785
Islamic Bank of Bangladesh, Dhaka 8/1983	3/1983	26.00	19.2	9	2.8	14	32.1	11	24.5	11	4.95 - 14.13
Albaraka Islamic Investment Bank, Manama	2/1984 6/1984		200.0	2	50.0	2	125.1	8	70.2	10	6.60/8.48

Note: There are no data available for items marked n.d.

SOURCE: *Akfar Inquiry*, 2, no. 12 (December 1985).

TABLE 4.3

Bank Islam Malaysia Berhad: Customers' Deposits*

Period	Current Account		Saving Account		Investment Account		Other Deposits		Total	
	Number of Depositors	M$ Million	Number of Depositors	M$ Million	Number of Depositors	M$ Million	Number of Depositors	M$ Million	Number of Depositors	M$ Million
December 1983	2,345	47.11	17,515	9.62	2,636	34.41	3	0.01	22,499	91.05
June 1984	4,392	40.70	32,012	26.12	4,658	101.22	24	3.59	41,086	171.63
December 1984	5,625	42.00	43,441	34.79	6,976	188.06	39	4.76	56,081	269.61
June 1985	7,488	46.11	55,507	46.48	8,832	173.24	72	5.27	71,899	371.10
December 1985	7,862	61.62	72,309	61.09	10,520	346.37	58	3.93	90,749	473.01

* The figures exclude short-term deposits of institutional customers which the bank accepted under the Special Investment Account deposits.

SOURCE: BIMB.

Investment Account deposits are accepted under the principle of trust financing (*mudaraba*) with obligatory distribution of profits between the depositors and the bank. In this contract, the bank acts as the entrepreneur and the customers as the providers of capital.

The rates of return for the Saving Account deposits and various categories of Investment Account deposits are presented in Table 4.4. The BIMB rates of return were a little lower than the rates offered by the commercial banking industry, as presented in Table 4.5.

TABLE 4.4
Bank Islam Malaysia Berhad: Rate of Profit Actually Paid to Depositors
(Percentage per annum)

Type of Deposit	June 1984	Dec. 1984	June 1985	Dec. 1985
Saving Accounts	4.96	5.14	5.46	5.18
Investment Accounts				
1 month	—	5.76	6.11	5.80
3 months	—	6.12	6.11	6.17
6 months	6.25	6.48	6.88	6.53
9 months	6.60	6.84	7.26	6.89
12 months	6.95	7.20	7.64	7.25
15 months	—	7.56	8.02	7.62
18 months	—	7.92	8.40	7.98
24 months	—	8.28	8.79	8.34
36 months	—	8.64	9.17	8.70
48 months	—	9.00	9.55	9.07
60 months & above	—	9.36	9.93	9.43

SOURCE: BIMB.

It is also important to note that about 90 percent of the total Investment Account deposits are for a period of two years and below. To encourage the depositors to put their money in the Investment Account deposits for a period of more than two years, a new policy was introduced in July 1985. According to this policy, the corresponding account holders will be paid interim profits every six months based on the prevailing rate of profit, and on the expiry date they will receive the remaining part based on the realized rate of profit.

The bank's deposits can also be viewed from the various categories of depositors, classified as follows: (1) the general public/individuals; (2) government departments and statutory bodies; and (3) various entities from the corporate sector.

The first category of depositors is considered the most important group that will determine the success of the bank in the future. However, the saving ratio of the Muslims, who are the main potential customers of the BIMB is much lower than the national ratio of 24.3 per cent,[14] partly because of their unwillingness to associate themselves with interest-based banking operations. This factor is more obvious among the Muslims living the rural areas. Thus, it is important for us to analyze briefly this category of depositors in relation to the BIMB.

TABLE 4.5
Interest Rates of Commercial Banks
(Percentage per annum)

Time Period		Fixed Deposits Period in Months: 1	3	6	9	12	Savings Deposits
December 1982	Lowest	8.57	7.50	8.00	8.00	9.25	5.00
	Highest	10.50	9.50	9.50	10.00	10.50	8.50
	Mode	9.00	9.00	9.25	9.50	10.00	6.50
December 1983	Lowest	6.25	6.75	7.00	7.00	7.50	5.00
	Highest	10.00	9.75	9.75	9.75	9.50	8.00
	Mode	8.25	8.50	8.50	8.75	9.00	6.00
December 1984	Lowest	9.00	9.25	9.25	9.50	9.50	6.00
	Highest	10.50	10.75	10.75	10.75	11.00	9.25
	Mode	10.00	10.50	10.50	10.50	10.75	7.50
December 1985	Lowest	7.50	7.75	7.75	8.00	8.00	6.00
	Highest	9.00	9.25	9.50	9.50	9.75	9.25
	Mode	8.00	8.50	9.00	9.00	9.00	6.50/7.50

SOURCE: Bank Negara Malaysia, *Monthly Statistical Bulletin*, November 1985.

In terms of the number of depositors, individuals accounted for the largest proportion of the bank's customers. About 98 per cent of the present depositors from this category are Muslims. The Muslim depositors can be further classified into two categories: (a) those who already have had contacts with commercial banks before coming to the BIMB; and (b) those who were yet to have any bank account at all and who were saving some of their income not by depositing money in banks, but by buying real assets. The latter group constitutes only 5 per cent of the total depositors of the bank.

The first category of Muslim depositors (a) is said to be very sensitive about the rate of return on investments. It is believed that quite a large number of them will continue to be the bank's customers only if the bank can maintain a reasonable rate of profit. It appears that the present rates of profit distributed by the bank are acceptable to them so that they seem indifferent in their choice between the BIMB and other banks for depositing their money. This conclusion, however, seems too general and hypothetical, and a detailed empirical work is needed to verify it.[15] It is also important to note that there are some among this category of depositors who come to the bank because they fully accept the Islamic principles regardless of the rate of profit. Nonetheless, the majority of these depositors, it is believed, still maintain contact with conventional banks as well, at least by holding current account deposits.

The second category of Muslim depositors (b) is motivated mainly by commitment and conviction. These depositors put their money mainly in Saving Account deposits. Their number, which is presently very small, is expected to increase especially when more branches are opened throughout the country. Obviously, this category of depositors consists mainly of rural Muslims who may well become the main supporters of the bank in the future.

Financing and Investment Activities of the BIMB

As at 30 June 1984, the BIMB's financing and investment amounted to M$161.1 million. This increased to M$322.0 million a year later. About 15 per cent of the available funds (depositors' plus shareholders') were channelled on *mudaraba* and *musharaka* bases. About 65 per cent of the funds were channelled under the principles of *bai'bithaman ajil* and *ijara*, while trade financing, mainly under the principle of *murabaha*, accounted for about 15 per cent of the total.

However, if we look at the financing and investment of depositors' funds independently, as at the end of 1984, out of the total new financing and investment granted, 77.6 per cent were granted under the principle of *bai'bithaman ajil*, 9.7 per cent under *murabaha*, 5.4 per cent under *ijara*, and 1.7 per cent under *mudaraba*. Thus, both *bai'bithaman ajil* and *murabaha* constituted about 87.3 per cent of the financing and investment granted. This figure increased to about 95 per cent by the end of 1985 (71.2 per cent under *bai'bithaman ajil* and 23.8 per cent under *murabaha*).[16]

It is obvious that the bank's pattern of financing and investment has a somewhat close semblance to the practices of other commercial banks. No doubt, this line of techniques will enable the bank to achieve the normal objectives of conventional banks such as profitability, safety, and liquidity; but this is rather inconsistent with the proposed involvement of the bank mainly with the first-line of techniques identified as *mudaraba* and *musharaka*. As the bank is largely engaged in the second-line techniques, that is *murabaha* and *bai'bithaman ajil*, there are doubts in the minds of the people as though the bank is allowing interest through the back door.

As mentioned earlier, the bank pools the funds from various accounts together and then grants financing and undertakes investment. The bank keeps 30 per cent of the profits and leaves 70 per cent for its depositors. The share devoted to depositors is divided into various accounts based on certain weightage. The lowest weightage is given to Current Account and the highest to Investment Account deposits. In the case of Investment Account deposits, different weightage is assigned depending on the time frame, that is duration of the deposits: the longer the time period, the higher the weightage.

The sectoral allocation of funds disbursed covers nearly all the major sectors, including agriculture, mining, quarrying, manufacturing, construction, wholesale and retail trade, transport and storage, business services, and real estate and housing. It is of interest to note that about 90 per cent of the bank's funds have gone to Muslims. As at 30 June 1985, there were 1,415 accounts of financing and investments with customers, involving amounts ranging from less than M$1,000 to over M$5 million. A large number of accounts involved relatively small amounts, with nearly three quarters falling within the category of M$100,000 or less.

Liquidity Requirements and Other Investments

Like other commercial banks, the BIMB is also required to maintain statutory reserves with the central bank. As at 30 June 1984, the bank's statutory deposit with the Central Bank amounted to M$11.610 million or about 4.7 per cent of the bank's total liabilities. The ratio fell to slightly less than 4 per cent by 30 June 1985.

In addition, the bank is also required to maintain the minimum liquid assets[17] ratios as follows: (a) 10 per cent of its total eligible liabilities, excluding Investment Account liabilities; and (b) 5 per cent of its Investment Account liabilities.

The bank had short-term investments in the Government Investment Certificates to the tune of M$71.2 million as at 30 June 1984. Cash and balance with other banks and agents amounted to M$8.67 million, and statutory deposit with the Central Bank amounting to M$11.6 million. All in all, total liquid assets of the bank equalled M$91.47 million or 38 per cent of the total deposits received. This ratio is very much higher than the ratio required by the Central Bank and that maintained by other commercial banks (around 25 per cent). To supplement its liquidity, the bank also had short-term investment in stocks of commodities traded on the basis of "cash-and-carry operations" with various agents totalling M$60.0 million.

By mid-1985, the ratio of liquid assets to total deposits dropped to 21.3 per cent which was still higher than what was legally required by the Central Bank. In addition, the bank also had short-term investments in stocks of commodities amounting to M$75.0 million, an investment of M$6.9 million in quoted and unquoted shares in Malaysia, and investments of M$6.1 million in its own subsidiaries. Most of the bank's last two investments took the form of joint-ventures (*musharaka*) with other parties.

Obviously, the high liquidity ratio maintained by the bank will affect the profitability of its operation. This high ratio of liquid assets, however, is considered prudent, the BIMB being a pioneer in Islamic banking. Nevertheless, the ratio might be reduced in the future to the level required by law, as the bank needs to invest more in order to generate a reasonable rate of profit for its shareholders and depositors.

Staff Recruitment and Development

The BIMB has placed considerable emphasis on recruitment, training, and development of its staff, not only to ensure technical efficiency, but also to familiarize them with the *Sharia* principles relating to banking and finance. For this purpose, the bank runs special in-house training programmes. Thus, every batch of new recruits (about thirty persons per batch) undergoes a rigorous training programme.

The staff strength of the bank as at 30 June 1984, was 272, including 109 officers. By 30 June 1985, this number had increased to 366 of which 152 were officers. The bank is expected to continue recruiting more staff to reach the target of 1,000 by 1990, with officers accounting for one-fourth of the total.

Subsidiaries and Branch Network

The bank formed three subsidiary companies during its second financial year (1 July 1984 to 30 June 1985). For the purpose of acquisition of immovable and movable fixed assets, the bank formed a wholly-owned subsidiary company with a paid-up capital of M$1 million under the name of Syarikat Al-Ijarah Sendirian Berhad. Another wholly-owned subsidiary company with a paid-up capital of M$25,000, known as Al-Wakalah Nominees Sendirian Berhad, was formed to act as a nominee for the BIMB and its clients.

A third subsidiary company was the Syarikat Takaful Malaysia Sendirian Berhad in which the bank holds a 51 per cent equity, valued at M$5.1 million. The company began its Islamic insurance (*takaful*) operation in the financial year 1985/86.

The bank has also given serious attention to branch expansion. As at 31 December 1985, the total number of the bank's branches was eleven, and it is expected that the number will grow at the rate of six branches per year. In general, initial capital required per branch is about M$1.5 million, with a staff strength of about eighteen to twenty. The bank has plans to open at least one branch in all the fourteen states in Malaysia (including the Federal Territory) during the first phase.

Total Assets and Financial Results of the BIMB
As at 30 June 1980, the total assets of the BIMB, excluding contra items, stood at M$325.5 million. Including contra items, the total assets amounted to M$550.7 million. The corresponding figures increased to M$514.2 million and M$778.8 million, respectively, a year later. The bank incurred a net loss of M$1.3 million in the first financial year ending 30 June 1984. After the payment of *zakat* (obligatory payment or tax for charitable purposes) of M$483,547, the accumulated losses carried forward were about 1.8 million. However, during its second financial year ending 30 June 1985, the bank made a profit of M$4.4 million before *zakat* and taxation. After deducting the payment of *zakat* and taxation, the total profit available for appropriation stood at M$2.56 million (3.2 per cent of the shareholders' funds). After taking into account the 25 per cent transfer to the statutory reserve and the M$1.8 million accumulated loss brought forward, the bank showed a retained profit carried forward of M$0.15 million (0.33 per cent of the shareholders' funds). A more detailed financial analysis of the bank is presented in Appendix B.

Issues and Problems

There are several issues and problems pertaining to the establishment and operations of the BIMB. We shall address some of them in this section.

The Question of Approach
There were groups of people who openly expressed their worries about the viability of Islamic banking in a non-Islamic financial and juridical environment. To them, a proper Islamization process of the economy should begin with the formulation of an Islamic constitution in the country. This argument stems from the fact that the existing inherited Constitution limits the application of the *Sharia* by the Muslims in the country. The status of Islam as an official religion of the Federation, as stated in Article 3 of the Constitution does not give full recognition to Islam as a complete system of life in which the *Sharia* principles govern all aspects, economic, political, legal, social, and cultural. There are certain provisions in the existing Constitution that directly limit the application of the *Sharia*, particularly those in Sections 3(1) and 5 of the Civil Law Act 1956.[18]

Thus, it has been argued that the proper approach to Islamization would be to introduce and implement the *Sharia* which will automatically foster the applications of Islamic principles in all economic activities of the people. This argument, however, lacks credibility. The establishment of the BIMB is in actual fact a continuation of the efforts of the modern Islamic banking movement which first started in the Middle East countries. Based on the experiences of earlier Islamic banks established in Middle East countries, there is enough evidence to erase doubts about the viability of Islamic banks.

In the Malaysian context, the fact that the Islamic bank is directly supported by the government has given the project an additional strength. However, viability in the financial sense alone will not be sufficient, if we view the implementation of Islamic banking as only a part of the Islamization process. Accordingly, the criteria of success for an Islamic bank need to be widened. Islamic banking is thus seen as an instrument for establishing an economic order that is both efficient and equitable.

Furthermore, to insist on an Islamic constitution for the country and a complete understanding of Islamic principles on the part of the Muslims as pre-conditions to start Islamic banking would be tantamount to postponing and even avoiding the process of Islamization of the economy.

There is evidence to show that the establishment of the BIMB has inspired many Muslims in the country and triggered off an education process to rediscover Islam. In addition, following the introduction of Islamic banking, the institution of Islamic insurance has also made its appearance in the country. Such efforts, as they gather momentum, will cause the existing legal provisions which contradict the *Sharia* principles to be reviewed and amended.

However, it is important that the Islamization process proceeds in a phased manner so that it does not disrupt the smooth functioning of the economy.

Over-Dependence on "Second-Line Techniques"

Another issue raised concerns the excessive reliance of the BIMB on the second-line techniques of operation, that is *murabaha*, *bai'bithaman ajil*, and *ijara* in the disbursement of funds. These secondary techniques are seen by some as counterparts to the institution of interest as practised by conventional commercial banks. This is so because the mark-ups charged by the Islamic bank are about the same as the rates of interest, if we were to convert these mark-ups into a ratio of the principal sum of money provided by the bank. Some people therefore simply accuse the BIMB of charging interest in a disguised form. Consequently, the cost of finance advanced by the Islamic bank under the various modes is still high and is comparable to the cost of funds provided by other banks based on interest; hence, the basis for some people to question the real status of the bank, whether it is really an "Islamic" bank in both letter and spirit or just another commercial bank albeit without the interest label.

There is also apprehension among the Muslim scholars that *bai'bithaman ajil* and *murabaha* sales may deteriorate into purely financing arrangements with the agreed profit margin being no more than a camouflage for interest. Thus, it is expected that there will be basis for such criticism unless the Islamic bank ceases to depend on these modes of finance.[19]

The bank has been accused of being only concerned with making profits and neglecting the welfare elements in its operations. The latter argument, however, stems basically from the tendency of some people to equate the bank with *bait-ul-Mal* or welfare house, which it is not. The bank belongs to the realm of *tijari* (commercial sector) and not to that of *siasi* (public sector), nor to that of *ijtimai* (welfare sector).[20]

Therefore, it can be argued that the Islamic bank should concern itself with doing business rather than undertaking welfare activities, as it has a responsibility to protect the interests of the depositors and shareholders by maintaining a reasonable rate of return on their investment.

However, the fact that the bank needs to make profits cannot justify its over-dependence on the second-line techniques of operation because possibilities for making even more profits through the first-line techniques such as *mudaraba* and *musharaka* are not absent. Besides, the bank's over-dependence on the second-line techniques may also lead to inequitable distribution of gains between the users and the providers of capital. Otherwise, the bank cannot contribute significantly to changes in the distribution of income as encouraged by Islam. In this context, it is relevant to note that many customers of the bank prefer to get *murabaha* rather than *musharaka* finance, as they make more profits after paying a fixed sum of mark-up as agreed in the contract. Clearly, the first-line techniques of *mudaraba* and *musharaka* will be more just in terms of profit distribution between the users and the providers of capital. The success of the bank in expanding its activities along these first-line techniques of operation, however, will depend on certain conditions.

The BIMB, as an Islamic commercial bank, should play the role of an intermediary between the surplus units and the deficit units. The bank should act as an entrepreneur and promoter, encouraging people to invest and to take calculated risks. In other words, it means that the bank should finance the projects of those direct investors under the principles of *mudaraba* and *musharaka* and refrain from starting its own projects. This would help not only broaden the equity base in conformity with the Islamic ideals, but also minimize undue risks for the bank.

Be that as it may, there are several reasons why the BIMB relies heavily on the second-line techniques of operation. Firstly, from the *Sharia* point of view, we cannot deny there is nothing un-Islamic about these financing modes. Secondly, such financing is considered less risky than *mudaraba* or *musharaka*.[21] Thirdly, the bank must listen to the market which needs all sorts of financing, including the so-called second-line techniques. Fourthly, the bank's over-dependence on the second-line techniques, to some extent, may be attributed to the profile of its senior staff members the majority whom have had conventional commercial banking rather than merchant banking experience; it is the latter which has greater relevance to the first-line techniques of Islamic banking.

Nevertheless, whatever the reasons one could give to justify the BIMB's over-dependence on the second-line techniques of operation, there can be no excuse for not actively promoting the first-line techniques which would reflect the true spirit behind Islamic banking. The first-line techniques can help achieve the ultimate objectives of Islamic banking, that is alleviation of economic injustice as manifested by excessive concentration of wealth and inequitable distribution of income. In addition, "moral" risks associated with dishonest entrepreneurs can be reduced if not eliminated in the long term.[22]

Saving and Investment Mechanisms

Another issue of serious concern refers to the mechanism used by the bank in the mobilization of deposits. It is reasonable to assume that depositors are sensitive to the rates of return on their capital. That an Islamic bank cannot give any promise on the rate of return to its depositors, it is sometimes argued, might discourage savers from depositing their savings in interest-free banks. Obviously, there is an urgent need for these banks to find new mechanisms to mobilize deposits. However, it is important to note that the rationale for Islamic banking is based on the premise that there exists a Muslim society that is genuinely interested in eliminating *riba*, even at the cost of bearing all the inconveniences and difficulties that will be unavoidable in the initial phase.[23] One possible avenue would be to invoke the Islamic value system that encourages moderation in spending (*infaq*) one's wealth (*mal*) and prohibits hoarding. This may be a good approach in the long term, as it will take a long time to influence people's behavioural patterns, but it cannot immediately fulfil the urgent needs of Islamic banks. One solution would be for the bank to build a loss-offsetting reserve from their annual profit, which can be used to ensure a fairly stable rate of return to the depositors. An individual's decision to save or invest with the bank is presumably determined by the previous rates of profits distributed by the bank in the past. This will serve as a guide for potential depositors to compare various investment alternatives. Thus, for instance, the Muslims in Malaysia may compare the rates of return usually offered by the Pilgrims' Management and Fund Board (see Table 4.6) with what the BIMB has been giving, although the past rates are not necessarly good indicators of the future rates.

Islamic banks, especially those in other Muslim countries, have collected small amounts of deposits from a large group of depositors and channelled the funds to a limited number of entrepreneurs. It thus seems that they are gathering funds from small-time depositors for the benefit of a few rich, big-time investors. However, this is not a problem with the BIMB, as 74.2 per cent of the bank's accounts of financing and investment with customers involve amounts ranging from less than M$1,000 up to M$100,000. As at 31 December 1985, the average amount per depositor in the Saving Account deposits of the BIMB was about M$845. In addition, many of the BIMB financing and investment ventures have been granted to business institutions that directly represent the interest of the Muslims in the country such as the PMFB and religious agencies.

Like other Islamic banks, the BIMB is also facing problems relating to the short-run instruments for mobilization of its resources as well as disbursement of its short-term funds. In the case of conventional commercial banks, these instruments take the form of interbank and money market operations involving treasury bills, government bonds, banker's acceptance, and bill discounting. But all these are clearly interest-based. There are, however, other ways to resolve liquidity problems. For example, the bank may enter into bilateral arrangements with other banks for mutual credit facilities on a profit-sharing basis, or alternatively there could be an interbank co-operative arrangement to extend reciprocal accommodation on condition that the net use of this facility is zero (mutual borrowings cancel out mutual lendings) over a given period.

TABLE 4.6

Pilgrims' Management and Fund Board: Percentage Rate of Bonus Paid to Depositors, Number of Depositors, and Size of Deposits

Year	Rate of Bonus (%)	Number of Depositors ('000)	Size of Deposits (M$million)
1980	8.5	51	108
1981	9.0	58	150
1982	8.0	66	183
1983	8.5	75	196
1984	8.5	133	210

SOURCE: *Annual Report*, Pilgrims' Management and Fund Board, 1984.

Conclusion

Progress made by the BIMB so far is encouraging and the experience is somewhat similar to Islamic banking experiments in other countries. The bank is expected to continue its progress remarkably in the future, at least in achieving the conventional banking objectives of profitability, liquidity, and safety in view of it being the only Islamic bank granted permission to operate in the country. However, the ultimate criteria for judging the success of the bank should not be confined to just the degree to which *riba* is eliminated from its operation and the size of profits earned in the process. Far more important is the extent to which the bank helps achieve other desirable goals of the Islamic economic system, such as eradication of poverty, optimum utilization of resources, maintenance of economic stability, and equitable distribution of income and wealth.

Available evidence clearly suggests that the BIMB has been successful only in so far as the conventional banking objectives are concerned. The bank's over-dependence on the second-line techniques of operation of *bai'bithaman ajil* and *murabaha* imply that its operation is not structually very different from that of conventional banks. Thus, the bank has been unable to influence the pattern of the distribution of profit between the providers and the users of capital in a more equitable manner as enjoined in Islam. It may be argued that more meaningful outcomes could have been achieved, had the bank placed greater emphasis on the first-line technqiues of *mudaraba* and *musharaka*

Be that as it may, the accusation that the BIMB has failed to alleviate economic injustices prevailing in the economy, owing to its over-dependence on the second-line techniques, seems unfair in view of the fact that the bank is still an infant, operating on a small scale in a hostile interest-based capitalistic environment. In any case, such failures are no indications of the inability of the Islamic system to provide practical solutions to modern-day problems, as the BIMB is operating in isolation in an inhospitable environment and does not represent the system itself. In other words, BIMB efforts amount to no more than the struggle of an embryo to survive in difficult circumstances without proper support systems.

Thus, it is obvious that no single element of the Islamic system, however important, cannot produce the desired results, if it is forced to operate in isolation. For an Islamic bank to contribute significantly to the fulfilment of Islamic objectives, its implementation must lead to other complementary changes to complete the process of eliminating *riba* from the economy, such as the establishment of Islamic non-bank financial institutions, specialized credit institutions, deposit insurance corporation, and investment audit corporation.[24]

However, it is also important to note that if the establishment of an Islamic bank is considered as part and parcel of the process of Islamization of the economy, as it was claimed in the case of Malaysia, a mere replacement of *riba* by a profit-sharing or equity-based system, will not suffice. Elimination of *riba*, after all, is only one aspect of the Islamic economic reforms, as it is not the only virtue that Islam stands for. Thus, the achievement of the rich and wholesome fruits of the Islamic economic system requires a complete realignment of the economy in line with the Islamic economic paradigm.[25] In other words, it requires that the process of elimination of *riba* must be accompanied by, and strengthened through, other motivating and structural changes. The introduction of Islamic banking is only a part of the process, and not the be-all and end-all of the process.

The trend of economic thinking at present tends to support the superiority of the Islamic profit- and loss-sharing principle. The fact that several valid and constructive criticisms have been levelled by many leading economists[26] at the whole banking system of Malaysia indicates that the static

Anglo-Saxon model of banking is outmoded and that there is a need for a more dynamic and developmental approach. Islamic banking provides such an alternative approach, hence the interest shown in its experiment.

APPENDIX A

Bank Islam Malaysia Berhad
Organization Chart

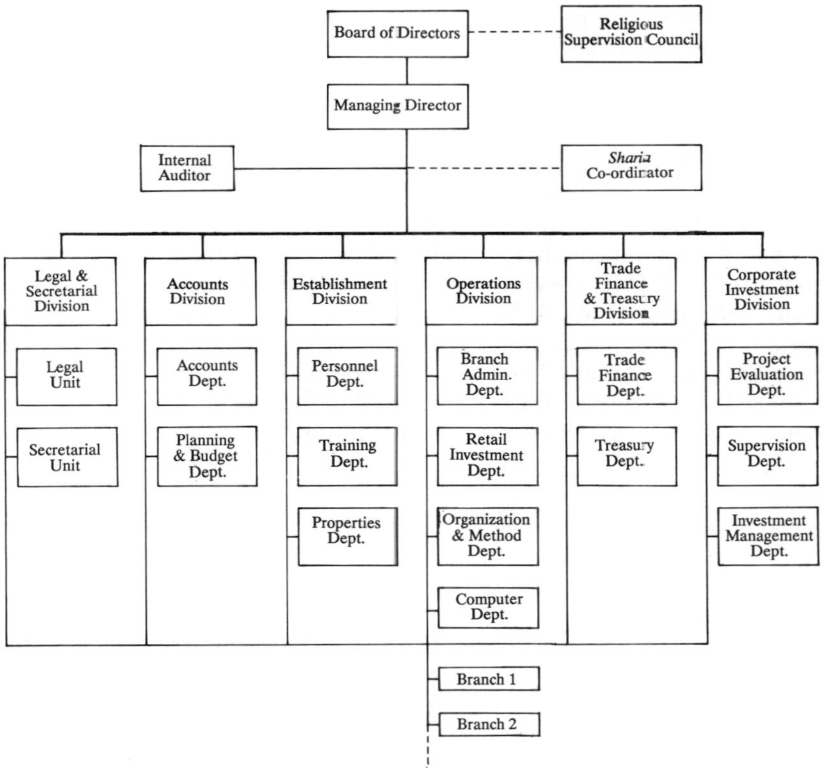

SOURCE: BIMB.

APPENDIX B

Financial Analysis of BIMB

Introduction

This financial analysis of the BIMB is basically a gross comparison of various selected figures and ratios between the BIMB and the overall commercial banking industry (domestic and foreign) in the country. It is realized that this comparison might not produce accurate and appropriate results; nonetheless, it can provide us with some indications of the performance of the BIMB *vis-à-vis* other commercial banks in the country. The selected data and ratios of BIMB and commercial banking industry for the period of 1984 and 1985 are shown in Appendix C.

The BIMB, when compared to other commercial banks of Malaysia, is rather small. Its total assets represent only about 0.8 per cent of the total commercial bank assets in Malaysia. Its deposits account for only about 0.5 per cent of the total commercial bank deposits. Even though the assets and deposits of the BIMB are considered relatively small, the bank has shown a remarkable performance. It has managed to make a profit within two years of operation. The net profit stood at M$2.56 million at end of June 1985, after deducting *zakat* and tax. The returns on equity for 1985 was 3.2 per cent as compared to -2.0 per cent in 1984. The return on assets has also improved from -0.32 per cent in 1984 to 0.33 per cent in 1985.

Capital Structure

The capital of the BIMB is more than adequate to support its operation. The ratio of financing and investment of customers to capital accounts, and the ratio of customers' deposits to capital accounts of the BIMB are much lower than the industry norms — which seem indicative of inefficient use of funds. However, this should not be taken too seriously, as the bank was admittedly very cautious in its approach in the early stage of operation.

The proportion of capital account to total assets of the BIMB is more than twice the industry average, giving much coverage for its shareholders.

Assets and Deposits Structure

The ratio of financing and investment of customers to total assets has increased from 29 per cent in 1984 to 41 per cent in 1985. In comparison with the industry average, this ratio is far below that of the industry. This is undertandable since the BIMB is still new.

Looking at the composition of accounts, the proportion of Current Account to total deposits of the BIMB is at par with the industry norms. This shows positive performance of a young bank.

The ratio of financing and investment of customers to total deposits, which measures the collection and disbursement of funds for the BIMB, increased from 67 per cent in 1984 to 78 per cent in 1985. This is very much lower than the industry norms of 93 per cent and 96 per cent in 1984 and 1985, respectively. This suggests that the BIMB has a large amount of funds lying idle and not used efficiently.

Liquidity

The liquidity ratio of BIMB has decreaed from 63 per cent in 1984 to 40 per cent in 1985. The bank is still considered highly liquid, compared with the industry norms. The proportion of liquid assets to total assets of BIMB was 28 per cent in 1984 and 21 per cent in 1985.

Conclusion

(i) The BIMB has not utilized its full potential capabilities; it should increase its financing and investment of customers to the industry norm [*sic*].

(ii) The bank is very liquid as many of its funds are lying idle, the utilization of which will generate additional revenue for the bank.

(iii) The BIMB has shown a remarkable performance even though it is a young bank. It has the potential of getting better returns in the future, as it enjoys monopoly status, being the only Islamic bank in Malaysia.

APPENDIX C
Selected Data and Ratios of the BIMB and Commercial Banking Industry

Data	1984 (M$million)		1985 (M$million)	
	BIMB	Industry	BIMB	Industry
Total assets	550.7	66727.4	778.8	72,972.9
Liquid assets[1]	151.5	10,395.2	164.5	10,773.5
Earning assets[2]	317.3	61,390.0	512.2	67,480.8
Financing & investment of customers	161.1	42,504.3	322.0	48,297.3
Total deposits	241.4	46,907.8	410.2	5,033.65
Ratios				
A. *Capital Structure*				
Capital accounts to total assets (%)	14	5.4	11	5.7
Customers' deposit to capital accounts	3.09 times	13.1 times	5 times	12.2 times
Financing & investment to capital accounts	2.1 times	12.1 times	3.9 times	11.7 times
B. *Assets and Deposit Structures* (%)				
Financing & investment to total assets	29	65.2	41	66.2
Current accounts to customers' deposits	17	17	11	14
Financial & investment to total deposits	67	93	78	96
Earning assets to total assets	57.6	92	65.8	92.5
Liquid assets to total deposits	63	25	4	24
C. *Profitability* (%)				
Return on assets	(0.32)	—	0.33	—
Return on equity	(2)	—	3.2	—

Notes: 1. *Liquid Assets*:
BIMB = Stock of Commodities + Statutory Deposits with Central Bank + Investment in Government Investment Certificate (GICs) + Cash balances with banks and agents
Other commercial banks = Statutory Reserve + Money at Call + Treasury Bills + Government Securities + Private Securities + Cash and balance with Central Bank

2. *Earning Assets*:
BIMB = Total Assets – Fixed Assets – Intangible Assets
Other commercial banks = Total Assets–Fixed and other assets

3. For comparative purposes, financing and investment of BIMB customers is assumed to be defined in a way similar to loans and advances in other commercial banks.

SOURCE: BIMB, *Financial and Statistical Bulletin*, week ending 1 February 1986.

NOTES

* I gratefully acknowledge comments, suggestions, and assistance provided by Br. Sheikh Ghazali Abod and Br. Azmi Omar. I also owe a particular token of gratitude to Dr Abdul Halim Ismail, Managing Director of the BIMB and Mr Haizir Yahya, Bank Negara Malaysia, for their kind co-operation and assistance in the collection of data for this study. The responsibility for all errors is my own

1 Stated so in one of the most quoted books on the concept of Islamic Banking; M.N. Siddiqi, *Banking Without Interest*, 2nd ed., (Lahore: Islamic Publications, 1973), p. xiii.

2 Qur'an (2: 275) meaning: "But God hath permitted trade and forbiden usury".

3 An exception is the practice of Islamic banking in the Islamic Republic of Iran.

4 The other two accepted approaches are the phased process of Islamizing the entire banking system as implemented in Pakistan and the overall Islamization of the economy as implemented by the Islamic Republic of Iran.

5 M.N. Siddiqi, "Muslim Economic Thinking: A Survey of Contemporary Literature", in *Studies in Islamic Economics*, edited by K. Ahmad (Leicester: ICRIE and the Islamic Foundation, 1980), p. 219.

6 Ibid., p. 220.

7 Ibid., p. 222.

8 R.K. Ready, "The March Toward Self-Determination" (Paper presented at the First Advanced Course on Islamic Banks, International Institute of Islamic Banking and Economics, Cairo, 28 August-17 September 1981).

9 Bank Negara Malaysia, *Money and Banking in Malaysia*, Silver Anniversary Edition 1959-1984, (Kuala Lumpur, 1985), p. 318.

10 Banking Act 1973, Section 31.

11 Islamic Banking Act 1983, Section 5.

12 Bank Islam Malaysia Berhad, Articles of Associations, Article (3).

13 Dr Abdul Halim Ismail, "Bank Islam Malaysia Berhad: Structure and Functions" (Paper presented at the Seminar on Current Trends and Development of the Banking Industry in Malaysia, 6-7 June 1983.

14 *Mid-Term Review of the Fourth Malaysia Plan 1981-1985*, (Kuala Lumpur: Government Printers, 1984), p. 69.

15 The proposition made in this analysis is basically based on the interview with Dr Abdul Halim Haji Ismail, Managing Director of the BIMB.

16 Bank Negara Malaysia, *Annual Report*, 1984 and 1985, p. 76 and p. 91, respectively.

17 These consist of notes and coins (legal tender in Malaysia) balances with the Central Bank

(excluding statutory reserves) and Federal Government Investment Certificates.

18 Ahmad Ibrahim, "Legal Impediments in the Islamization of the Malaysian Economy with Special Reference to Banking and Insurance" (Paper presented at the Seminar on Issues in Islamic Economics, Economic Society, International Islamic University, Petaling Jaya, 27-29 December 1985).

19 M. Umer Chapra, *Towards a Just Monetary System* (Leicester: The Islamic Foundation, 1985), p. 171.

20 Abdul Halim Ismail, "Islamic Banking in Malaysia: Some Issues, Problems and Prospects" (Paper presented at the seminar on Issues in Islamic Economics, Economic Society, International Islamic University, Petaling Jaya, 27-29 December 1985).

21 It is often argued that the *mudaraba* and *musharaka* modes of financing entail two types of risks, i.e. "moral" risks and business risks. The former arises from *mudarib* (the entrepreneur) declaring a loss or profit lower than the actual value because of lack of integrity, while the latter arises from the behaviour of the market forces being different from that expected. In addition, it is also argued that financing under the first-line techniques of operation involves a longer period of time and thus tends to be more risky and inconsistent with the short-term nature of deposits received by the bank. As the bank is newly established and needs to build up people's confidence in its operations, it has to ensure reasonable returns or profits to its depositors. *Murabaha* and *bai'bithaman ajil* are therefore considered the safest modes of financing under the present circumstances.

22 For example, when the user of the bank funds realizes that his ability to secure funds from the bank depends on the profit that his business generates, there would be an automatic check on his tendency to cheat. Thus, market forces would have the effect of almost eliminating such a risk. Moreover, a system of properly audited accounts, accompanied by special random audit of the accounts of the users of bank funds, can help minimize cheating.

23 Dr Muhammad Uzair, "Some Conceptual and Practical Aspects of Interest-Free Banking", in *Studies in Islamic Economics*, edited by K. Ahmad, (Leicester: ICRIE and the Islamic Foundation, 1980). p. 37.

24 M. Umer Chapra, op. cit., p. 147.

25 M. Umer Chapra, ibid., p. 81, and S.N.H. Naqvi, *Ethics and Economics: An Islamic Synthesis* (Leicester: The Islamic Foundation, 1981), p. 110.

26 See, for example, V. Kapanathy, "The Banking Industry: Appropriate Strategic Responses Needed", *Banker's Journal* (Malaysia), December 1986: 21-24.

5 ISLAMIC BANKING: THE PHILIPPINE EXPERIENCE*

Michael O. Mastura

Introduction

Minority banking is not a new development but the rise of Islamic banking is a significantly more recent phenomenon in the Philippines. The major impetus behind the convergence of minority banking and Islamic banking in the Philippines makes therefore an interesting study. The advent of minority banking can be said to have taken root with the establishment of the Philippine Amanah Bank (PAB) in 1973. Due to the Muslim minority groups' aspiration to get into the economic mainstream, the movement to adopt Islamic banking principles into the PAB's operation has continued to be discussed since 1974.

This article discusses the historical forces that led to the establishment of the PAB and the extent to which its dealings have been carried to respond to the "north-south" relations in the Philippines. It reviews the capital structure, economic performance, and relative position of the PAB *vis-à-vis* the Central Bank and other banks, and focuses on the gradual shift to Islamic profit- and loss-sharing (PLS) operations.

Historical Perspectives

The crisis of the 1970s, which centred around some kind of a national dichotomy in "north-south" relations in the Philippines, must be reviewed in proper historical perspectives.[1] The most important aspect of institutional development in Muslim Mindanao thus far can be seen in the creation of the PAB as a specialized model of banking to propel socio-economic reforms. The discussion in this section gives the background.

The PAB as a Specialized Government Institution

A new provision of the General Banking Act of the Philippines classifies banking institutions into the following general categories: (1) commercial banks; (2) thrift banks; (3) rural banks; and (4) expanded commercial banks. The reformed law provides for the specialized and unique government banks which are not covered by the preceding classifications, but are subject to the supervision and regulation by the Central Bank pursuant to the provisions of the Central Bank Act.[2] As noted in the financial structure, the PAB is classified as a "specialized bank" along with the Development Bank of the Philippines and the Land Bank of the Philippines.

The PAB was chartered, at first, as a specialized government institution without reference to its Islamic banking operations. Its establishment on 2 August 1973 by virtue of Presidential Decree No. 264, came at a time of serious national challenge and dilemma. Originally designed to serve the special banking needs of the Muslim areas in the Southern Philippines, it became evidently a part of the government's response to the Muslim rebellion. Its first primary task was to get involved in the rehabilitation and reconstruction work in the strife-torn regions of Mindanao, Sulu, and Palawan.

The corporate character of the PAB may be gleaned from its charter. It is provided in the statement of purposes according to which the bank shall "provide credit, commercial, developmental and savings banking facilities at reasonable terms to the people of the primarily Muslim provinces of Mindanao" (Sec. 4, P.D. 264). The bank is mandated by its charter to invest 75 per cent of its total loanable funds in medium and long-term loans for economic development purposes in the region (Sec. 4, para. (j), P.D. 264).

The charter specifies that the principal place of business of the PAB shall be in Zamboanga City, Mindanao; and that it shall establish such branches and agencies in the dominantly Muslim provinces of Mindanao and Palawan (Sec. 1 and Dec. 2, para. (g), P.D. 264). Aside from the head office, there are branches in Cagayan de Oro City, Cotabato City, Davao City, General Santos City, Iligan City, Jolo, Makati, and Marawi City. Preference to employ officers and personnel is given to the Muslim population in Mindanao, Sulu, and Palawan as may be necessary to carry out its business (Sec. 2, para. (f) and Sec. 9, P.D. 264). As of June 1986, the PAB had a total office plantilla of 213, out of whom 120 Muslims and 66 non-Muslims constituted the personnel complement.

The major government financial institutions own the controlling stock of the PAB. However, the stockholdings of the government in common and preferred shares may be sold at par value at any time to citizens of the Philippines who are registered stockholders. There is an offer of preference to Philippine citizens "who are residents of the provinces served by the bank before the shares of stock may be publicly offered by listing in the stocks at any stock exchange" (Sec. 15, P.D. 264). The government has a total subscription of P30 million and another P20 million comes from four government financial institutions, namely the Government Service Insurance System (GSIS), Social Security System (SSS), Philippine National Bank (PNB), and the Development Bank of the Philippines (DBP), at P5.0 million each.

The authorized capital stock of the bank is P100 million divided into one million par value share of P100.00 each. The shares are divided into four classes: Series A and Series B to be subscribed by the government and the government financial institutions; Series C to be subscribed as common shares by Filipino citizens and domestic corporations and entities, 70 per cent of the equity of which is owned by citizens of the Philippines; and Series D to be subscribed by foreign nationals, their corporations and/or associations (Sec. 3, P.D. 264). This capital structure indicates that the government was to hold a substantial portion of the initial paid-up capital to give it the needed commitment of the national leadership. The capital subscription of the government financial institutions was envisioned not only to make up the built-in institutional shareholdings, but more importantly to complete the required P50 million paid-up capital.

In Table 5.1, the capital structure of the PAB is shown with the relative ratios of stocks subscribed and paid-up. Table 5.2 indicates the number of stockholders from the common shares (Series C) and the corresponding number of certificates of stock issued from September 1974 to June 1986.

A unique featue of the PAB is that its charter provides for a compulsory clause on retention of earnings. Thus,

> ...all profits assigned as dividends to the shares of the government, and all remaining net profits of the bank after the payment of the dividends to stockholders other than the government of the Philippines, its agencies or instrumentalities, if there is any, shall be transmitted to the Muslim Development Fund of the Philippine Amanah Bank (Sec. 15, P.D. 264, as amended by P.D. 542).

Formative Stages of Organization

The details of the formative organization of the PAB were contained in two Letters of Instructions (LOI) which were issued as accompanying documents to the bank's charter. These LOIs were directed to the governor of the Central Bank and the Secretary of Finance, the Executive Secretary, the Secretary of National Defence, and the acting chairman of the PAB.

Letter of Instruction No. 144. The President of the Philippines by virtue of LOI No. 144 designated the governor of the Central Bank as acting chairman of the Board of Directors of the PAB. As such, he was ordered to accomplish the following organizational tasks in a period of not more than two months.

TABLE 5.1
Capital Structure and Subscriptions, 1974-86
(In million pesos)

Series	Amount	Paid-up & Subscribed	Authorized Subscriber	Remarks
A	30	30.0	National gov't.	Fully paid
B	20	20.0	GSIS, SSS, PNB	Fully paid
C	30	0.2	Filipino citizens	Partial public subscription
D	20	None	Foreign nationals	Open for subscription
Total	100	50.2*		

* As of year end 1985, the capital surplus and undeclared dividends amounted to P18.896 million.

SOURCE: Administration and Finance Department, PAB.

TABLE 5.2
Number of Stockholders under Series C Covering September 1974 to June 1986

	No. of Stockholders*	Certificates Issued	Par Value (P)
Muslim	996	1,663	166,300.00
Non-Muslims	154	344	34,400.00
Total	1,150	2,007	200,700.00

* From September 1974 to June 1986.

SOURCE: Office of the Corporate Secretary, PAB.

First of all, the governor of the Central Bank was to formulate by-laws for the PAB in the implementation of its charter subject to the approval of the Board of Directors. He was also directed to prepare and finalize the organizational structure for the bank, placing emphasis on the establishment of offices, creation of positions and corresponding salaries, and all other relative administrative matters.

Next, the governor of the Central Bank was tasked to prepare the lending procedures for the PAB to implement the provisions of P.D. No. 264 on loans and investments and lending limits. The task was to be accomplished with the end in view of absorbing and implementing all government financing and capital assistance programmes undertaken by government financing institutions. The strategy was then to ensure that the PAB actively participated in the Task Forces for rehabilitation and reconstruction of the Muslim South.[3]

Finally, the governor of the Central Bank was instructed to prepare the scheme of loaning assistance to supplement its capital from government financing institutions at nominal interest rates subject to the agreement of the parties and made against the security of the PAB or any of its stockholders. The strategy was to augment and supplement the capital of the PAB mandated under Section 4, paragraph (h) of the charter. This provision specifically allowed the DBP, PNB, and other financial institutions to extend loans to the PAB repayable in the amortization period. The conditions set forth for the PAB to avail of this provision were: (1) that the said government financial institutions should be convinced that the resources of the PAB are inadequate to meet the legitimate credit requirements of the locality wherein the bank is established; (2) that there is dearth of private capital in the said locality; and (3) that it is not possible for the private stockholders to increase the paid-up capital thereof (Section 4, para. (h) P.D. 254).

Letter of Instruction No. 144 recognized the importance of capital formation in the additional tasks directed at the chairman of the bank, who was to include "an investment scheme for the direct purpose of crude oil, its refining and distribution of refined oil and its by-products in behalf of the government of the Republic of the Philippines" (LOI No. 144, para. (e)). For this purpose, the governor of the Central Bank as acting chairman of the PAB was authorized to enter into contract with foreign governments or corporations in behalf of the government. This part of the instruction was not carried out because the Philippine National Oil Corporation (PNOC) was later organized to assume this contracting function.

Letter of Instruction No. 182. The constitution of the Board of Directors and election of officers of the PAB was much delayed, although LOI No. 144 directed the Central Bank governor to nominate the nine members and to designate an officer-in-charge. Thus, LOI No. 182 dated 8 April 1974 was issued designating an executive vice-president who was empowered to establish the offices and employ the necessary personnel to man the PAB's operation.

The first branch was set up in the town of Jolo. It was a place completely devastated during the encounter between forces of the government and the Moro National Liberation Front (MNLF) in March 1974. Pursuant to LOI No. 182, the executive vice-president of the PAB was instructed to prepare and implememt a policy for emergency loans to the residents of Jolo, in co-ordination with the chairman of the Inter-Agency Task Force for the rehabilitation of Jolo. In doing so, the PAB had to consider the unusual circumstances affecting the residents of the strife-torn Muslim provinces. Accordingly, the PAB had to effect a modification of its standard lending procedures in order to meet the emergency situation.

A type of financing now recognized as "social grants" under the Inter-Agency Task Force Guarantee Fund was worked out. These consisted of: (a) unsecured loans for rehabilitation of hard-hit areas of conflict; (b) land purchases for the resettlement and rehabilitation of rebel returnees and evacuees; and (c) advances for financing consultative and negotiation activities. This non-banking practice gave the PAB its political expediency image which subsequently proved difficult to overcome. And yet, no "compensatory subsidy" was given to the PAB for such "counter-insurgency strategies".[4]

Even as the crisis situation gave birth to a specialized Muslim minority banking, the PAB was also required to provide impetus to social policy needs in the Southern Philippines. Establishing the credit policies for the PAB to fulfill its commitment to the Muslim community entailed new institutional structures. This brings us to the *Sharia* (Islamic law) framework of avoiding *riba* (interest) and undertaking *mudaraba* (partnership) operations.

Institutional and Corporate Thrust

This section begins with the consideration of the move toward adopting an Islamic framework for banking operations of the PAB. In an earlier work,[5] certain constraints facing the PAB were discussed, but here, some concrete observations on Islamic banking business will be made. Here, we assume a policy conclusion that the PAB has decided to operate two "windows" for deposit transactions. The idea is therefore to maintain the deposits outstanding to run their course on an interest basis but at the same time encourage the holders of such accounts to shift to the PLS scheme. The review of the economic performance of the PAB as a commercial bank is limited to a comparative analysis (see Table 5.3).

Clarification of Issues Relating to Islamic Banking

There was another major impetus behind the establishment of the PAB as an autonomous financial structure. In fact, LOI No. 144 directed the governor of the Central Bank to prepare and implement a programme for the subscription of Series C and Series D shares of the PAB. This meant that the completion of the capitalization of the PAB had depended on the offering of shares to some leading Muslim business personalities or institutions.

Primarily due to this consideration, the charter of the PAB was amended by P.D. No. 542 dated 20 August 1974. The set of economic principles that make up an Islamic paradigm for financial transactions was spelled out in broad terms as follows: "The Philippine Amanah Bank shall be based on the Islamic Concept of the banking, following the no-interest and partnership principle."[6] The axiological frameworks are essentially expressed by this amendatory clause but the Philippine monetary authorities and the Board of Directors of the PAB have little understood its operative objectives. As an autonomous financial institution, the PAB has envisaged its corporate mission to include the implementation of the economic provisions of the Tripoli Agreement of 1976.

For a better understanding of the peculiar aspects and universal operational methods of Islamic banking the first study team was sent to some Middle East countries. In 1979, under Board Resolution No. 1032, the study team conducted researches and observations of existing Islamic banks in Egypt and the Arab Gulf states. In the report of the team to Dr Cesar A. Majul, who was then chairman of the Board of Directors, two recommendations were highlighted:

- o The need to design an Islamic system for every banking activity undertaken by the Philippine Amanah Bank; and
- o The need to fit this Islamic system into the organization and/or operational structure of the Philippine Amanah Bank.[7]

The study team was correct in its assessment that the first aspect was a technical one and called for the creation of a Technical Task Group to be given the responsibility of designing the Islamic banking system for the PAB. It was even pointed out that the system should provide an "operational module" that would include procedures, forms, accounting and control management, and an information system.

The second phase of the study and planning was conducted in 1981 when this author became president and chief executive officer of the bank. A review of the bank's performance after its ninth year of operation was conducted in order to undertake new action plans. The second study team's Status Report of 1982 helped to determine and answer the following basic questions:

- o Why has the Philippine Amanah Bank progressed on a rather slow basis compared to investment opportunities in the region?

TABLE 5.3
Philippine Amanah Bank Comparative Data on Growth for Commercial Banking, 1975-85
(In million pesos)

	1985	1984	1983	1982	1981	1980	1979	1978	1977	1976	1975
Resources (end of year)											
Cash and other check items	6.962	6.176	4.566	4.446	3.518	5.352	4.519	6.792	2.273	0.874	0.461
Due from banks	10.606	24.488	22.755	9.026	16.487	20.283	6.463	7.792	7.274	3.041	2.940
Loans and discounts	130.047	136.879	152.630	153.672	126.336	59.805	50.862	39.052	30.091	21.387	13.195
Investments in bonds and other securities	82.798	62.599	21.775	34.096	26.178	53.373	6.820	7.059	20.651	19.486	28.501
Other resources	73.259	52.379	61.992	39.426	39.029	16.631	17.895	9.828	7.835	7.618	6.914
TOTAL	303.672	282.521	263.718	240.666	211.548	155.444	86.559	70.523	68.124	52.406	52.011
Deposit Outstanding											
Savings	22.178	21.311	22.985	20.967	118.472	60.936	10.081	7.299	11.031	1.353	0.660
Demand	17.663	22.883	21.794	16.405	21.971	26.234	17.107	6.931	2.557	0.543	0.395
Time	146.745	142.681	123.896	116.036	4.527	2.641	4.083	2.966	1.274	0.052	—
PSSD	0.736	0.900	0.469	—	—	—	—	—	—	—	—
TOTAL	187.322	187.775	169.144	153.408	144.970	89.811	31.271	17.196	14.862	1.948	1.055

TABLE 5.3 (cont'd)

	1985	1984	1983	1982	1981	1980	1979	1978	1977	1976	1975
Capital Accounts											
Paid-up Capital	50.189	50.188	50.170	50.128	50.115	50.111	50.106	50.101	50.089	50.055	50.035
Surplus	18.896	12.837	9.274	5.270	4.463	3.496	1.645	1.054	(1.054)	(0.755)	(0.800)
TOTAL	69.085	63.025	59.444	55.398	54.578	53.607	51.751	51.155	49.035	49.300	49.235
Earnings and Expenses											
Earnings	40.256	40.639	30.738	25.766	15.656	10.065	7.000	6.712	5.437	4.535	3.412
Expenses	34.198	37.074	27.252	24.959	14.690	8.214	6.409	5.657	4.683	4.491	4.237
NET PROFIT	6.058	3.565	3.486	0.807	0.966	1.851	0.591	1.055	0.754	0.044	(0.825)

SOURCE: Administration and Finance Department, PAB.

- o Why has the Philippine Amanah Bank not fully performed as an Islamic bank?"[8]

The concerns of the Status Report were matters of business and not of law. It was indicative of the type of problems that had to be altered, short of legislative means, by management objectives and corporate strategies. The study team was convinced that the PAB's leverage capital had little impact on the make-up of the economic structure in Muslim areas.

An Appraisal of the PAB's Catalytic Corporate Role

The Negative Factors of Minority Banking. The Status Report of 1982 indicated that there was inadequacy of capital to pursue development banking goals. The capital structure of the PAB was seen by Muslim foreign investors as too small to warrant an attractive investment opportunity. This had constrained the bank's capability to conduct international banking transactions.

In discussing the negative factors, the consensus of the managers of the PAB was that one of the contributory factors to the slow growth of the bank had been its inadequate infrastructure facilities. The PAB's equipments were mostly outmoded and acquired from the closed Philippine National Co-operative Bank then under receivership of the Central Bank. The poor image of the PAB was accentuated by such hardly serviceable equipment facilities and poorly maintained bank premises. The annual budget had not reflected any capital outlay since 1974. Thus, the 1983 Annual Budget carried an appropriation of P1.157 million for the improvement of its facilities.

The Status Report noted the PAB's problem of assembling a qualified personnel complement. This was attributed to the low salary structure of the bank which had resulted in the low morale of its staff and Muslim minority feeling of being discriminated against and treated as "second rate" citizens compared to the non-minority bank civil servants. Nor were the working conditions self-fulfilling. The PAB banking entailed more working hours than has been the case with the PAB's major bank competitors. In short, the PAB staff found that minority banking was time-consuming.

The Status Report revealed that the bad loans made during the first few years of operation haunted the management in later years. These unsecured loans totalling P4.8 million had to be recommended for writing off. Not only was it an expensive experience but it also turned out to be a burden on current operations during the second decade of operation. A correlation analysis between the problems attendant to the PAB's operations in highly depressed areas of Mindanao and Sulu and the inadequacies of its credit delivery system proved critical to its profitability margins. The Manila and Marawi branches exceeded the break-even deposit level as against loans outstanding while branches in Cotabato, Jolo, and Iligan, including the Zamboanga head office, had not fared well. The three branches in Davao, Cagayan de Oro, and General Santos, which are not predominantly Muslim cities, were below par. These three branches which reflected negative returns had indicated a higher administrative cost for Mindanao operations due to slow loan recovery.[9]

In aggregate form, comparative data on investment exposures to Muslim and non-Muslim borrowers by branches are presented in Table 5.4.

TABLE 5.4
Beneficiaries of Loans Granted from 1974 to July 1986 by Branches

Name of Borrowers	Total No. of Muslim Loan Borrowers	Total Amount Granted (P)	Total No. of Non-Muslim Borrowers	Total Amount Granted (P)
Cotabato	752	7,233,120.00	181	5,218,080.00
Cagayan de Oro	17	539,000.00	224	10,204,659.00
Iligan	96	2,550,256.00	192	6,703,436.46
Zamboanga-A	349	18,711,300.00	702	34,928,500.00
Metro Manila-A	21	4,095,947.73	110	118,373,644.22
Davao	33	12,374,500.00	259	13,374,000.00
Gen. Santos	42	1,248,500.00	165	5,047,499.00
Marawi	1,921	14,179,103.37	78	261,507.88
Jolo	264	4,909,000.00	34	311,200.00
Total	3,495	65,831,727.10	1,945	194,422,526.56

SOURCE: Branch Supervision Department, PAB.

Of the 3,495 loan borrowers who are Muslims, only 1 is a corporate entity owned and controlled by Muslims. Nearly all of the borrowers are either single proprietorships or partnerships. This observation is even more pertinent, in view of the fact that of the 1,945 loan borrowers who are non-Muslim clients, 6 are big public institutions, namely the Manila Electric Company, the Philippine Long Distance Company, the Philippine National Bank Sugar Crop Loan Program, the Iligan City government, and the General Santos City government. Out of the P194,422,526.56, the aggregate amount of P84,100,000.00 (43.26 per cent) corresponds to these 6 loan portfolios; the remainder is spread over areas where Muslims are not predominant in Mindanao. Roughly, the aggregate sum of P65,831,727.10 (or 33.86 per cent of the total) was channelled to Muslim recipients with geographic concentration at the head offices in Zamboanga City, Marawi City, and Cotabato City and the town of Jolo, Sulu. The only equity investment of the PAB is with the Marawi Resort Hotel to the tune of P500,000. The equity contributions were originally raised by the Ayala Corporation, the Mindanao State University, and the Southern Philippines Development Authority. This development financing was not, however, carried out on a *mudaraba* basis but on a turnkey basis.

The Positive Factors of Minority Banking. The Status Report of 1982 did not overlook the significant fact that the PAB is a fresh community-oriented service industry. Thus, the accent on negative factors in making socially desirable but economically unsound investments could not obscure the gainful experience of the Muslims in asset management. The opportunities for financing the new business lines in the Muslim community and in offering retail banking services all the more accentuated the "catalytic corporate role" of the PAB in developing its highly depressed area of operation.

Notwithstanding its low acceptability as a specialized banking institution, the PAB's depositors grew from barely a thousand in 1974 to 27,391 account holders by the end of 1981. The bank's heavy dependence on government deposit could be taken also as a positive factor at work in the otherwise uneasy business environment of the Southern Philippines. This was a service function performed by the PAB as an official government depository under Central Bank Circular No. 1349 and as the officially designated depository of the autonomous government of central and western Mindanao.

The Status Report discussed the structural bottlenecks and suggested the practical means to overcome them. So far, the legislative means and regulatory needs to operationalize the Islamic banking business lines for the PAB have not been effected. But, the common stock ownership in the bank was identified as a potential step to help market its new capital formation programme. Our recent study shows, as can be seen from Table 5.2, that the bank had on record 1,150 individual shareholders whose contributions accounted for an insignificant aggregate amount of P200,700.00. These figures do not reflect the disaggregated PSSD deposits (see Table 5.5), which are also indicative of the broader category of investors – holders of PLS accounts. The idea of widespread stockholdings, coupled with an action programme for widespread profit-sharing investment accounts, was thus conceived as a captive Muslim market for banking services.

The re-thinking of strategies contained in (a) the Pilgrims Special Savings Deposit (PSSD) and (b) the Inward Remittance and Investment Program (IRIP) launched in 1983 and 1984 have brought to focus a number of unresolved issues. The long-run implications of these programmes spell out the gradual shift to the *riba*-free PLS account. Such programmes practically eliminate interest rates still figuring on both the deposit liabilities and loans and discounts sides of the bank's ledgers. Thus, in practice, the framework would allow the performing assets of the PAB to be shifted to *mudaraba* forms.

TABLE 5.5
Comparative Statement of PSSD Deposits for the Years 1983, 1984, and 1985
(In pesos)

	1983	1984	1985	Increase/ Decrease (₱)	Increase/ Decrease (%)
January	—	667,300.17	845,114.98	177,814.81	21.040
February	13,259.94	662,684.22	751,846.58	89,162.36	11.859
March	41,717.50	851,852.98	644,635.14	-207,217.84	-32.145
April	323,834.50	1,075,034.13	574,215.49	-500,818.64	-87.218
May	327,709.24	1,324,598.560	775,286.840	-549,311.72	-70.853
June	391,226.24	1,580,648.92	700,400.10	-880,248.82	-125.678
July	345,328.08	1,487,211.810	590,485.100	-896,726.71	-151.863
August	416,455.47	403,051.55	522,952.46	119,900.91	22.928
September	476,742.58	650,912.640	440,198.900	-210,713.74	-47.868
October	381,499.32	765,449.58	1,015,582.750	250,133.17	24.630
November	367,719.30	797,694.070	806,937.540	9,243.47	1.146
December	469,184.47	900,445.090	735,699.370	-164,745.72	-22.393
Monthly Average	323,152.42	930,573.64	700,279.60	-230,294.04*	-32.886

* The difference is between the 1985 and 1974 figures.

SOURCE: Administration and Finance Department, PAB.

Special Corporate Policy Considerations

Despite some structural obstacles, an important point can be made for policy consideration with respect to systems for producing Islamic banking services. Operations and systems for generating interest-free deposit accounts and profit-sharing investment portfolios have taken footage at the PAB. This needs to be elaborated under two headings.

Pilgrims Special Savings Deposit Account
Under the non-interest system, only the Pilgrims Special Savings Deposit (PSSD) account was launched to operationalize the PLS account. The rationale behind its establishment was to enable the Muslims to save and be assured of the opportunity to increase the depositors' funds through investment in all spheres of trade, commerce, and industry that are lawful in Islam. The undertaking of pilgrimage (hadj) represents for the average Muslim a form of mobilizing resources within the framework of certain moral

and social priorities. In economic terms, the travelling costs for such a journey can be regarded as expenditures from accumulated surplus income, or as one study puts it, "the expenditures may be entered as transfer payments for invisible imports or travel".[10]

The PSSD accounts are kept absolutely separate from interest-bearing accounts of the bank. The salient features of PSSD accounts are as follows:

(i) The accounts can be opened by individuals in their own single or joint names. A PSSD account can be opened with a minimum amount of P100.00. Any withdrawal must not be less than P10.00, except when the account is being closed. However, to participate in the profit and loss sharing a minimum balance of P100.00 must be maintained in the PSSD account.

(ii) Upon the opening of the accounts, the depositors are issued a deposit book (passbook), in which the bank will record all deposits/withdrawals made. Under no circumstances must a depositor make entries in the passbook. If the passbook is lost/mislaid/stolen, the depositor must immediately report it in writing, stating the circumstances surrounding said loss/theft/misplacement. Replacement of lost/stolen/mutilated passbooks shall be governed by existing bank rules and regulations at the time of loss/theft/mutilation of the passbook.

(iii) As required by the Central Bank of the Philippines, a service fee of P0.50 per month shall be imposed on PSSD account if:

a. There has been no deposit or withdrawal for a continous period of at least five (5) years, and

b. The balance of the account is P10 or less. A notice shall be sent to the depositor thirty (30) days prior to the imposition of such charge.[11]

The investment, computation, and distribution of profit/loss are governed by the following rules:

(i) Profit and Loss Sharing (PLS) funds will be invested by the Philippine Amanah Bank at its absolute discretion in any non-interest-bearing transactions. The bank shall determine and identify the avenues for investment of PLS deposits. The investment in these avenues would be made either on the basis of participation in profit/loss or on the basis of mark-up in prices, which implies that the bank would acquire relevant assets and sell them to the concerned clients with a mark-up in price on deferred payments basis. Other set of terms for investment shall be contracted by the bank with clients seeking financial support and such terms may vary on a case to case basis depending upon the requirements of each transaction. However, in no case shall the bank employ any part of its PLS funds in any interest bearing transactions.

(ii) On a semi-annual basis at the end of June and December each year, the bank management shall determine the income from the PLS funds of the bank. A proportionate expenditure, excluding interest expenses relating to interest bearing deposits based on the ratio of PLS deposits to total deposits of the bank, shall be deducted from such income. Thereafter, an amount to be determined by the bank shall be appropriated and transferred to a Reserve Fund and the balance will be distributed in an equitable ratio between the bank and the PLS depositors.

(iii) In accordance with the requirements of the Shariah, the depositors shall participate not only in the profit but also in the loss of the PLS operations of the bank. However, present indications and based on their professional expertise, the bank strongly hopes that insha-Allah, it would be able to return reasonable profits in PLS operations.[12]

The PAB involved co-operating agencies and organizations in the hadj savings movement based on the following basic understandings:

(i) The Philippine Amanah Bank Head Office and branches in consonance with its charter shall be the sole depository bank of the Tabung Hajj [Pilgrimmage Fund] and shall invest the funds under the Islamic banking concept of no-interest and partnership principle.

(ii) The Philippine Amanah Bank shall also provide the necessary organization and management and formulate policies in cooperation with the Philippine Pilgrimage Authority, the Ministry of Muslim Affairs and other government and private agencies to attain an efficient servicing and handling of the Tabung Hajj.

(iii) The Philippine Pilgrimage Authority (PHILPA) and the Ministry of Muslim Affairs shall assist PAB in the marketing and dissemination of information to the individual Muslims on the nature of the Pilgrims Special Savings Deposit. In addition, PHILPA may be allowed to identify areas of investment and be a partner thereto.[13]

By launching the PSSD accounts, the PAB has taken another step in the experiment on the shifting of its operations from conventional banking to Islamic banking. As of 30 June and 31 December 1983, deposit generated from the programme amounted to P0.883 million and P0.469 million respectively. For the first semester, this innovative "pooled funds" yielded a gross income of P0.029 million. The profit rate of this form of PLS deposit mobilization amounted to P0.021 million or an earnings of P0.10185 for every peso deposit (that is, 10.2 per cent). This compared above par of the return on regular savings account.

Aggregate changes in PSSD deposits, relative to handling of the annual hadj between 1983 and 1985 are reflected in Table 5.5. The average monthly balance is used as the basis for determining the PSSD return on investment. If meaningful policies are to be designed to expand the PSSD deposit base, the investments in non-*riba* transactions have to show a fair return. Table 5.6

indicates the return from foreign exchange transactions.

In terms of its overall performance, Musib M. Buat, who evaluated the Tabung Hajj savings movement, has summarized the major problems and constraints as follows:

- o The general lack or absence among the Muslims of the habit or practice of capital formation through cash savings in depository institutions.
- o Lack of sufficient capital among the Muslims to avail of the PAB equity/partnership venture.
- o Lack of sufficient capital on the part of the PAB particularly its loan portfolio due to its authorized capital limitations, to expand its loan/investment operations.
- o Lack of adequate skills among the Muslims, particularly the prospective entrepreneurs, in project development and management, thus affecting their credit standing in the community.
- o Skepticism of some people, including some Muslims, on the viability of adopting Islamic banking in the Philippine scenario, due to the inability of the PAB to (fully) implement the Islamic banking system.[14]

It was recommended, therefore, at the Symposium on Islamic Banking in December 1983, conducted jointly by the PAB and the SGV Development Center, that the propagation of the Islamic values of economics and finance would be *a priori* steps for forging public commitment to the concept of Islamic banking.

TABLE 5.6
Comparative Statement of Foreign Exchange from Pilgrimage Operations for the Years 1982, 1983, 1984, and 1985
(In pesos)

	1982	1983	1984	1985	Total
Foreign exchange profit	119,176.33	385,729.15	531,449.57	648,234.64	1,684,589.69
Service charge	75,527.98	5,294.00	484.81	—	81,306.79
Total	194,704.31	391,023.15	531,934.38	648,234.64	1,765,896.48

SOURCE: Finance and Administration Department, PAB.

The Inward Remittance and Investment Programme

Developing the banking habits of Filipino Muslims constitutes a dynamic motivation for the PAB's corporate mission. To improve the channels of overseas employees' earnings, the PSSD account was given a special function of fund transfers by Muslims who have relatives working abroad to defray pilgrimage costs. A unique feature was introduced to allow the opening of the account in the name of Muslims who intend to undertake the hadj, and the account number being provided to his relatives working abroad who would then remit regular accounts to the PAB for credit to the said account.

From all these, we may draw some empirical generalizations. In fact, negotiations in Jeddah for an arrangement to provide remittance and an investment programme tie-up between the PAB and the Islamic Investment Company of the Gulf (IICG) were broached in 1984. This resulted in the exchange of a draft Memorandum of Agreement which, after being submitted to the Central Bank of the Philippines, dragged on. As a source of legal documentation for the expanding global operations of Islamic banks, the draft agreement illustrates the extent of progress made in business linkage by the PAB.[15]

Exchange of proposals dated 17 and 25 January 1984 at Jeddah, Saudi Arabia, between the PAB president, Michael O. Mastura, and IICG general manager, Hassan Ali Abdelkader, covered the subject of servicing overseas Filipino workers' remittances and servicing the foreign exchange needs of Filipino pilgrims to Mecca foreign exchange requirements. The operating procedures were based on the Guidelines on Foreign Exchange Remittances of Filipino Overseas Workers approved by the Central Bank, Ministry of Labour and Employment, Ministry of Foreign Affairs, and the President of the Republic of the Philippines.

The following extracts of the correspondence linkage between the PAB and IICG define the areas of activities.

Activity 1: Remittance Programme

PAB	IICG
a. PAB opens account through IICG in US dollars for establishing correspondence and clearing of hajj funds of Filipino pilgrims.	a. IICG opens an Islamic account with PAB in US dollars for establishing correspondence and clearing remittances. Conditions of such Islamic account shall be agreed upon between the parties.
b. PAB arranges to the opening of individual, group or corporate accounts for effecting payments and/or crediting to the account of workers.	b. IICG arranges individual, group or corporate accounts for deposits and/or collections of remittances to PAB together with the transmittal slip.
c. Standard fees or charges against remittances are defined in Annex	c. Standard fees or charges against remittances are defined in Annex

I hereto and are shared between PAB and IICG in a percentage ratio according to Shariah principles of profit/loss sharing.

(I) hereto and are to be collected by IICG to be shared with PAB, computed monthly, quarterly and consolidated annually according to the agreed percentage ratio.

d. PAB in consultation with IICG, hires Investment Adviser (and/or Investment Supervisor) to be seconded to IICG in the required locations with a view to servicing and promoting the PAB remittance program.

d. IICG makes available its facilities to PAB and provides servicing and promotion of the PAB remittance program.

Activity 2: Investment Programme

PAB

a. PAB assists in promotion and marketing of the following:

   i. IICG Mudarabas, in particular The Fourth Mudaraba, for Current Investments;
   ii. IICG institutional Reserve Mudaraba;
   iii. Any other financial instruments introduced by DMI group including the IICG Group Savings Scheme.

b. PAB makes available its facilities to Filipino investors in IICG Mudaraba, when necessary, in the Philippines.

IICG

a. Subject to scrutiny and approval thereof by the Religious Board and other competent organs, IICG makes available its facilities for the promotion and marketing of the following:

   i. PAB Tabung Hajj Savings Scheme;
   ii. PAB Equity Stock Subscriptions;
   iii. PAB Islamic Mudaraba in the Philippines.

b. IICG advises PAB for business development or financial techniques based on Sharia when and where necessary in the Middle East, etc.

Activity 3: Administrative Service Cooperation

a. PAB transmits annual mutawiff fees/drafts and hajj funds via IICG correspondence relations,

a. IICG ensures the provisions of servicing of foreign exchange requirements of Filipino pilgrims at subject to existing rules of the Saudi Ministry of Hajj and Endowment.

b. PAB provides servicing of foreign exchange requirements of Filipino pilgrims, subject to the Philippine Central Bank rules, with provisions for IICG participation according to Sharia principles.

c. PAB shall have opportunity to send its personnel for On-the-Job (OJT) training.

the hajj terminal Jeddah, in Mecca and Medina branches of IICG.

b. IICG has the option, subject to the Central Bank approval to participate or ensure participation in the US dollar or Saudi rial foreign exchange requirements of Filipino pilgrims according to percentage ratio.

c. DMI-IICG shall allow the training of PAB personnel at its offices on terms and conditions to be agreed upon between the parties.[15]

The agreement also contained an understanding to allow representatives to be seconded and to assign investment/deposit agents at a fixed remunerations as well as account executives. In the event of any dispute between the parties that is not amicably resolved, regarding the agreement or the implementation thereof, on notice of either party, the dispute would be submitted to arbitration in accordance with the rules of the International Chamber of Commerce in Paris, provided that such rules do not contradict the Islamic *Sharia*. The draft agreement states that each party would name an arbitrator and the two so named shall nominate a third. If they fail to so nominate a third, or if any party fails to nominate his own arbitrator, within thirty days of such notice, such arbitrator shall be nominated by the Religious Board of the Dar Al-Maal Al-Islami (DMI) Group.

In its evaluation of the draft Memorandum Agreement, the Central Bank suggested the inclusion of specific provisions, among others, as follows:

(1) That the participation of PAB in the remittance of salaries of Filipino overseas workers shall be strictly in accordance with the Guidelines on Foreign Exchange Remittances of Filipino Workers approved by the Central Bank ... as well as the conditions for the approval for its participation in the said program;

(2) The specific terms and conditions under which funds of Filipino workers abroad are to be invested including –
   a. which institution, PAB or IICG, will receive the funds, be liable and keep books and records therefor; and
   b. documents to evidence the investment.

(3) That foreign exchange earnings of PAB from the program shall be inwardly remitted, while outward remittances of the share of IICG from fees and charges earned shall be subject to prior approval by the Central bank.[16]

And, to determine the viability of the proposal in relation to the financial condition of the PAB, the bank was required to submit a projection of the income and expenses from the remittance/investment programme for Filipino workers abroad together with the assumption used for such projection. It was also made to state the terms for which fees or charges earned from the programme should be shared between the PAB and IICG.

Progress in Implementation: A Review

Questions from the Central Bank

In reviewing the Philippine experience in Islamic banking, lessons can be learned from the questions raised by the Central Bank.[17] Taking broad hints from the PSSD programme, the Supervision and Examination Sector of the Central Bank sought the clarification on the following points.

Investment of PLS Funds. The PAB's guidelines on PLS deposits provide that profit and loss funds will be invested at its absolute discretion in non-interest bearing transactions determined according to the *Sharia* law. The obvious questions which the Central Bank examiners sought to clarify were: Is the *Sharia* law already in existence? If so, what are the pertinent provisions of the *Sharia* law governing Islamic investments?

Presidential Decree No. 1083, which was promulgated in 1977, recognizes Islamic law as part of the Philippine legal system. But, in its scope of application, P.D. 1083 is limited to family laws, property relations, and inheritance of Muslims. The legal aspect of *mudaraba* contracts is something else; in fact, there is a need to form within the bank a *Sharia* supervisory body to verify the implementation of the *Sharia* to all the PAB's business activities. For its part, it was suggested that a Central Bank Islamic banking desk could monitor compliance with a special Chart of PLS Accounts and the principles of accounting underlying it.

The second set of questions is more specific. What is the PAB's interpretation of "non-interest bearing investments"? Does this mean that PLS funds will never be utilized for loaning operation? For instance, one of the investment activities which the PAB planned to engage in for its PLS funds is the acquisition of "relevant" assets and selling them with a mark-up in price as its profit. The Central Bank examiners were interested to find out what these trade-related assets were all about. Based on studies of existing Islamic banks, there are up to fifteen Islamic precepts governing financial techniques, but the PAB was planning to concentrate at first on *murabaha* (cost-plus) sales instruments. It was envisaged that a composite method would gradually be applied to include transactions based on *mudaraba*, *ijara* (lease financing), and *musharaka* (equity participation) in financing the working capital requirements of industry, agriculture, construction, and commerce.

The Central Bank recognized such scope of transactions as falling under the business lines for expanded commercial banks (universal banking) and required therefore the recapitalization of the PAB. The Central Bank missed the point so that the real issue was sidetracked. The point to be made here is that there was no practical scope for a deliberate policy to implement Islamic banking other than that *profit* rather than *interest* would form the basis for working out the PLS investment. It was an issue not dependent on the capital requirement of the PAB.

Credit Control of PLS Funds. The other sets of questions are related to the scope of credit control affecting PLS funds. The direct investment of these funds may be invested in the equity of a prospective borrower-firm, or used for financing a project on a joint venture basis. In such cases, the Central Bank examiners were interested to know whether or not the PAB would take an active part in the management of the business project financed by PLS funds. If not, what would the PAB's safeguard be against possible record manipulation of records or distortion of the financial statements, which may be resorted to by the investee to show losses or reduced profits?

Direct participation of banks in "allied undertakings" and in "equity capital" participation are allowed by the major banking reforms of the 1970s and 1980s. Thus, banks have been allowed to nominate a representative to sit in the boards of affiliate or client companies under a supervised credit arrangement. In an analogous practice, the PAB has envisaged its participation to be not by direct management of projects but rather by a directorship or controllership arrangement for its direct investment in commercial and productive ventures. As a *mudarib* (partner) and provider of "risk capital" the PAB would thus extend another kind of bank credit which may be conveniently designated as "capital credit". Compared to "equity capital", this type of credit risk has an appreciable monetary significance; hence, the practical objectives of PLS investment control would be needed to supplement monetary policy.

Distribution of Profit/Loss. The formula for computing net profits for distribution to PLS depositors engaged the scrutiny of the Central Bank examiners. A cursory review of the questions manifests the practical problems involved in implementing the PLS system. For example, it was asked: In what instances or transactions will PAB funds (capital) be employed insofar as the operation of PAB accounts is concerned? How then are the earnings on PAB funds determined and computed?

At present, the formula appears complicated considering that the PAB maintains a "two-window" transaction. As a general practice, Islamic banks are careful to distinguish between the management of funds for investment on a PLS basis, that is funds of different parties which are not co-mingled and funds of several parties which are co-mingled but accepted as the equivalent of a bank deposit. The principle of great legal import in *mudaraba* contracts is that the bank may directly invest as a shareholder, partner, owner, or in any other capacity for its commercial operations. For this purpose, the PAB has to allocate from its ordinary capital funds or the Muslim Development Funds to augment or match the PLS funds. In any case, the share of PLS depositors and that of the PAB in the net returns on investments are determined on the basis of the proportion of each of the deposit accounts and their corresponding periods in months as well as the financing provided by the PAB from its own resources. For long-term investment, pending the approval of the special chart of PLS accounts, the historical method of determining the amount of PAB funds employed through the use of the control account as "Due from Commercial Operations" was suggested by the Central Bank.

Under the approved PLS scheme the cost of legal reserves is one of the deductible items to arrive at the net profits for distribution. For this reason, the Central Bank examiners were curious to be informed whether PAB funds would be employed to cover the required reserves for PLS funds. The answer of course is in the negative. How then is the cost of legal reserves on PLS funds determined? Does the PAB use a specific formula for this purpose? What is the nature and composition of the Reserve Fund? Is it also a deductible item from total profits from PLS investments?

The PAB management follows, in particular, the formula adopted by the Faisal Islamic Bank of Egypt. Apart from the statutory reserve required for deposit liabilities by the General Banking Act, an amount in general reserve equivalent to 10 per cent of the net distributable profit is provided for. By its nature, if the reserve funds are to be linked to the "divisible profits", it makes up a part of the net distributable profits but not of the "net profits" available for stockholders as dividends.

Some Observations

Many questions are still left unanswered because of procedural considerations. Much of the underlying clarificatory points can be discussed as either primarily an internal operational strategy or as a series of "exception" procedures. The next paragraphs will review some of the more important considerations.

Philippine Deposit Insurance Corporation. Are PLS savings deposits also insured with the Philippine Deposit Insurance Corporation (PDIC)? Given the nature of deposit insurance under Republic Act No. 3591, as amended, the covering premiums are connected with participation in the system-wide risk safeguards. As such, payments of deposit insurance claims by the PDIC are made only after many other safeguards have been exhausted. A special function of the PDIC derives fundamentally from the supervisory efforts to prevent the loss of public confidence in the banking system as a whole. As it is the reserve system rather than the deposit insurance system that specifically absorbs liquidity problems, an Islamic bank has to build up a Reserve Fund. This is done by retaining a certain percentage of the annual profits from PLS investment returns.

Reserve Fund. If the losses on PLS funds/investments were atttributed to the PAB's negligence, will PLS depositors share in the losses? As is the current practice of Islamic banks, an amount of at least 10 per cent of the bank's share of profits is set aside to form the Reserve Fund. This annual retention is allowed to accumulate until it becomes equal to the capital of the PAB. Such Reserve Fund is to be differentiated from the Statutory Reserves imposed by the Central Bank against liquidity and deposit liabilities. Where negligence on the part of the PAB or breach of contract in a manner prejudicial to operations is established, and thereby losses are incurred, the bank becomes liable to compensate the participants in investment from such Reserve Fund.

Simply stated, the Reserve Fund system provides better risk finance over time than the deposit insurance system. As the insurance business is interest-based, it does not conform to the principles of the *Sharia*. The element of *gharar* (defined as risk probability leading to uncertainty of the final outcome of the insurance contract) makes it unlawful in Islam. However, pending the complete shift to the Islamic chart of account, the PAB has complied with the PDIC coverage.

Dormant Account. Do the PLS savings deposits which become inactive still share in profit and loss distribution? The matter of dormancy of accounts is another supervisory effort to induce fund mobility. Strictly construed, there can be no "dormant account" under Islamic banking operations because there is no principal and interest to speak of. Earnings and losses computed periodically help to determine the balances in PLS deposits. When the deposit balance ceases to participate in the profit and loss scheme, a service fee is charged as required for dormant accounts by Central Bank regulation. Inactivity then presupposes a discontinuance through withdrawal of the share from PLS deposit investments. And yet, a PLS deposit account totally withdrawn four or five months after the end of the calendar semester will still earn its proportionate share, if the account was closed before the declaration of profit shares, since we have considered the time value of exposure to risk in the profit share computation.

Discounting. Without entering into the controversy over the validity of time preference as a basis of discounting, we have allowed the use of treasury bills as a transitory measure because the true yield is greater than the nominal discount basis. Treasury bills are traded on a bank discount basis so that the income derived therefrom are actually trading gains. For comparative purposes, there has been virtually no opportunity to invest interest in treasury bills as in high-yielding Central Bank coupon issues. During the past few years, the PAB experienced excess liquidity peaks marked by extremely volatile swings in interest rates. This, in turn, had justified the use of different variations in interest-bearing issues known as "Jobo Bills" which the Central Bank utilized to mop up the excess liquidity.

Speculation. At the other extreme of inflationary pressures, the speculative element had mounted an attack against the Philippine currency. Practical problems cropped up in the matter of short-term investment of PSSD accounts throughout the period of 1983-85 because of economic and political uncertainties. The black market rate for foreign exchange climbed to P27: US$1 when the official rate was P14:US$1. The speculation against the peso widened the differential between the official and the black market rates, while organized dollar salting activities set in.[18] This meant simply that the Muslim pilgrims, who needed the dollars beyond what the Central Bank made available, had to source their allocation outside of the banking system. Speculative practices and forward transactions impinged upon the currency swap operations of PSSD accounts.

Accounting. The application of the PLS account at the PAB has paved the way for alternatives to simple lending operations. But the task of reformulating its "credit system" along Islamic modes of *mudaraba* investment and *musharaka* commercial operations has stood at a tentative approval level. Nor has the PAB's investment policy following the Islamic trade financing under *murabaha* sales received the stamp of official action pending evaluation of the proposed charter amendments and Islamic chart of accounts. This explains why short-term investments where the PAB's own funds have been employed in PLS accounts are booked as "Deferred Credits" rather than through the use of a control account such as "Due from Commercial Operations" earlier suggested by the Central Bank.

Taxation. Are PLS earnings not subject to the 5 per cent gross receipt tax? For taxation purposes, all transactions and income taxes on the bank's profit shares plus fee income are withheld in line with the existing withholding tax rule. Once the profit distribution has been determined, the remainder is taken up as the bank's own income subject to the 5 per cent gross receipt tax, and the income distributed to depositors are then subjected to the final withholding tax. Most state-owned or controlled banks are tax-exempted but not the PAB.

Lending. This discussion would not be complete without touching upon investment strategy. As Islamic banks neither grant loans nor advances, its major activity lies in investment participation by itself or in partnership with others through legitimate means prescribed by the *Sharia* law. This is itself part of the overall question of the extent to which the operation of PLS accounts should promote business lines and services.

A case in point was the PAB's attempt to adopt the *qirad* principle in project development in the Kilusang Kabuhayan at Kaunlaran (KKK) livelihood movement of the past government. The PAB had planned that variations in investment of assets underlying PLS accounts could be extended to the KKK Puhunan Fund (so-called interest-free capital) being the capital owner (that is, a sleeping partner). Thus, in a memorandum dated 27 May 1983, the PAB identified the KKK Puhunan Fund to be utilized for investment participation in *mudaraba* contracts with small farmers and commercial users.[19] By design it was also intended that the PAB would participate in the government's Quedan Financing Programme for food production together with the National Food Authority under *ijara* financing agreements for the acquisition of fixed asset requirements such as farm implements and supplies. Partly because the KKK programme arose in a somewhat unusual political environment, the PAB proposal received a mixed response. But, there are already signs that a modified Quedan programme in which the Quedan Guarantee Fund Board together with the PAB could offer a type of farmer's commodity financing facility under *murabaha/musharaka* agreements.[20]

Proposed Guidelines on Islamic Banking Operations

The imperfections of the PSSD/PLS account were to bring to focus the ineffectual legal framework and the inadequacies of the PAB's accounting mechanism for its Islamic banking operations. It was the consultative questionnaires prepared by the Supervision and Examination Sector of the Central Bank that took the PAB to task, from which the 1985 Proposed Guidelines emerged.[21] This proposal was submitted to the Special Commission on Reorganization of Banks and the Central Bank of the Philippines.

Proposed Amendments to the Charter. The present charter of the PAB has been found to be ineffectual in comprehending the operational requirements of carrying out Islamic banking business. Although the proposal was not intended to make the PAB a model Islamic bank, it was envisaged that the bank's charter would conform to the concept and philosophy of Islamic banking, while its other corporate character as a commercial bank would remain.

The following outline sets out the material contained in the proposed Executive Order amending the PAB's charter:

1. The draft amendment contains a definition of terms such as depositor, Islamic bank, Islamic banking business, Islamic current account, Islamic participation account, share, the *Sharia*, *riba*, and *zakat*. These terms have their meanings based and adopted from the

Model Islamic Banking Act, the Islamic Banking Act of 1982 of Malaysia, the Law of Establishment and Statutes of the Faisal Bank of Egypt, and the Islamic banking laws of Pakistan.

2. New provisions are inserted expanding the corporate powers of the PAB to authorize it to engage in Islamic commercial operations and banking services. It empowers the PAB to accept certain types of PLS accounts and to act with full legality on behalf of the depositors' group in investing such deposits on a profit- and loss-sharing basis.
3. The authorized capital of the PAB is increased and its recapitalization is to be undertaken by a Private Offering and Public Offering of the unsubscribed shares. The capital account of the PAB is restructured to establish a clear separation between the Ordinary Capital Resources and the Islamic Share Capital Resources.
4. A new provision details the rights and guarantees of investors. Another amendatory clause is added to govern the disposal of shares which changes the control or ownership of the PAB.
5. A proposal is made to create within the PAB a *Sharia* Supervisory Council to offer advice and to undertake reviews as regards the application of the principles and rulings of the Islamic *Sharia* on the PAB's transactions.
6. A new provision relates to accounting and distribution of profit/loss and the imposition of the *zakat*. Another amendatory clause provides for a dividend policy of the bank.

Proposed Chart of Accounts

In what follows, the general criteria and accounting policies set up in the Tentative Chart of Accounts are outlined:

1. The modification adopts the generally developed Islamic principles and accounting rules on the basis of which the Balance Sheet and Profit and Loss Statement and the provisions for the *zakat* shall be prepared.
2. The main accounts are so charted as to include the asset structure and the liability entries which embody the Islamic deposit accounts and forms of *mudaraba/musharaka* investments for commercial operations and documentary credit transactions.
3. The accounting mechanism observes the statutory requirement for reserve settlement and for clearing transactions of PLS accounts consistent with Central Bank regulations and monetary policy directives.
4. The accounting system represents an understandable record from which the Auditor and *Sharia* Supervisory Council of the bank can

effectively examine the bank's practices and procedures in order to ensure that all transactions yield legitimate (*halal*) profits.

The Islamic method of accounting has been standardized over the years. The varying degrees of experience of Islamic banks and differing effects of regulatory measures have contributed to the discussion on movement toward greater uniformity. Alternative ways of treating certain accounting transactions however continue to be debated. The designed accounting forms are best condensed in the Balance Sheet and Statement of Profit and Loss.

Prospects and Doubts on the Proposals

In order to focus the effect of the legal framework, we end this section with a summary statement of the prospects and doubts on these proposals. The practical considerations involved in implementing them was suggested by Armand Fabella, chairman of the Special Commission on Reorganization of Banks, who argued for a phase-in system for two transacting "windows" modelled on the Pakistan scheme. The general points agreed upon were drawn into the following solutions:

- o Absolute minimum requirements to strengthen Islamic banking as concerns the applicable changes in Central Bank regulations, statutory and charter amendments; and
- o Interim limits in international banking operations pending full recapitalization and expansion of domestic commercial banking license.[22]

It is necessary to reconsider the second point since international banking transaction is essential to the correspondence linkages of the PAB with other Islamic banks. These interest-free banks are hardpressed to find avenues for investments which have been cleansed of interest. Thus, the PAB would be put at a disadvantage if it does not utilize the considerable advances in trade-related financing for PLS deposit accounts. Mutilateral joint ventures are, after all, already an accepted mode of transaction for profit-and-loss-sharing.

Two representative views from the Board of Directors of the PAB will serve to illustrate the sceptical questioning that has to be continously addressed. The Chairman of the Board, Cesar Zalamea, for instance, has expressed his reservations on the Proposed Guidelines on Islamic Banking operations in general terms:

> I have my reservation on the feasibility of undertaking Islamic Banking Operations (premised on profit sharing principles) and traditional commercial banking operations (where fees and interests are imposed) in one organization — Amanah Bank. The possible rechannelling of funds to and from these two operations, particularly from traditional commercial banking to Islamic banking may be looked upon by traditional banking depositors of the bank as a source of higher

> investment risk on their part. Internal bank policies on who would be eligible to borrow under the Islamic Banking operations may be a sensitive issue.[23]

This apprehension practically echoed what Prince Muhammad Al-Faisal, chairman of Dar-al Mal al-Islami, and his associates had already reasoned out in personal conversations with the author in mid-February of 1982 in Jeddah. Perhaps even more significantly it was on this score that Prince Faisal sponsored the PAB research team to look at the legal framework and operative principles of the Faisal Bank of Egypt model. The objection to the two transacting "windows" was found valid insofar as there was business anxiety over accounting for returns which are not to be tainted with interest (*riba*).

The comments of the chairman of the PAB's Executive Comittee testify to the merits of such views which were eventually reflected on the draft legislation. The prospective aspect was emphasized by Alicia Li. Reyes as follows:

> As soon as possible, Philippine Amanah Bank has to be given the license to operate as an Islamic bank. It is the only way it will be able to operate as envisioned under P.D. Nos. 264 and 542 and it is the only way it can attract capital funds from the big successful Muslim banks in the Middle East. Over the past few years, two groups from these Middle East banks did actually visit PAB, to study the feasibility of investing in PAB. Unfortunately because PAB is not yet operating as an Islamic bank, both groups decided to defer action on the proposal for them to invest in PAB's equity.
>
> But as soon as PAB is given the permission to undertake Islamic banking, I agree with the Chairman that PAB should no longer be allowed to contine doing regular banking activities, except for the already existing accounts which will have to be handled under their old terms and conditions until fully repaid.
>
> However since Islamic banking is believed to be a "riskier" banking proposition, PAB should not be allowed to go into it unless its organization shall have been beefed up with conservative, more professional and experienced personnel.[24]

In the proposal itself, recommendation was made to the effect that the Islamic banking operations of the PAB be placed under the supervision of a special unit of the Central Bank. It was further recommended that the Central Bank and the PAB should send some officers and employees for training in actual banking operations either in Pakistan or Malaysia within the first quarter of 1986.

Recent Developments on the Profit-Sharing Plan

The sluggish pace in the implementation of the full Islamic banking operations of the PAB was overtaken by the 1986 February revolution. In a major policy speech before the opening meeting of the Asian Development Bank board of governors, President Corazon C. Aquino set three broad economic goals which her new government intended to pursue: (1) alleviation of poverty; (2) generation of employment; and (3) equitable sharing of the fruits of development. In the banking sector, the plan was to reorganize the Government Financial Institutions (GFI) by divesting their assets from "the paralysing and wasteful effects of state control". The independence of the Central Bank was to be preserved with measures that "defend its mission to safeguard the integrity of the financial system and (Philippine) currency".[25]

What these imply for the PAB can be mainly featured in the ways that Islamic banks have adopted a policy for approaching the poorer, grass-roots sections of society. Islamic banks have, ever since their inception, tried to reorganize the financial life and forms of capital participation on the basis of the alternative system of profit-sharing. This is a very different perspective from the profit-sharing arrangement under which a corporate employer merely facilitates distribution of shares and dividends.

Profit-Sharing under Central Bank Circular No. 810

The profit-sharing programmes of banks and non-bank financial intermediaries authorized to perform quasi-banking functions (NBQBs) are operationally governed by Central Bank Circular No. 810 dated 26 June 1981. This guideline was issued as part of the banking reforms which allowed profit-sharing schemes among bank directors, officers, and employees of NBQBs and banks engaged in expanded commercial banking. Investment in allied undertaking provided appeals to profit-sharing. The financial allied undertakings on which investment could be made apparently has provided the basic foundation for policy provisions on investment banking. Nevertheless, apart from the divisible profits being interest-based, the return on investments on a profit-sharing basis under Central Bank Circular No. 810 are computed not in accordance with the Islamic parameters of appropriation account.

Labour-related Proposals for Profit-Sharing

There has been public discussion about labour-related proposals for profit-sharing as a strategy to equitably distribute the fruits of enterprise. But the process of turning this pro-labour pronouncement, as advocated by Labour Minister Augusto Sanchez under the Aquino government, into legislative fiat that would require companies to share profits with their workers came under much criticism. The compulsory profit-sharing scheme was looked upon by those who are opposed to it, "as a disincentive to investment or reinvestment for improvement and expansion" goals.[26] In the past regime, there was even a move by former Labour Minister Blas Ople to organize a Workers' Co-operative Bank, but its organization was tied to the overseas workers fund and not to the workplace, so that its importance in social legislation was not incorprated in the banking reforms suggested by the Council of Financial Associations of the Philippines to the Central Bank.

Profit-Sharing in Corporate Structures

The current focus of debate on profit-sharing is not just coming from labour; even the management service sector has its own views. Progressive views on profit-sharing are articulated in corporate structures more on the basic goal of participative management. As David Sycip has recently observed, "a profit-sharing arrangement in a fairly run enterprise is a step towards a broader capitalism" in which "the labour's value is in effect capitalized, not just purchased as an input required by enterprise". However, the right perspective must be kept on the following general propositions worked out by Sycip:

> (1) A fair profit-sharing formula should be based on a sharing of the profits after both employees (including executives) and shareholders have received their basic compensations for the inputs they have contributed respectively to the enterprise, and the sharing should be in proportion to the value of their respective inputs.
>
> (2) The contribution of the employees, of course, is the value of their work, while the contribution of the shareholders is the usage value of the capital used by the enterprise.
>
> (3) The value of the work rendered by the employees for a given period equates with the compensation paid to them for the period. On the other hand, the usage value of the capital contributed by the shareholders should be equated with the opportunity cost of providing the capital. This could be taken as the interest the shareholder could have earned if he had merely loaned his money out.
>
> (4) The profit that would be subject to profit-sharing therefore should be the after-tax profit of the enterprise after it has set aside an appropriate amount to cover the opportunity costs of its shareholders (the compensation paid to the employees will have already been taken into account in the after-tax profit).[27]

At the bottom of it all, such profit-sharing arrangements seek merely a fair material interest of the executives and employees in the corporate after tax profits. The rate of return in this instance is still based on the concept of "opportunity cost" and its application would signify that the shareholders are limited to the opportunity created. In a comparative way, as already argued by Monzer Kahf, "Islamic economics does not assume any correspondence between exchange value and the amount of labour".[28] In yet another context, the business logic of *mudaraba* profit- and loss-sharing schemes derives from a very different set of value premises. Practical banking has allowed the use of devises to supplement profit-sharing arrangements such as buying assets on a *murabaha* cost-plus basis. For this reason, Islamic banks are also reorganized as commercial corporate structures for direct investments.[29]

Future Outlook

In the above presentation, we have driven home the point that even under a "hostile" business environment the PAB has made a breakthrough in its conduct of Islamic banking and services. However, the bank continues to use profit-sharing mechanisms alongside interest not simply to substitute one technique over another, but as a transitory measure pending the approval of the Profit- and Loss-Sharing (PLS) Chart of Accounts. In the light of certain gaps in the charter of the PAB, a policy board backed up by the monetary authorities has initially put into effect the limited Islamic banking experience of the PAB.

The proposals discussed in the article have called into the open the legislative means and regulatory needs that should be considered for a meaningful PLS approved scheme consistent with the universally accepted *Shariah* principles. We have explored the general policy conclusions in which Islamic banking operation is legally possible under the two PLS programmes of the bank. Procedural considerations were reviewed as well, insofar as these comply with the generally accepted practices of other Islamic banks.

Quite recently, a study committee of the Presidential Commission on Government Reorganization (PCGR) has recommended in principle to privatize the ownership of the PAB. In effect, the PAB can place the PLS system of banking in its proper context once the privatization of the bank is worked out. The PAB management is sympathetic to the PCGR recommendation and has given two cogent reasons for it.

First, at present the shareholders do not provide any real control over the policy and managerial decisions of the bank's activities. The capital structure needs to be infused with private capital of entities or persons who are committed to fulfil their financial dealings in complete respect for the ethical demands and social values of the Islamic *Sharia*.

Secondly, the future prospects of PLS in corporate structure lies with a broader base of investors rather than in the government sector. This company-based profit-sharing scheme eliminates the problem of interlocking directorates and the issue of preferred shares in favour of any controlling vested interests. However, it is safe to say that the government support is still necessary for the public to have confidence in the bank.

In conclusion, we consider that the monetary authorities in the Philippines will be more receptive to the PLS operation if and when they see that it has a comparative advantage. But it was not the PAB's intention to show just that; it was also reckoned that the strategic importance of such an Islamic-based PLS system is to gain access to the petrodollar market in recycling wealth. In fact, some pointers in the evolution of the PLS accounts of the PAB could well guide the structures of an autonomous economic and financial system envisaged for the "north-south" relations in the Philippines. In addition, the Islamic banking industry is likely to provide the institutional linkage between the Philippines and the Islamic world of business and trade.

NOTES

* In revising this paper, I was assisted by Abdillah E. Hashim, PAB Vice-President for Finance and Administration who supplied the data in the tables.

1 See Michael Mastura, "Comparative Analysis of the General Banking Act and the Model Islamic Bank: The Philippine Amanah Bank as a Case Study" (unpublished) and "Legal and Regulatory Framework for the Islamic Banking Operations of the Philippine Amanah Bank", 1984 (unpublished).

2 Republic Act No. 337, as amended by P.D. No. 71, Section 6-A. For an excellent overview, see Gabriel C. Singson and Manuel G. Abello, "Domestic and Offshore Financing and Syndicated Loans" in Workshop Papers, ASEAN Law Association 214 (1980).

3 Memorandum Order No. 411 dated 11 March 1974 created an Inter-Agency Task Force of the Rehabilitation of Jolo. Memorandum Order No. 426 dated 29 April 1974 was issued to restructure and specify the responsibilities of the Working Groups under the Inter-Agency Task Force. A Task Force based in Manila provided the planning and logistical support for the rehabilitation effort, and a Task Force based in Jolo was the implementing arm in which Amanah Bank became involved.

4 "Philippine Amanah Bank Status Report on its 9th Year of Operations", (hereafter "The Status Report of 1982") 6 September 1982, prepared by Michael O. Mastura, Lito Simba, Sumulong Sadala, Lina Dumlao, and Juhan Abdurasad.

5 Ibid. Sources on the subject in general are easily available.

6 "Banking Laws and Other Laws Relating to the Philippine Financial System" compiled by the Central Bank of the Philippines, 177 (1982).

7 "Copy of the Report of the Study Team (1979)" is found in "The Status Report of 1982" as an Annex. The first team was composed of Mr A. Karim Sidri, PAB director; Mr Ricardo Sadac, PAB corporate secretary; and Mr Tirso Antiporda, Sr., CB representative.

8 See the author's letter addressed to Finance Minister Cesar E.A. Virata on "The Status Report of 1982".

9 The "Review of Agricultural Financing in the Philippines" by the Technical Board for Agricultural Credit dated 17 July 1981 showed that the regions of Western, Central, and

Northern Mindanao received merely between 1 and 3 per cent of bank loans.

10 Cf. Abdul Kadir Haji Din, "Economic Implications of Moslem Pilgrimage to Malaysia", *Contemporary Southeast Asia* 4, no. 1 (June 1982).

11 Materials contained in the "Guidelines on the Pilgrim Special Savings Deposit Account (Tabung Hajj) of the Philippine Amanah Bank (1982)".

12 Ibid.

13 Ibid.

14 Musib M. Buat, "Islamic Banking and Finance: Implications on Economic Planning and Project Development" (Paper presented at a symposium on Islamic Banking and Finance, Manila, 13 December 1983, sponsored by the SGV Development Center and Philippine Amanah Bank).

15 "Draft Memorandum of Agreement covering the Philippine Amanah Bank Remittance Program with linkage to Islamic Investment Company of the Gulf -Sharja, a wholly owned subsidiary of Dar Al-Maal Al-Islami Trust", (1984).

16 Letter dated 29 August 1984, Deputy Governor Carlota P. Valenzuela of the Central Bank to Mrs Alicia Li. Reyes, vice-chairman, PAB Executive Committee.

17 Letter dated 8 June 1983, Director Castro, Central Bank Supervision and Examination Sector, Department I to Michael O. Mastura, president of the Philippine Amanah Bank.

18 See the article of former Trade Minister Roberto V. Ongpin, "The Binondo Central Bank" in *Business Day* (Manila), 25 April 1986, explaining the events that led to the creation of Task Force Luntian under the Presidential Anti-Dollar Salting Task Force under the Marcos government.

19 The "Memorandum for the Ministry of Muslim Affairs" was prepared by this author together with Director Musib M. Buat and Ustadz Abdelbaset Bansil. An expanded concept paper was later submitted by Director Buat to the Policy Review and Evaluation Office of the Ministry of Human Settlements in support of the proposal.

20 Proposals to Deputy Minister Emil Ong of the National Food Authority are under study by the PAB. A new Quedan programme was approved in April 1986 by the Quedan Guarantee Fund Board.

21 "Proposed Guidelines on Islamic Banking Operations of the Philippine Amanah Bank", 12 November 1985. Abdillah Hashim, Napoleon Malbun, Rodolfo Ocampo, and Tupaan Datu Imam collaborated with this author in the preparation of these guidelines.

22 Summary points of the meeting between Armand Fabella, Chairman of the Reorganization Commission and officials of the PAB, including EVP Asgari Aradji, Abdul Karim Sidri, and the author.

23 Comments dated 13 December 1983 of Dr Cesar C. Zalamea, chairman of the PAB.

24 Comments dated 6 January 1986 of Mrs Alicia Li. Reyes, vice-chairman of the Executive Committee of the PAB.

25 Economic policy speech of President Corazon C. Aquino delivered before the opening meeting of the Board of Governors of the Asian Development Bank at the Philippine International Convention Center on 30 April 1986.

26 Reaction of Aurelio Periquet, Jr., president of the Philippine Chamber of Commerce and Industry as reported in the *Manila Bulletin*, 22 April 1986.

27 The views of David Sycip are culled from his article "Profit Sharing", *The Manila Times*, 16 April 1986.

28 Monzer Kahf, The Islamic Economy 35 (1978). A more recent work by Mohsin S. Khan of the IMF Research Department, "Islamic Interest-Free Banking: A Theoretical Analysis" assumes that real income goes to capital rather than being divided between capital and labour.

29 This issue is answered squarely in "Progress Report on Implementation of Islamization Programme in Pakistan", Government of Pakistan, Finance Division 9 (1985).

6 THE QUESTION OF ISLAMIC BANKING IN INDONESIA

M. Dawam Rahardjo

Introduction

The absence of an Islamic bank in Indonesia has invited questions as to why such an institution does not exist in a country with the largest Muslim population in the world. In 1983, a leading Indonesian Muslim magazine, *Panji Masyarakat*, issued a special report on the "Islamization of the Economic System" in which a discussion on Islamic banking was included.[1] A similar report also appeared in *Infobank*, a banking magazine issued by Bank Duta Ekonomi, one of the major private banks in Indonesia.[2] Such articles are demonstrative of the fact that there is an interest in the topic of Islamic banking in Indonesia.

According to the *Infobank* editorial, the business community and government circles have begun discussing interest-free banking partly because of the acceleration of commercial bank interest rates which have recently become very high. A number of factors are important in determining the feasibility of a non-interest bank in Indonesia.

In the present development circumstances, it seems that the possibility of creating an Islamic bank in Indonesia will depend on whether or not the society and the government could be convinced of the utility and role of Islamic banks in the economic development process. The non-interest banking model and other forms of business financing related to an Islamic banking system, such as *mudaraba* (profit-sharing) and *musharaka* (equity participation) are commonly discussed as "alternative" solutions to recurrent economic problems. Therefore, the discussion on the prospects of establishing an Islamic bank in the Indonesian context will be viewed from the perspective of the present ongoing development process.

The Intellectual Tradition

Hatta's Opinion

A very early discussion on the question of bank interest can be found in Mohammad Hatta's numerous articles published before the Second World War and in the early fifties, one of the most important of which was an article entitled "*Kedudukan Bank Dalam Masyarakat*" (The Place of a Bank in Society).[3] In that article, Hatta, a leading economist, described the *mudharat* (evil) of *rente* (interest) or *riba*, which he described as a high percentage of additional charge on money lent for consumption purposes. The *rente* levied upon borrowing for consumption needs could lead to a loss of somebody's freedom. For him, *riba* is strictly forbidden by religion, and therefore, its legal status is *haram*. "Riba remains *haram*", Hatta said, "And it is that kind of *riba* that is outlawed by religion".

However, he defined *riba* as "consumptive *rente*", that is, additional money to be included in the repayment of principal lent for consumption. "Productive *rente*", defined by Hatta as additional money to be paid with the principal of a loan given for a productive purpose, was different. The money that is lent constitutes "capital", which in nature is productive, and which can produce income for the borrower. In this case, the *rente*, would be the price to be paid for the opportunity to use the capital of others. For Hatta, the "productive *rente*" was part of the profit made on borrowed money. That kind of *rente*, in his opinion, was not *riba*, provided the rate charged was low. To support his stand, he quoted the opinion of a leading Minangkabau *ulama* (jurist), Syeikh Haji Abdullah Ahmad, who stated that *rente* was not *riba*, if it was announced publicly beforehand, so that anybody who wished to borrow already knew and agreed with it. On the basis of this *ulama*'s liberal view, Hatta drew the conclusion that banking interest, the rate of which is open, was not *riba*.

In another article entitled "*Melawan 'mindering'ataukah Konkurensi 'mindering'*" (Against Money Lending, or Competing with Money Lending?),[4] Hatta specifically criticized a report in the magazine *Dunia Dagang*[5] covering *"Bank Pasar"* (Market Bank) which was reported as business efforts against *mindering* or money lending activities in society. The Market Bank, which provided small loans on short-term credit, in his analysis, was disclosed as charging too high an interest rate. He referred to the interest levied by the Market Bank, at the rate of 40 per cent every forty days or 360 per cent annually, as an example of *riba* even though the money was used in a productive way, that is, for trading. He also objected to the view that the Volks Credit Bank, established by the Dutch colonial government, which had an 18 per cent interest rate, was collecting *riba*. Hatta argued that the Market Bank was not fighting against *riba*, as was stated in its constitution, but was instead perpetuating the practice of *riba* and was only competing with the *mindering* or money lending traditionally practised by the Chinese. Hatta, therefore, agreed to the issuance of a social law prohibiting *riba*, even to the extent that it should include sanctions against practitioners.

Hatta was a socialist who believed in the ideal of a socialist or collective society based on a co-operative system. According to Hatta, there would be no *riba* in such a society; a productive *rente*, however, would remain in existence.

> In a collective society, a *rente* accrues to the public, collected by a public representative, such as the State, and is used for meeting public needs. In the present society, the *rente* falls into the hands of wealth-owning individuals, who can lend it or invest it in a house or land or other things.[6]

From this assertion, it can be inferred that Hatta wanted a banking institution to be established, owned, and managed by the State or a body regarded as representing the public interest, such as a co-operative. This view was expressed in his article "*Islam dan Rente*" (Islam and Interest).[7] But, here again, Hatta affirmed his view that not all *rente* was *riba* and not all *rente* was *haram* or prohibited.

In an article entitled "*Bank dan Rente*" (Bank and Interest),[8] he advocated the establishment of a bank by the Muslims, because he viewed banks as a mark of the progress of a society, without which a society could not possibly develop its economy. But, he had in mind a conventional bank that openly charged interest to finance economic activities.

In his writing called "*Keperluan Kredit Dalam Masyarakat Indonesia*" (The Need for Credit in the Indonesian Society), he accused banks in operation of being "credit enterprises" which he deemed as nothing more than "*riba* collecting bodies" which should not be termed as banks. On the other hand, he refused the idea current in the Muslim community of developing a non-interest bank. A bank, according to Hatta, could not exist without charging interest. Furthermore he said:

> Oddly, among Muslim groups who refuse interest, some people actively advocate the importance of a bank. Several types of Muslim banks have been established announcing 'without interest'. So they try to run a bank without incurring interest.[9]

Hatta was in fact a devout Muslim despite his Western education. However, he is known more as a nationalist and a socialist than as a Muslim intellectual. As an economist, he failed to understand how a bank could possibly survive without interest, because he believed that a bank could not obtain savings or deposits, and consequently could not possibly mobilize capital. He observed that those who rejected receiving money interest, tended to invest their capital in houses and land and receive rents which according to him was nothing but interest in essence.

Furthermore, he criticized Muslim banks as stating that they charge no interest when in fact they do. He reasoned that a bank needs an income to pay wages to its staff and dividends to its shareholders. As long as its staff needs salaries and its clients expect a profit in the form of dividends at the end of the year, the bank which "does not incur interest" is forced to seek profit from the money lent. The money received in return is more than the money paid. "The surplus is *rente* and it proves itself to be interest". But, because *rente* is considered *haram*, people try to eliminate the face of *rente* by calling it an "administration fee", as a source of income to pay its staff. About this term, Hatta comments:

> Up to this point, their theory to eliminate the interest charge is right. But the practice? In practice, the amount of the administrative fee is calculated according to the sum borrowed, by quoting a certain percentage of the amount borrowed. There are one or two Muslim banks that discount 1 1/2 per cent from the sum of money borrowed per month for an 'administration fee', or the same as 18 per cent a year. Repayment calculated in percentage from the amount borrowed is but *rente*, although it is called the 'administration cost'.[10]

From the quotation cited above, it seems that the idea of an Islamic bank was already being debated even before World War II. Even the Indonesian Muslims had established the so-called "Muslim Bank" that did not charge interest, but took a fixed administration fee and gave a dividend on profit. But in such cases, Hatta thought, the dividend distributed to the clients as well as the administration fee charged were both interest in essence, as was the case with house and land rents. Therefore, Hatta did not reject the concept of bank interest for productive loans or interest which was not excessively high, although he conceded that interest charged on consumption credit and high rates of interest amounted to *riba*. A productive loan interest, that was neither very high nor very low, was not *riba* but *rente* the legal status of which according to Hatta was *halal*. In fact, Hatta argued that interest was a necessity required in the establishment and operation of a bank which was much needed by society to advance its economy.

Hatta's Influence

Today, the establishment and operation of banking institutions in Indonesia are more or less based on Hatta's theory of legitimization of interest. *Riba*, which has the legal status of *haram*, is declared prohibited by State law. The *riba* referred to is an illegal charge on money lent by an individual or an institution operating a banking business unlawfully without government licence. But a bank charging interest on money lent is permitted to operate as long as it is licensed by the government according to the holding regulations. Private groups, foreign or domestic, may be given licences to establish banks. However, around 75 per cent of the present banking institutions, excluding rural banks, are State banks. This is in line with what Hatta wished to happen, that money or capital lending activities should be in the hands of a body or group representing the public. Among commercial banks, around 70 per cent are government banks. In terms of credit extension, almost 90 per cent credit extended is supplied by State banks.

With regard to ownership, there are four categories of banks, namely the state banks, domestic private banks, foreign private banks, and co-operative banks. The State banks engage in various functions as commercial banks, development banks, savings banks, and secondary banks or credit institutions and lending-saving institutions that are managed by government, private, and cooperative groups, covering 5,000 offices, such as the *badan kredit desa* (BKD, village credit body) or *badan kredit kecamatan* (BKKK, sub-district credit body) or *perkumpulan simpan pinjam* (credit union), *pergadaian* (pawnshop), *koperasi* (co-operative), *lumbung desa* (village food reservation house), etc. All these primary and secondary banking institutions are mostly engaged in productive or business credit. Only a few provide consumption credit, and even then the proportion of this credit is limited. As a result, consumption credit operates in an unorganized money-market.

However, various non-bank and non-financial organizations have provided consumption credit to various offices, including bank offices, and credit to their own staff or clerks on special interest terms or at very low interest rates. But, in the rural areas, consumption credit is furnished by money lenders (of course, operating illegally) and retail traders, or through the *arisan* system (rotating group credit system) or saving-lending associations. All these institutions, organizations, associations, and individuals give and take interest. Interest, in short, has become institutionalized.

Besides putting into effect a commercial credit system, the government has also been executing a low-interest credit policy, and even implementing a subsidized interest rate policy. Such credit is provided to encourage production and activate small business, and recently also to stimulate exports. To promote investment, the government provides medium- and long-term funds with low interest rates; low interest rates are charged likewise to increase agricultural production, especially of food, and small industries and businesses in rural areas. Interest rates for export production and trade are also lower than the normal commercial rates. For food procurement, the government also provides low-interest credit to co-operatives. Only recently, to overcome housing problems, especially in big cities or more densely populated towns which are confronted with housing shortages, the government has also supplied concessionary credit through a housing programme and a savings bank programme. The National Savings Bank and the government, through the Central Bank (Bank Indonesia), have been giving credit without interest to promote housing for the poor.

Today, the credit and saving-lending activities at different levels, both formal and informal, have grown very rapidly, especially since the start of the

New Order Government in 1967, to keep pace with the increasing rate of production and consumption activities in the public and private sectors. The development of credit and saving-lending has increasingly categorized and institutionalized banking and bank interest notions. Banks in this case, in accordance with Hatta's view, have become useful institutions. Ironically, banks are viewed, based on Hatta's framework, as institutions that are actively eliminating *riba* or at least reducing much of the *riba* activities in the form of money lending businesses within the society which charge illegally high interest rates. In this process of institutionalization, the opinions and attitudes of the public toward *riba*, with reference to religious prohibition, have become more and more indifferent and permissive, until they seem to regard the notion as a normal phenomenon.

The influence of Hatta's thoughts on the development of banking institutions in Indonesia is clear enough. Since 1967, the government of the New Order has expanded this process of institutionalization down to the village level and has brought about a rather dramatic change, as reflected in the increase not only in the number of banks and non-bank institutions, the volume of funds mobilized, the expansion of credit volume and type, but also in the number of bank clients, depositors, as well as individuals and enterprises receiving credit. Judging from this development, one can conclude that the institution of interest on capital appears to have been accepted by the general public.

Alternative Views

However, it remains questionable as to whether Hatta's argument, government policies, and all the changes which have occurred in the institutions of credit and banking have been able to circumvent the opinion that *riba* is *haram*, and that interest charged by the banks in saving-lending activities is *riba* and therefore *haram*. In 1960, a masters thesis, "*Bank dalam Islam*" (Bank in Islam), was written by Achmad Khatiba, now a high-ranking government official in the Department of Religion.[10]

According to Achmad Khatib, there are four main views offered by the leading *ulama*s on this problem. The first is the one represented by H. M. Bustami who holds the view that interest in whatever form, including the so-called "administrative fee", is *haram*. The opposing view, pronounced by A. Hasan, another leading *ulama* from *pesantren* Bangil, argues that what is prohibited is only mutiple rate interest, while low interest is not only *halal* but also necessary to advance the economy and to give help to those in need. Hasan goes even as far as to say that Muslims are obliged to develop banks and co-operatives if they intend to eliminate *riba*. More moderate views are taken by Syeikh H. Abdullah Achmad, a prominent Minangkabau *ulama*, and K.H. Mas Masur. Abdullah Achmad, who is one of those who initiated the idea of establishing Minangkabau Bank, argued that interest that was publicly made known and agreed to by the borrower, was permissible. Meanwhile,

K.H. Mas Mansur contended that any bank interest whatsoever is *haram*. Nevertheless, it was felt that there was a public need and desire to have a bank that worked on the basis of interest. Therefore, it was considered permissible to establish, manage, and run a banking business. In conclusion, the *halal* character of the interest and banking business is only temporary. On the basis of this argument, he then suggested that Muslim societies and experts should investigate and undertake further studies on how to solve the problem of credit needs in relation to bank interest.

A semi-official opinion was expressed by the present chairman of Majelis Ulama Indonesia (MUI) or the (Indonesian Council of Ulama), K.H. Hassan Basri. According to him, the status of the time deposit interest or saving-deposit interest was *halal*, while other types of interest still remained debatable. The former chairman of the MUI, the late K.H. Syukri Ghozali, expressed another view. To him what was clearly prohibited was the multiple interest drawn by the money lenders, while bank interest, for the reason of "emergency conditions", was *halal* or permissible. K.H.E.Z. Muttaqien, one of the MUI chairmen, opined that *riba* was any profit on borrowed money containing an element of exploitation. He argued that banking interest, the rate of which was only 16 per cent per year or 3 to 4 per cent above the inflation rate, was not *haram*, as he saw no exploitation element in it. He even argued that it was banking in fact which was in conformity with the Islamic system. This was so because Islam strictly forbids the personal accumulation of wealth or hoarding and the banking system was seen as a means of allowing wealth to circulate. For that reason he advocated that all Muslims who possessed surplus money should deposit or save it in a bank or co-operative, or use it to purchase stocks or bonds and other valuable notes. What was important to him was whether or not any interest or its equivalent contained elements of exploitation. By this token, an "administration fee", if the rate is high, could be regarded as containing an exploitative element and should therefore be categorized as *riba*.

It seems clear from the above discussion that social and economic developments have contributed to the changing views of the *ulama* and the public about *riba*. The need for banking institutions in economic development is seen in the light of the credit demand of the society for consumption purposes and production activities and the implementation of government policies to increase production. In addition, price increases entail inflation and erode the real value of money. All these are considered when judging the legal status of interest charged or received, as reflected in the opinions of the various *ulama*s cited above.

The Banking System and Development

Since the New Order came about, there has been an expansion of bank credit.

Many types of credit have been created for various purposes. Broadly speaking, there are two kinds of credit: (a) ordinary commercial credit with a normal rate of interest applied to business enterprises in general; and (b) various special credits with low or subsidized interest rates.

As can be seen in Table 6.1, in the early 1970s, credit allocation was concentrated in the trade sector, which marks the onset of a foreign trade liberalization period. This situation continued until 1974. Since the oil shock of 1974, credit allocation shifted to the mining sector where it reached 30 per cent. In the meantime, the growth of credit volume in the manufacturing sector, which had already been at a high level from the beginning, continued to grow. In 1981, the manufacturing sector credit allocation exhibited the highest portion, accounting for 32.4 per cent of the total credit extended. During the period 1972-81, allocation of credit to the manufacturing sector was the largest, accounting for 30 per cent of the total on the average, followed by the trade sector which accounted for 25 per cent of the total. It appears here that the expansion of credit facilities, which constitutes large-scale and and medium- or long-term credit, occurred mostly in the modern sectors. Meanwhile, the agricultural sector, representing the more traditional sector, has shared only 7 per cent of the total credit. However, its growth rate is reasonably high, averaging 28 per cent in the 1972-81 period, although this is still below the total average of 32 per cent.

Besides normal commercial credit, the Indonesian government since the fiscal year of 1973/74 has also provided credit for small-scale businesses, particularly for increasing agricultural output. The government, through BRI or Bank Rakyat Indonesia (Indonesian People's Bank)provides soft loans distributed down to sub-district level offices. This small business credit is well known under the name of KIK or *kredit investasi kecil* (small investment credit) and KMKP or *kredit modal kerja permanen* (permanent working capital credit). The development of KIK and KMKP is featured in Table 6.2.

From the above table we see that in the first year of operation, the KIK and KMKP funds lent amounted to Rp30.8 billion, or 2 per cent of the total bank credit (see also Table 6.1). In the beginning, 48 per cent of this loan was directed to investment and 52 per cent for working capital. Every year the amount increased at the rate of 57 per cent for KIK and 20 per cent for KMKP. The number of clients also increased at the rate of 44 per cent and 70 per cent respectively. The fund for this small credit grew not only in absolute but also in relative terms, starting from 2 per cent in 1972 to become 8 per cent in 1981. The proportion also shifted more towards working capital, so that in 1981, 74 per cent was alloted to working capital.

The government also implemented other small credits, smaller than KIK and KMKP, namely *kredit mini* (mini credit) ranging from Rp10,000 to Rp200,000 and *kredit midi* (medium credit) ranging from Rp200,000 to Rp500,000. Both were addressed to encourage small business through the provision of fixed or working capital. Another even smaller credit was

TABLE 6.1
Banking Credit Allocations to Economic Sectors
(In billion rupiahs and percentage)

Sectors	1972	1973	1974	1975	1976	1977	1978	1979	1980	1981	Total 1972-81
Agriculture	62	87	117	220	266	270	345	438	526	557	2,887
	(9.1)	(8.2)	(7.4)	(8)	(7.4)	(6.9)	(6.4)	(7)	(6.7)	(6.8)	(7.0)
Mining	7	8	11	741	1,036	1,062	1,699	1,893	1,866	1,896	10,319
	(1)	(0.7)	(0.7)	(29.9)	(29.9)	(27)	(31.5)	(30.2)	(23.7)	(23.3)	(24.8)
Industry	178	278	359	719	990	1,156	1,624	1,933	2,563	2,641	12,441
	(26.1)	(26.3)	(22.9)	(26.1)	(27.8)	(29.4)	(30.1)	(30.8)	(32.5)	(32.4)	(30.2)
Trade	299	428	627	766	858	911	1,114	1,338	1,977	1,046	10,364
	(43.9)	(40.4)	(49.9)	(27.9)	(24.1)	(23.1)	(20.7)	(21.3)	(25.1)	(25.1)	(25.1)
Services	48	79	122	172	260	319	389	422	482	529	2,822
	(7.1)	(7.5)	(7.7)	(6.3)	(7.3)	(8.1)	(7.2)	(6.7)	(6.1)	(6.5)	(6.8)
Others	87	179*	381*	132	156	219	223	244	466	484	2,528
	(12.8)	(16.9)	(21.5)	(4.8)	(4.4)	(5.6)	(4.1)	(3.9)	(5.9)	(5.9)	(6.1)
Total	681	1,059	1,573	1,750	3,566	3,937	5,394	6,268	7,880	8,153	41,261
	(100)	(100)	(100)	(100)	(100)	(100)	(100)	(100)	(100)	(100)	(100)

( ) These figures are percentages of the totals in their respective columns.

* This includes credit in foreign value for agriculture, transportation, industry, business (excluding exports and imports), and other unknown factors.

SOURCES: 1972-75: *Statistik Keuangan dan Perbankan, 1970/80*, BPS Jakarta.
1976-81: Bank Indonesia, *Laporan Tahunan*.

TABLE 6.2
Development of KIK and KMKP, 1974-81

Kind of Credit	1974	1975	1976	1977	1978	1979	1980	1981	Average Growth Rate (%)
1. KIK									
a. Client (000p)	9.6	16.6	27.8	39.7	55.0	72.1	114.5	125.4	44
b. Value (bil. Rp)	15.2	28.1	49.6	74.2	105.8	163.1	361	336	57
c. % of total	48	49	43	39	38	35	37	36	
d. Av/Client/mil. Rp	1.6	1.7	1.8	1.9	1.9	2.3	2.8	2.7	—
2. KMKP									
a. Client (000p)	14.5	24.1	166.1	322.4	420.5	644.0	889.8	953	82
b. Value (bil. Rp)	15.6	28.7	67.1	115.0	177.2	304.5	569	656	70
c. % of total	52	51	57	81	62	65	63	64	
d. Av/Client/mil. Rp	1.1	1.2	0.4	0.4	0.4	0.5	0.6	0.68	—
Total 1b + 2b	30.8	56.8	116.7	189.2	282.0	467.6	900.0	1,022.0	
KIK + KMKP as percentage of total credit	2	2.1	3.3	4.8	5.2	7.5	7.2	8.0	

SOURCES: *Statistik Keuangan dan Perbankan, 1979/1980*, BPS and *Statistik Ekonomi-Keuangan Indonesia*, Bank Indonesia, Januari 1981.

introduced, *kredit candak kulak* (KCK), or fast trading credit. Channelled through co-operatives, this type of credit averaged from Rp3,500 to Rp15,000 and was alloted especially for petty trading.

In Central Java, the local government also launched another type of small credit. It was channelled through the *badan kredit kecamatan* (BKK) or sub-district credit body and provided loans ranging from Rp5,000 to Rp200,000. It was also meant to provide working capital for petty traders from the smallest to the bigger ones. The new credit programmes seem to be developing rapidly in terms of volume of credit extended – from Rp442.6 million in 1972 to Rp7.7 billion in 1981 or at an average annual rate of 43 per cent.

By looking at the inflation rate annually, we can roughly estimate the real interest rate of various credits. In the beginning of Five Year Plan I (FYPI), the inflation rate dropped quite drastically from 85 per cent in 1968 to only 10 per cent in the following year and went down further to become only 9 per cent and 2.5 per cent. During 1972-74, it was rising before it began to fall gradually from 1975 onward reaching the bottom point at 6.9 per cent in 1978, but it went up again in 1979 and 1980. Since then the inflation rate has been under control at a one-digit level or a little over.

With the rate of inflation going up and down, the government issued fund mobilization policies beginning in 1971 through the TABANAS programme (Tabungan Pembangunan Nasional or National Savings Programme), TASKA (Tabungan Asuransi Berjangka or Insurance Time Deposit Saving), and Certificates of Deposit with varied rates of interest, depending on the length of time. In the beginning, the interest rate fixed for TABANAS was 18 per cent yearly and 15 per cent for TASKA, but subsequently it was revised down in 1972, 1973, and 1977. The interest rate for the Certificates of Deposit also varies according to the amount and length of time , but monthly interest rates have fluctuated between 0.5 and 6.0 per cent (Table 6.3).

In 1969, the time deposit interest rate went down along with the decline of the inflation rate. From 1968 to 1977 the government granted high interest rates ranging from 6 per cent to 15 per cent to depositors to encourage saving. The inflation rates during 1972-75 were high, reading 33.3 per cent in 1974.

From the experience of the fund mobilization programme, a conclusion can be drawn that the savings interest rates went up and down, depending mainly on the inflation rate. If the inflation rate was high, the government banks were prepared to pay higher rates of interest. By providing an interest incentive, the government and the banks have been able to mobilize funds from the public.

We can infer from Table 6.4 that the government has been successful in mobilizing funds through various types of deposits. The current account, time deposit, saving, TABANAS, and TASKA, have mutiplied 20.7 times, 12.8 times, 17.2 times, 17.4 times, and 3.1 times, respectively, within a ten-year period, during which time the total deposits multiplied by 16.9 times. It is relevant to note that the erosion in the value of money during that period was as high as 1,664.2 per cent.

TABLE 6.3
Interest Rates of Time Deposit, 1968-78

Start of Validity	Less than 3 months	3 months	6 months	12 months	18 months	24 months
1 October 1968	$1\frac{1}{2}$	4	5	6	—	—
17 March 1969	$1\frac{1}{2}$	3	4	5	—	—
1 May 1969	1	2	3	3	—	—
10 July 1969	1	$1\frac{1}{2}$	$2\frac{1}{2}$	3	—	—
15 September 1969	1	$1\frac{1}{2}$	2	$2\frac{1}{2}$	—	—
1 January 1970	1	$1\frac{1}{2}$	$1\frac{3}{4}$	2	—	—
31 May 1972	$\frac{3}{4}$	1	$1\frac{3}{4}$	$1\frac{1}{2}$	—	—
12 April 1974	$\frac{1}{2}$	$\frac{3}{4}$	1	$1\frac{1}{2}$	—	—
9 April 1974	$\frac{1}{2}$	$\frac{3}{4}$	1	$1\frac{1}{4}$	2	$2\frac{1}{2}$
28 December 1974	$\frac{1}{2}$	$\frac{3}{4}$	1	1	$1\frac{3}{4}$	2
13 January 1977	$\frac{1}{4}$	$\frac{1}{2}$	$\frac{3}{4}$	$\frac{3}{4}$	—	$1\frac{1}{2}$
1 January 1978	—	—	$\frac{1}{2}$	$\frac{3}{4}$		$1\frac{1}{2}$

SOURCE: Bank Indonesia, *Statistik Ekonomi-Keuangan*, March 1978.

The high interest rate policy for savings was meant to mobilize funds for financing development and economic activities through banks and financial institutions, especially state banks. At the same time it was also intended to absorb community funds which otherwise could be used for speculative purposes and push up the inflation rate. On the other hand, with high interest rates for savings, credit costs could become prohibitive. However, the government, in order to encourage production activities, has also applied a cheap credit policy by subsidizing interest rates at times. For instance, the government has provided liquidity credit to the implementing banks at low rates of 3 to 6 per cent annually, so that the banks can in turn lend their funds to the public at low rates, ranging from 9 to 21 per cent per year. For small credit, the government has provided loanable funds with interest rates even lower than 12 per cent (Table 6.4).

Table 6.4 also demonstrates that, in order to promote food production and small business, particularly in the rural areas, the government has provided very cheap credit facilities. Mini-credit and KIK, for example, were available at the interest rate of only 10.5 per cent per annum. For BIMAS and INMAS (food production increase programmes), KCK, midi-credit, and KMKP, the interest rate applied was only 12 per cent. For food procurement, the government has provided credit to co-operatives at a 9 per cent interest rate. If we compare all these with the average rate of inflation of 16.5 per cent during the period of 1969-80, (except for several credit types, such as for imports) the interest rates would still be below the inflation level, although for several years (1969, 1971, 1974, 1977, 1979, 1978, 1981, and 1982) the inflation rates were lower. More often than not, with the inflation rate remaining relatively high, the real interest rates were either low or negative. In such a situation, the depositors would lose while the credit receivers would gain.

On the basis of the Indonesian experience it may be argued that an interest rate system has played a useful role by compensating the depositors for erosion in the value of money in times of inflation. Nevertheless, we conclude that an interest rate system can hardly be just. For, when the inflation rate is high, the depositors lose while the debtors gain. Such a situation is obviously unjust. If the interest rate system was not applied it would seem that debtors would have gained at the expense of depositors. This, however, does not necessarily mean that in interest-free Islamic banking the depositors would lose because of inflation, as they would have a share in the profits made by the bank.

With a high inflation rate, demand for credit has been growing at a fast rate. In Indonesia, the number of small businesses and self-employed people is very large and accordingly the applicants for small credit are numerous. It is understandable that they cannot be adequately served by the existing banks, so that many do resort to informal traditional sources.

There are two possibilities with regard to developing an Islamic bank: (a) Islamizing the existing system; and (b) fulfilling the credit needs of those who have up to now gone only to informal credit sources. It seems evident that the first is hardly possible in the Indonesian context, since the formal credit institutions are subject to rigid central and regional governmental regulations. The profit-sharing model, however, could be tried out within the informal sector.

Traditional Credit Practices

There are various traditional ways by which people solve their credit needs. Generally speaking, in rural areas the role of money lenders is significant,

TABLE 6.4

Types of Small Credit by Source of Fund, Client Group, Purpose, Size, Interest Rate, and Requirements

Type of Credit	Funding Source	Client Group	Loan Purpose	Loan Size (In rupiahs)	Nominal Interest Rate (%)	Requirements
Rice production programme	Bank Indonesia	Farmers	Purchase agri inputs	50,000	1/month	No collateral recommendation from village head and extension workers
KIK	Bank Indonesia	SS entrepreneurs	Investment	Max 10 mil	10/year	Collateral: Up to 50% of loan and assets from loan
KMKP	Bank Indonesia	SS entrepreneurs	Working capital	Max 10 mil	12/year	Collateral: Up to 50% of loan and assets from loan
Kredit mini	Central government budget	Mini-scale enterprises	Working capital and investment	10,000 – 200,000	12/year	Good purchased with the credit
Kredit midi	Bank Indonesia	Larger mini-scale enterprises	Working capital and investment	200,000 – 500,000	10.5/year	Good purchased with the credit
KCK	Central bank budget	Petty traders	Working capital	3,500 – 215,000	3/month	No collateral recommendation from village head
BKK	Provincial government	Petty traders	Working capital	5,000 – 200,000	3.4 – 4.8 plus forced saving	No collateral recommendation from village head
Food procurement	Central government	Co-operatives	Working capital	According to the need	9	No collateral credit guarantee from department of co-operation

SOURCE: Susan Goldmand and Jay Rosengard, "Credit to Indonesian Entrepreneurs: An Assessment of Badan Kredit Kecamatan Program", Development Alternative Inc., 1983.

especially for consumption needs. Such credit takes the form of money or commodities, the interest rate of which varies from 3 to 40 per cent per month. Credit paid daily in small amounts bears even higher interest rates of up to 10 per cent per day.

A second form is the well known *ijon* which involves the sale of agricultural produce to marketing agents before harvest when the crop is still "green" or not yet ripe. This practice is widespread among small farmers prior to harvest time, caused by a lag between consumption and income schedules. When the crop is still "green", the price tends to be very low, below the market price. In fact, the price during the harvest time is also low, but the traders can always postpone their selling until after the price has gone up again. This is actually another credit system paid for by harvested crops. According to law, this system is strictly forbidden but control of this unlawful practice can hardly be implemented. The most effective way to get rid of this system is to create an alternative system.

A third way for farmers to get cash is to mortgage their valuables, including their land, to pawnshops – which are always owned by the government – against their credit. In the case of land pawning, the interest is calculated on the repayment of debt in the form of land rent. Likewise, in the pawn system, the borrowing farmer pays the debt after the harvest in money or in kind.

Other credit suppliers are trading agents, direct traders, or commodity traders. They are most often found in small industrial clusters scattered in many regions and sub-districts, acting as business monopolists in the rural areas. The credit suppliers extend their credit by or through the purchase of commodities in advance. Here, when the commodity is still in production, the producers often need money. In such a situation, the traders can purchase the said product beforehand by giving an advance payment. The interest payments involved in such deals are in the order of 10 to 15 per cent per month; one report even says that interest rates charged can be as high as 50 to 300 per cent per month.

The role of debt payment in kind markedly characterizes this traditional credit system. As the general and main problem of the farmers is lack of cash, they redeem their debt with their produce. Sometimes they repay partly with money and partly with commodities. A farmer who does not own land will have to repay his debts by working to earn the money to do so. There is evidence to show that interest rates in such cases usually vary from 10 to 60 per cent per month.

Various groups within the community have tried to create alternative credit systems that are more equitable. One of these is popularly known as *arisan* (rotating credit). In this system, each member has to regularly contribute a certain sum which is pooled. By lot, one or two persons will get a turn to use the money collected. But, this method is usually practised among higher income earners who are capable of paying their instalments. The *arisan* system usually does not incur any interest. This is one form of traditional interest-free borrowing which is practised not only among consumers but also among producers in relation to their business needs.

The *arisan* system theoretically and practically can be developed to become a saving-lending group. This kind of group usually emerges among craftsmen, small entrepreneurs, and petty traders who need cash to purchase raw materials or trade commodities. But, in the case of the saving-lending groups, the members agree to pay 3 to 5 per cent interest. The group, therefore, creates a common fund which in turn can be lent to other members.

Such operations have at times and in many places developed to become formal saving-lending organizations in the form of co-operatives. The Koperasi Simpan Pinjam (Saving-Lending Co-operative), better known as KOSIPA, established by a veterans group, had emerged in many provinces. It was subsequently merged into the present KUD (Koperasi Unit Desa, or Village Unit Co-operative). This co-operative used to exist in Central Java and engage in short-term consumption credit, sometimes charging exhorbitantly high interest rates. Although it called itself a co-operative, KOSIPA was similar to the *Bank Pasar* that was criticized by Hatta.

Another effort to eliminate usury practices in the community is by further developing the saving-lending group to become a so-called *usaha bersama* or common enterprise. The difference between this and the *arisan* is that *usaha bersama* does not only engage in saving and lending. It also undertakes common production and common marketing, or it co-operates in certain parts of the production process. The saving-lending activities here serve to support the primary activities, that is production and marketing. The fund lent is the common saving fund. A person can borrow after having saved a certain amount, and the amount of the debt is in proportion to the money he has saved. But, *usaha bersama* charges interest at the rate of 5 per cent per month, as it also gives interest to the depositors. Some *usaha bersama*s and saving-lending groups have been initiated by and have received extension services from various non-governmental organizations (NGOs), one of which is the Credit Union of Indonesia.

An Assessment of the Present Situation

From the above description, it is clear that some credit or financial institutions do extend small credit and mini-credit services both for consumption and production purposes. Firstly, we have identified primary credit institutions, most of which are supported by government banks. These institutions serve to promote agricultural production, especially in food, and to help food procurement which presumably deserves cheap credit facilities. The channelling agency is the BRI (Bank Rakyat Indonesia) which maintains offices down to the sub-district level. Besides promoting agricultural activities, the government, through a broader banking network, also provides funds for KIK and KMKP to help small businesses which are offered low interest rates, as they represent a priority sector.

One thing worth noting with regard to formal credit services is that although the formal rate of interest is low, in practice the effective interest rate including other costs is as high as 20 to 22 per cent per month. The procedure is also too complicated and time-consuming for the rural folks. Moreover, as the loan is given in a lump sum and not in instalments according to the borrower's needs and the time within which he must repay the loan, he finds finds it difficult to use the money effectively and economically. In reality, the farmers experience considerable difficulty in repaying the loan.

Secondly, there are the secondary credit institutions, co-operatives channelling KCK, the *bank desa* (village bank established locally with local funds), village rice granary system (*lumbung desa*), and the pawnshops or BKK in Central Java. As shown in Table 6.5, the rates of payment in these secondary credit institutions are surprisingly high.

Table 6.5 shows the growth of credit volume of three formal secondary credit institutions. The largest credit volume is through pawnshops (83 per cent) which is drawn generally for consumption purposes, while *bank desa* and *lumbung desa* account for only 15.8 per cent and 0.2 per cent, respectively. The repayment rates, however, are quite impressive: 93 percent, 80 per cent, and 97 per cent respectively. This indicates that the secondary credit system has run smoothly. A *bank desa* operates at a 6 per cent interest rate, while a *rumah gadai* (pawnshop) charges a 5 per cent interest rate within a maximum period of six months and a *lumbung desa* imposes a 15 per cent interest rate per quintal within one season. Although these forms of credit operations are meant to eliminate the exploitative system embedded in the money lending credit and monopolist trading practices, their interest rates are still quite high. However, as shown in Table 6.5, all the three credit operations, especially the *lumbung desa*, had a high rate of growth in real terms (based on 1971 prices).

Another matter which deserves attention is the use of credit itself. Generally speaking, the credit extended by formal credit institutions is for production purposes. It is difficult for these institutions to justify consumption credit. For one thing, consumption credit usually occurs among people who have financial problems and who are likely to have repayment difficulties. For another, it is considered immoral to charge a high interest rate on those who have consumption problems, which according to Hatta's view is *riba*. However, the consumption problem is a real one. Moreover, the consumption credit need does not always come from those who are facing severe financial problems, as the need for such credit is also felt by those who have current cash-flow difficulties. As an example, one may mention financial help to buy expensive goods such as houses, motorized vehicles, television sets, etc. Since it is difficult to borrow from the bank, the people will naturally go to a secondary credit institution, money lenders, or other informal sources.

TABLE 6.5
Development of Credit through *Bank Desa* (Village Bank), *Lumbung Desa* (Village Rice Granary), and *Pegad Ean Negara* (State Pawnshop)
(In million rupiahs)

Institution	1972	1973	1974	1975	1976	1977	1978	1979
Village Bank								
No. of active banks	2,443	3,420	3,326	3,323	3,328	3,323	3,267	3,329
Credit extended	2,667	2,010	2,325	2,832	2,710	3,202	3,788	3,971
Repayment	2,554	1,917	2,131	2,603	2,592	2,978	3,541	3,709
Repayment Rate (%)	95.7	95.4	91.6	91.9	92.9	93.0	93.5	93.4
Village Rice Granary								
No. of active banks	2,019	2,021	2,215	2,212	2,212	2,204	2,202	2,136
Credit extended	4.4	9.0	11	13.3	14.8	32.6	54	72.4
Repayment	1.8	6.6	8.7	11.1	10.2	25.2	42	65.5
Repayment Rate (%)	90	73.3	77.3	83.3	69.0	75.6	78.6	87.7
State Pawnshop								
No. of active banks	437	437	440	441	441	441	446	448
Credit extended	10,532	9,847	11,991	13,417	13,730	15,207	18,150	23,037
Repayment	9,726	9,058	10,932	12,877	12,461	14,597	17,316	20,929
Repayment Rate (%)	92.3	92.0	91.8	74.3	92.8	95.9	95.4	90.8

Table 6.6 shows that most of the formal credit (74 per cent) is utilized for production purposes. The table also shows that not the whole amount of credit is used for what is aimed at by the programme, as consumption and house renovation loans account for more than one-fifth of the total.

TABLE 6.6
Distribution of Responses according to the Utilization of KIK, KMKP, KACK, and Mini-Credit in Thirteen Research Villages

Type of Utilization	No. of Respondents	Percentage
Working capital in trading	24	44.4
Investment in agriculture	10	18.5
Investment in non-agriculture	6	11.1
Consumption	5	6.3
House renovation	6	11.1
Others	3	5.6

Unlike formal credit that is directed for production purposes, most of the informal credit is used for consumption purposes. There is a real need for credit for consumption but such credit is much less than that which is available for production. Thus, there is a need for some special institutions which can serve to meet this need.

In practice, the debtors of formal credit use part of their production credit to meet their consumption needs. Otherwise, they will have to turn to secondary credit institutions, which charge much higher interest rates. As a last resort, they may turn to money lenders or to various forms of informal credit systems such as *arisan* or they may borrow from friends and relatives. In the modern sector, some offices provide credit facilities to their staff on low interest rates.

If we agree with Hatta's argument that interest charged is not *riba* provided that it is used for production, then a bank's role is to provide credit for non-consumption purposes. The idea of establishing an Islamic bank is also directed at production. What, then, is the place of consumption credit, which is no doubt real? In certain respects, consumption credit is given as a special case, and if it is given, the interest rate tends to be rather high. But, then, according to Hatta, the interest rate for consumption credit should not be high or else it would be *riba*.

We must also consider the changes in consumption patterns and the changing real needs as a result of development. Consider, for example, the need for housing and transportation, and the consumption needs of the low-income group. To provide such a financial service, what kind of policy should be adopted? If the interest rate is high for consumption loans, then it will be considered immoral; but if it is made low, then there can be abuses. For example, someone might apply for consumption credit on low interest and then use it for production.

Nevertheless, consumption credit deserves attention, because if formal institutions cannot meet this need, the public would be trapped in an exploitative informal system that charges exhorbitant interest rates. However, production credit, if it results value-added production, can also help produce the means of consumption. Here, credit can be directed to help people to do business or create remunerative employment, and incomes generated can be used as means for consumption or as savings for future consumption. On the basis of the above economic logic, credit programmes carried out by groups of social activists are usually accompanied by savings activities of the community members derived from the surplus of business profits or wages. The borrowers or clients can use part of the surplus money for consumption, while part of the profit or capital can be saved. The savings fund can also be used as a contingency fund whenever needed. This approach is reflected in the BKK experience in Central Java, detailed in Table 6.7.

TABLE 6.7
Utilization of Surplus/Profits and BKK Savings

Utilization	Surplus/Profits (%)	Savings (%)
Working capital	58	36
Family needs	28	36
Housing improvement	4	3
Lebaran, selamatan	1	18
Equipment purchase	2	2
Gold, silver, jewelry	2	0
Start new activity	2	0
Sand investment, funerals, weddings, etc.		5

SOURCE: Goldmand and Rosengard, op. cit., p. 85.

It appears from Table 6.7 that not all the profit is used for consumption. The biggest portion of the profit is ploughed back to add to the working capital (58 per cent). Two per cent is used for the purchase of production equipment. The rest is used for family needs (28 per cent), house improvements (4 per cent), *lebaran* (festivities marking the end of Ramadan), *selamatan* (celebrations), and other occasions such as weddings and funerals (2 per cent). But, part of the money is also converted into savings. A larger part of the savings (38 per cent) is used as working capital for the purchase of equipment, but an even larger portion of the savings is finally used for consumption (64 per cent). This supports our earlier statement that encouraging savings created by production activity is one way to overcome consumption problems. It becomes clear that investment is not the only objective of saving; a portion of it can be set aside for future consumption. Thus, indirectly at least, production credit can help people solve their consumption problems.

For the above reasons, various NGOs engaged in community development try to help people solve their consumption problems by setting up saving-lending organizations, which can also help other people to produce something by using available credit. One of the successful cases in this movement is that promoted by the Badan Koordinasi Koperasi Kredit (BKKK Indonesia) or Credit Union of Indonesia (see Table 6.8).

During its fifteen years of operation, the BKKK has been able to mobilize 137,518 members in 1,234 saving-lending groups. Only 53 or 4.3 per cent of these groups are legally registered as such, the rest being considered informal organizations. The total money circulated reached Rp4.9 billion and the organization provided Rp5.3 billion loans in 1984, an average of Rp38,502 per person. This amount means something for low-income people in solving their consumption problems. This organization also provided reserves amounting to Rp183 million in 1984, charging an average monthly interest rate of 3.5 per cent. The interest income that makes up the reserve will finally be used as loan funds available to members. This experience might be applied in the search for a viable operational model for an Islamic bank. The programme fulfils credit needs for production and eliminates elements of exploitation by returning the interest earned to the group for group funds, while it also covers the administration or transaction costs.

Another experiment also opens possibilities for the development of an interest-free banking system. The LP3ES (Lembaga Penelitian, Pendidikan dan Penerangan Ekonomi Sosial or Institute for Economic and Social Research, Education and Information), Klaten Branch, has since 1982 been undertaking an experimental credit programme called the *qirodh* system. The programme began as part of the small-scale industry promotion scheme. This scheme takes three forms: (a) promotion of small-scale industry; (b) programme for developing productive activities of rural women; and (c) promotion of home-centred economic activities.

The programme adopts two models of operation. First it promotes lending and saving activities with an interest rate of 3 per cent per month. Second, it implements the *qirodh* model with a 1 per cent administration fee and profit-sharing wherein 60 per cent of the profit is shared by debtors or clients, 20 per cent is retained as group savings and operational costs, and 20 per cent is utilized for the administration of the programme.

TABLE 6.8
Growth of Credit Unions in Indonesia, 1970-84

Year End	No. of CUs	No. of Members	Total Savings	Loans Outstanding	Reserves	Total Assets
1970	9	739	1,259,187	710,756	62,257	1,342,570
1971	18	1,614	4,257,345	3,918,966	119,743	4,337,089
1972	35	2,084	8,049,032	7,604,721	298,052	8,347,084
1973	72	5,131	13,718,334	11,488,891	393,340	14,113,675
1974	116	8,495	36,154,920	30,826,184	611,232	36,766,152
1975	197	14,834	95,463,089	85,322,216	1,775,169	106,278,939
1976	239	16,969	149,605,974	135,887,818	2,705,668	161,810,455
1977	285	25,670	343,679,712	356,714,614	10,036,705	406,372,722
1978	347	30,038	410,556,373	427,676,184	12,040,962	572,795,512
1979	455	45,492	756,137,831	772,196,791	22,070,430	909,379,904
1980	535	56,805	1,189,080,516	1,267,077,140	43,129,025	1,456,763,401
1981	783	81,206	2,008,471,794	2,216,692,929	77,821,496	2,523,481,840
1982	992	104,161	2,944,555,635	3,187,923,441	106,699,546	3,540,685,877
1983	1,095	124,954	4,334,481,499	4,519,447,078	106,528,126	5,193,868,049
1984	1,234	137,518	4,913,575,640	5,294,784,303	183,732,601	5,933,896,347

At present, the programme has a Rp200 million credit turnover. The credit fund, which originally came from LP3ES through foreign funding agencies, is also now derived from local accumulation which now forms 35 per cent of the capital fund. The programme thus constitutes a secondary credit institution in the form of a co-operative and in the form of an NGO programme that operates on a non-profit basis aimed at utilizing the credit programme as a component of a small-scale development scheme. A similar programme has also been carried out by TEHNOSA, a co-operative group set up by a group of alumni and students of the Bandung Institute of Technology (ITB).

Conclusion

Based on these empirical and practical considerations, we can now turn to some factors that support or deny the rationale of establishing an interest-free Islamic bank in Indonesia. First, as we have observed, within the Indonesian society, where the majority of the population is Muslim, *riba* in the form of a multiplying interest rate, is still practised. This practice occurs not only in the informal or traditional credit institutions, but even in the formal credit institutions, both at primary and secondary levels. This credit system is utilized for both consumption and production purposes. This provides us with a good reason to eradicate the exploitative system through the operation of a credit system based on Islamic principles.

The second factor that lends support to the rationale of establishing an Islamic bank is the observation that, although the government has furnished the public with cheap credit facilities for food production and procurement, the amount and proportion of credit overdues and delinquencies are still significantly large. This leads us to the conclusion that this credit programme is still burdensome for the farmers because of the tied nature of the credit to the utilization of intermediate inputs such as bio-chemicals, which constitute the bulk of the production costs. In addition, there is the element of uncertainty in the harvest and sale of the products. No bank, however, is prepared to share the risk. This situation opens an opportunity to apply the *qirodh* system, where the lending bank participates in the sharing of risks in production and procurement.

The third reason is the big demand for credit, both for consumption and production purposes. If there is no bank that provides such credit facilities, people wanting credit will be forced to go to the informal credit systems, or even formal credit institutions which draw a high rate of interest. If an alternative system is not developed, people will continue to remain trapped in the exploitative system of *riba*. Viewed from Islamic perspectives, as interpreted by K.H.E.Z. Muttaqien, a banking system is imperative because Islam prohibits people from accumulating funds just for the sake of accumulation. The existence and operation of a bank will provide the public with ways and means to channel their surplus funds to beneficial uses such as savings, so that people in need can borrow from these funds for consumption and production purposes.

Fourth, there are still many people in Indonesia who do not participate in the banking system because they consider bank interest as *riba*. Therefore, an opportunity should be given to those Muslims to establish a bank or a financial institution that is free from *riba* in their terms. If Muslims desire to save without accruing *riba* (though they expect to get returns for their deposits in the form of profit distribution), they should be given the opportunity to do so by implementing the *qirodh* system and other aspects that are part of the Islamic banking model.

Given that permission is granted by the government to establish an Islamic bank, various theoretical and practical problems will have to be solved.

First of all, there is the contention of some leading *ulama*s and Muslim leaders that bank interest is not identical with *riba* or usury. If the interest rate is made public and is acceptable to the people who wish to borrow or if the interest rate is not high, it is contended, the bank interest is not *riba*. There is even an *ulama* who argues that conventional banks perform an Islamic function by serving to prevent people from hoarding money which is prohibited in the Qur'an. If that is the case, the existing state banks have a strong religious legitimation. Moreover, from empirical experience, we have found that the government sponsored banks and other secondary financial institutions were established with the clear purpose of eradicating usurious practices.

Second, from a theoretical viewpoint, a low interest rate applied over a certain period of time cannot be regarded as an usury. In nominal terms, the interest rate is positive but, in real terms, the level of interest rate may be zero or even negative in the face of a high rate of inflation. It may therefore be argued that the rate of inflation should be built into the interest rate. In an inflationary situation, interest-free banking might mean that the borrower profits and the lender loses. In other words, if an Islamic bank is to be established, the question of inflation should be addressed.

Third, an Islamic bank or any bank, as an enterprise or activity, needs a large amount of capital. Where can these funds be obtained? The administration fee which reflects the transaction costs could be as high as 10 per cent of the total. To be sure, administration fees are allowed in Islamic banking, but they should not be fixed in percentages. In an Islamic banking system, the retained surplus and distributed profit are calculated afterwards. This practice creates a disadvantage to depositors because they can only reap the benefit at the end of the year. Furthermore, it is not certain whether the bank will have a surplus or not, thus creating uncertainty for the depositors which might constitute an additional disincentive.

The fourth problem relates to practical considerations. If the *qirodh* system is implemented, many aspects of this problem will emerge, for example the problem of declaring profits, both on the part of client to bank and vice versa. The mechanics of all this will call for a more complex system than the one based on fixed interest rates.

The fifth problem has to do with consumption credit. If an interest system cannot be applied for consumption credit, then no bank can develop this source. Meanwhile, the concept of Islamic banking with its credit utilization and profit-sharing models is addressed to providing production credit. Does this mean that consumption credit can have no place in an Islamic banking system?

Another crucial consideration relates to the problem of legality. At present, avenues for establishing another new bank in Indonesia are closed. Therefore, an Islamic bank could only operate as a branch or part of an existing private bank. But this will call for additional banking regulations to protect the clients and public interests.

Another possibility proposed by Dr Ir. A.M. Saefudin, a former staff member of Bank Indonesia, is to open an "Islamic Counter" that receives savings without interest, so that the depositors also have the right to interest-free credit. This proposal too can hardly be put into effect, given the present banking regulations. Yet another possibility is to operate Islamic banking principles through co-operatives which are mostly subject to stringent government control. In order to implement such a scheme, co-operatives will first have to become autonomous institutions owned by the community where the members and the management can decide on their own policies and programmes, free from government intervention.

At present, therefore, the only avenue open for initiating an Islamic bank is through the NGOs and those co-operatives which are largely free from government control, that is, co-operatives outside the KUD (*koperasi unit desa* or village unit co-operative) in rural areas and the KSU (*koperasi serba usaha* or multi-purpose co-operatives) in urban areas. One example of this kind of co-operative is the one developed by the LP3ES in which the *qirodh* model forms part of the small-scale industry and community development programme. The operational costs of this credit programme is subsumed under the programme budget. This is also the case with TEHNOSA, although this programme has attained a higher stage of independence and self-reliance.

An Islamic bank operated through a community development approach needs several things. First, the operation of the bank must be based on the existing infrastructure, equipment, and operational costs of the NGOs that have already mounted small enterprise promotion programmes, community development programmes, rural and agricultural development programmes, etc. In other words, Islamic banking can become an integral part of the main activities of the NGOs. In this framework, the NGOs can provide not only capital but also managerial inputs. In production, finance, and marketing, NGO groups can become the targets for the services of the NGO-sponsored Islamic bank.

The starting capital of such a bank constitutes a serious problem. In Malaysia and some other Muslim countries, the governments have come forward to provide part of the capital. In other countries rich merchants and businessmen with religious commitment and conviction have been keen to take equity stakes in Islamic banks. In Indonesia it is rather difficult to expect Bank Indonesia, the government banks, or the Department of Finance to contribute their capital to an Islamic bank. However, one cannot rule out the possibility of the Department of Religion or the Department of Social Affairs showing some interest.

In the Indonesian context, an Islamic bank can operate well if it applies the principles of a co-operative system. The banking operation then becomes a part of the co-operative organization which itself runs other activities. In this context, the Islamic bank needs to give incentives to its depositors, for the saving activity is an essential element in Islamic banking. Here, becoming a bank client is like becoming a member of the co-operative, with the obligation to contribute an initial deposit. Some co-operatives give an interest incentive to depositors. Interest rewards can also be replaced by a distribution of co-operative income. If a fixed of return should be given, this may be done at the same rate as the inflation rate. In this system, those who have the right to borrow will be those who maintain a voluntary saving deposit, though non-members can also borrow under the *qirodh* system. After receiving credit, the client may be obliged to open a current account with the bank.

An Islamic bank should also perform a social function by providing consumption credit to those having immediate consumption problems. Here, there are two kinds of consumption: short-term and long-term consumption. For those who are facing short-term consumption problems, the bank can provide interest-free loans. But, in the long term, this group should be free from chronic consumption problems by obtaining production loans so that they can earn more.

The second kind of consumption need relates to people who are not necessarily poor. They usually belong to the middle class or lower middle class but they are at times in need of loans for, say, building a house, purchasing a vehicle, paying educational fees for their children, or paying medical bills, etc. They are in a position to pay their debts by instalments. Some of these problems have already been solved by some offices or enterprises which give credit to their staff on low interest. But for those who are self-employed, the problem still remains. One solution would be for the bank to acquire a house and lease it to the client who then pays a rent and an instalment until he acquires ownership of the property. Likewise, the bank could act as an insurance company that would pay educational, medical, or other costs and receive repayment in the form of instalments.

This kind of consumption service may not give a meaningful profit to the bank, but the point is that it is an important social function which the bank should not ignore. To compensate for this, the bank can run businesses which will pay for or subsidize this social function.

NOTES

1 "*Islamisasi Sistim Ekonomi*" [Islamization of the economic system], *Panji Masyarakat*, no. 411 (October 1983).

2 "*Bank Islam*", *Infobank*, no. 53 (May 1984).

3 Mohammad Hatta, "*Kedudukan Bank Dalam Masyarakat*" [The place of a bank in society], in *Beberapa Fasal Ekonomi* [Some economic Passages], vol. 2, Jakarta: Dinas Penerbitan Balai Pustaka, 1958, pp. 28-47. Hatta was a foreign trained economist and the most profilic writer on this topic to date. Besides his role as freedom fighter and statesman after independence, he is honoured as the Proclamator of Independence and the first Vice-President of the Republic. No less than fifteen articles, short and long, were produced by him, extensively discussing topics to do with money, bank credit, and the question of interest, all of which are compiled in his book *Beberapa Fasal Ekonomi* indicating his vast and technical knowledge of banking and its operations.

4 Hatta, "*Malawan 'mindering' ataukah Konkurensi 'mindering'*" [Against money lending or competing with money lending in *Beberapa Fasal Ekonomi* [Some economic passages], pp. 219-10.

5 Hatta, "*Bank Pasar*" [Market bank], *Dunia Dagang*, no. 2 (February 1939).

6 Hatta, "*Islam dan Rente*" [Islam and interest], p. 216.

7 Hatta, "*Islam dan Rente*", p. 218.

8 Hatta, "*Bank dan Rente*", pp. 203-209.

9 Op. cit., p. 205. Hatta said

Tetapi anehnya, dalam golongan kaum Muslimin yang mengharamkan rente, giat sekali orang menganjurkan bank. Berbagai macam bank Muslimin telah berdiri dengan mengumumkan 'tidak memungut rente'. Djadi mereka mencoba menjalankan bank dengan tidak memungut dan membayar rente.

10 Op. cit., p. 207. Hatta said

Hingga sekian benar teorinya untuk menghilangkan rupa pungut rente itu. Tetapi betapa praktiknya? Dalam praktik jumlah ongkos administrasi itu dihitung menurut besar pinjaman, dengan menentukan sekian persen dair pada djumlah yang dipinjamkan. Ada satu dua bank bank Muslimin yang menghitung "ongkos administrasi" itu 1 1/2% sebulan dari pada jumlah uang jang dipinjamkan, atau sama dengan 18% setahun. Pembayaran yang dihitung sekian persen dari pada jumlah pinjaman adalah rente, sekalipun disebut 'ongkos administrasi'. Lahirnya saja jang berubah, nama rente diganti dengan ongkos administrasi, tetapi buktinya sama saja, tidak berubah sedikit juga. Buktinya sebagai rente dapat disembunyikan kepada manusia yang tidak berpikir panjang, tetapi kepada Tuhan yang dapat menampak yang tersembunyi tak dapat dihilangkan. Disini lahir terpelihara, bathin tidak. Alangkah besarnya rugi dengan ichtiar semacam itu.

7 THE ISLAMIC BANKING OPTION IN THAILAND

Surin Pitsuwan

Introduction

The Muslim minority in Thailand has been a focus of attention among political observers for quite sometime now. There are approximately 2.2 million Muslims, mostly Malay stock, in a country of 52 million. Hitherto, literature on Muslims in Thailand has been limited to the political dimension, that is political integration, separatism, violence and tension, and conflicts between the mostly Buddhist government officials and the Malay-Muslims in the southernmost region. Very little attention has been given to their economic conditions and plans to elevate their social and economic standing within the context of Thailand's social and economic development plans.

Like in the Philippines, most of Thailand's Muslim population live in rural areas, with over 80 per cent concentrating in the five southern border provinces of Songkhla, Satun, Yala, Pattani, and Narathivat. The rest of them is distributed unevenly in the nation's capital and its environs, the urban centres of the northeast, and the north. The rural Muslims are, by definition, engaged in agriculture, most of them small-scale and very traditional in their production method. The average landholding size in the five southernmost provinces is less than fifteen acres. There is absolutely no large-scale plantation of any type owned by Muslims. Most of the cultivated land is inherited from ancestors, and not acquired by means of purchase. Thus, with landholding size becoming smaller as the size of the population grows and urban areas expand, the Muslims will be forced to migrate away into more rural and mountainous regions. An alarming number of landless labour is also rising among Muslims.

As the Thai government pushes ahead with its national development plans (1986 was the last year of the Fifth National Economic and Social

Development Plan), most of the rural Malay-Muslims are left further behind on the road to economic prosperity. As prices for agricultural commodities continue to be depressed in the world market, urban middlemen become more sophisticated in their operation, and the government price guarantee schemes fail miserably in the face of world-wide economic slowdown and rising agricultural self-sufficiency, real earnings among the rural Malay-Muslims of Thailand have been declining. Surplus rice crop, rubber, and coconuts, the main economic crops of rural Muslims, have become commodities of little value.

The Sixth National Development Plan (1987-91) calls for complete rural electrification and the promotion of rural industrialization. As capital for investment flows into the southern border region, where natural resources in the form of mineral deposits, forestry, and fisheries are abundant, the mostly uneducated Malay-Muslims will be driven even further into the economic backwaters. Already, the fishing piers of Songkhla and Pattani are full of large fishing boats from the coastal cities in the north. Large seafood factories are being established where the management fluently speaks the central Thai dialect and the unskilled labourers are mostly poor Malay-Muslim youths who can no longer be absorbed into the traditional agricultural-based economy. The government feels that the economic infrastructures that have been constructed, that is roads, telecommunications systems, electricity, and commercial aviation, can now be exploited to their full potentials for economic development. Unfortunately, the Malay-Muslims will not be ready to benefit from this major economic transformation.

In the capital city of Bangkok, where the Chularajamontri (Shaikh-ul-Islam) resides, the Muslims are engaged in commercial pursuits. The Muslim merchants of Indian or South Asian extraction are some of the wealthiest Thai nationals. Muslims of Indonesian and Malay stocks are also very well intergrated in all social, economic, and political senses. Their Islamic identity could be detected only when they are in their private homes. Like most Chinese in Thailand, the Muslims in Bangkok have been successfully absorbed by the dominant Thai culture. Their unique features remain only in the spheres of personal religious life. Aspirations for separate socio-political and economic facilities or institutions are not very much present among the Muslims in the metropolitan area.

While the Bangkok Muslims are more sophisticated in their manners and methods of modern social life, they are less interested in creating a coccoon within an Islamic social system for themselves than taking the full advantage of the existing economic and financial systems. The Islamic values that Muslims in Bangkok want to inculcate among their youth are of a personal nature, not of social scale. They are more concerned with the youth *Fardu Ain*, that is daily religious rituals, Muslim etiquette, morals, and ethics. And yet, they, the Bangkok Muslims, are in a better position both intellectually and politically to devise and demand for concessions from the government to establish their own

"Islamic facilities" so as to allow them to fully observe their "Islamic way of life" in an un-Islamic environment.

The Islamic national leadership, the Chularajamontri, the National Islamic Council (NIC) which he heads, the Bangkok Islamic Council, and the various Islamic centres and foundations in Bangkok have not shown any sign of interest in creating separate socio-economic institutions and facilities for the Muslims in Thailand. Their interests lie mainly in social welfare activities, education, fighting drug abuse among the Muslim youth, and other social functions. The social awareness and commitment for any major effort to create financial and banking facilities specifically for Muslims, based on Islamic principles, is not present.

Informal Arrangements

The Muslims in Thailand are not immune to the influence of Islamic resurgence of the last and present decades. They, too, are caught in the rising tide of Islamic fundamentalism, and the growing sense of Islamic identity has led to a desire to infuse Islamic values into their social life. Muslim student clubs at universities expand their membership. Muslim youth organizations have become more active at the mosques and other Islamic centres. Muslim girl students now cover their heads with scarves and follow the Islamic codes on dresses. Study groups grow in number around the country. Islamic studies literature explodes in volume and depth of analysis. Adoption of social, political, and economic values are being tried both in the metropolitan area and in the provinces. In this section, we shall explore some of the economic and financial models that are being experimented among the more committed Muslims in Thailand. They are the following:

1. The zakat and charity funds of the Office of the Chularajamontri;
2. Muslim co-operatives and financial clubs;
3. The hadj account; and
4. The Muslim investment establishment.

The Zakat and Charity Funds

When the present Chularajamontri, Haji Muhammad Prasert Muhammad, was elected on 10 August 1981, one of the many projects that he wanted to see prosper was a centralized Zakat and Charity Fund for the Muslims in Thailand. He rationalized that with over 2,000 mosques around the country, a Muslim population of over 2 million, and the annual *zakat mal* (wealth and property tax) and *zakat fitrah* (poll tax in the month of Ramadan), the Muslims of Thailand only need a better system of collection and management of these necessary religious taxes to make them beneficial to the entire society. Inspite of the existence of many *zakat* institutions around the country, poverty, illiteracy, and diseases remain common among the poor Muslim folks. Evidently, the society's wealth is not being used to its maximum potential. The Chularajamontri Office set the following as its objectives:

a. to prove to the Muslims that the only remedy to the problems of the needy and the poor is to centralize the Zakat Fund in order to enable it to function effectively and correctly in accordance with Islamic principles;
b. to eliminate poverty and hardship, which will result in narrowing the gap between the rich and the poor within the Islamic society;
c. to create a brotherly atmosphere within the Muslim *ummah* in each and every community, as it is the obligation of the rich to pay *zakat* while the needy and the poor have full right to receive it; Muslims should never be seen "begging from *kafir*" (non-believers) in Thailand; and
d. to ensure that the Zakat Fund assist Muslim children in their basic Islamic education, regardless of their parents' economic situation.

The Zakat Fund of the Office of the Chularajamontri represents the first attempt by the highest Muslim leadership in the country to organize a central fund to which Muslims from all over the country are encouraged to contribute. But, the manager of the fund, Dr Imron Maluleem, the secretary general of the NIC (who also serves as the personal secretary to the Chularajamontri), claims that most of the slightly over 1 million baht fund is from foreign donations. It is most interesting that the fund draws no interest from its bank account and is not being put into any form of investment. In Dr Maluleem's words, "There is still a conflict of opinion on what to do with and how to manage the Fund. We do not want to risk it. We receive the money in the form of donations, we distribute it to eligible individuals. The Fund only serves as a distributor of *zakat*."

Each Ramadan, the Chularajamontri sends out an appeal to the twenty-six chairmen of the Provincial Islamic Councils around the country to collect the *zakat fitrah* and send it to the central Zakat Fund. But, only a handful of the over 2,000 imams respond to the appeal for they too have their own poor and needy to take care of and they too need to better organize their collecting system. Oftentimes, travelling *fakirs* (wayfarers) and students from various Islamic institutions would beat the imams to the *zakat* payers. They have a priority over the far-away poor and needy of the metropolitan area.

What is interesting is the fact that the fund cannot be invested in a any commercial enterprises. It cannot draw interest. It only serves as a transit point between the *zakat* payers and the individuals eligible to receive it. The fund cannot be expected to be transformed into a major financial establishment such as a trust fund, an Islamic investment unit, or an Islamic bank, as its primary objective is redistribution. Little attention has therefore been given to what to do with the accumulated fund.

Another interesting point is that the original Zakat Fund is actually turning out to be a charity or *sadaqat* fund. The real *zakat* is being absorbed by provincial and local imams and *fakir*s. Foreign donors are now the major source of the fund. Less and less of its income comes from religious taxes.

Muslim Co-operatives and Financial Clubs

Both urban and rural Muslims in Thailand are now beginning to be aware of the fact that their dependency on outsiders for daily transactions of agricultural products and necessary items can only be broken through their unity and effective co-operative arrangements. The Muslim poor in the slum areas of Bangkok are now turning to the idea of a co-operative system to relieve themselves of the high prices of their daily needs purchased from Chinese merchants. In the rural areas of the south, Muslim folks get together to collect their agricultural products and sell in large quantities to the middlemen at higher prices than before. The same co-operatives also serve as a source of financial assistance to members in need of such relief.

In Bangkok, Muslim groups in the Yannawa District have formed a co-operative among the residents. Each share costs 300 baht and each member is entitled to buy their daily foodstuff and other items from the co-operatives at considerably lower prices. Profits are being used to help needy Muslim students as well as put aside for future interest-free loans to members. Mr Ramadan Abdul Kadir, a leading member of the Muslim Unity Club, the parent group of the co-operative of Yannawa, claims that the people are very supportive of the idea and that the co-operative is working very well.

In Nakorn Sri Thammarat, a group calling itself Jamaat Nasratul Muslimin has established a similar venture among the province's Muslims. The co-operative is called "Baitul Maal" and serves as both a co-operative and a savings club for its members. More mosques in the rural areas of the provinces are also experimenting with the idea. But, little is yet known about the result of these experiments.

The province of Trang, in the south, is probably a bit ahead of Nakorn Sri Thammarat in the establishment of a co-operative and savings entity for the Muslims. A group which calls itself "The Islamic Ethics Group" established a Fund for Muslim Co-operative in Trang on 5 January 1985. Within a year, it sold more than 2,000 shares at 300 baht each. It is now concentrating on co-operative activities with the hope of going into financial operations for its members. Its slogan is "Islam develops spiritual life, business develops human beings, capital formation develops both men and society."

What is interesting about these embryonic entities is the indication that the Muslims in Thailand are now aware of their potentials and the strength of their unity in economic terms. Socio-political and economic conditions are forcing them to adopt measures, protective and offensive, to protect and promote their economic well-being. It will take sometime before their skills and expertise could be developed to a level sufficient to launch major financial and business ventures. Clearly, they are aware of their deficiencies and they are determined to find solutions.

The Hadj Account

Muslims from Thailand have been going to Mecca for the performance of one of their religious requirements, the hadj (pilgrimage) for the past three hundred years. But the financial and logistic organization of the hadj for the Muslims in Thailand has remained unchanged and undeveloped. From the time of sea travel to the present-day air transport, the organization and the logistics of the Thai hadj organizers have worked to the disadvantage of the pilgrims. Each year there are approximately 2,000-3,000 pilgrims from all over the country passing through the Don Muang Airport in Bangkok on their way to Mecca. Each year the Muslims of Thailand spend approximately 150 million baht for often unreliable services related to the hadj pilgrimage. Corruption, outright cheating, and abandonment have often been associated with the hadj organizers in Thailand.

And, the pilgrims themselves are not always in the best and sound financial positions at the time of their pilgrimage. The majority of pilgrims have to sell their inherited pieces of land and other properties in order to raise the funds for the long journey. Many mortgage their lands with banks or other commercial entities through the intermediary of the hadj organizers. Upon their return, they find out that their lands or properties have been put up as collaterals for loans larger than the sum they required for their hadj trips in the first place. Ignorance and excessive desire for the fulfilment of the last Islamic pillar make the poor Muslims of Thailand vulnerable to cheating and exploitation. The end result is the loss of property to the banks and other commercial entities or wealthy individuals who are usually non-Muslims.

The Muslim leadership at the highest level has not been able to design a better plan for the hadj service for the Thai Muslims. The entire industry is full of exploitation, excessive profits, deception, and outright corruption. The government has set up a supervisory committee to oversee the hadj service, but so far hadj organizers have managed to escape supervision and control.

But the real problem lies much deeper than the rampant cases of exploitation. The Muslims themselves feel that the hadj is their religious duty and that outside authority, particularly the government, must not interfere. No attention is being given to whether the Muslims of Thailand can actually afford the expenses associated with the hadj pilgrimage. And, no one can decide on that question except the pilgrims themselves.

Most pilgrims spend their lifelong savings on their pilgrimage. The majority of them have to resort to the sale of their inherited property such as land before they could come up with the necessary capital. This last resort has a drastic negative impact upon their children's economic welfare. Each successive generation will have to spend most of its accumulated and inherited wealth for the hadj journey. Very little wealth is left within the community for future economic development and expansion.

Commercial banks operating in the Muslim-dominated areas of the south realize that there is a large sum of savings associated with the hadj pilgrimage. They designed, for example, a special account called *wang simpan untok buat haji* with the Bangkok Bank for potential pilgrims to put their money in. However, this is nothing new. It is but a typical "saving account" with full interest, except that the name is different.

A challenge to the Muslim leadership in Thailand comes from the creation of a hadj organization in Malaysia (Tabung Haji) with both savings and investment operations in accordance with Islamic principles. The establishment of a similar institution in Thailand can help develop attitudinal changes that will promote planning and saving for future consumption in the Muslim community of Thailand. The existence and success of such an organization will also ensure that Muslims do not lose their property to commercial banks and wealthy merchants outside the Muslim community as a result of the Muslims' desire to perform their religious obligation. A well-organized hadj institution can also help provide better hadj services for the Muslim pilgrims from Thailand in the future. The annual sum of 150 million baht is large and attractive enough for the Muslim leadership and the government to put their heads together and to make a thorough study of its feasibility.

Muslim Investment Establishment

As a result of a large number of Thai labourers working in the Middle East and an increasing volume of Thai-Middle East trade, Arab investment and financial firms have begun to expand their operations in Thailand. In 1985, Alirajni Commercial Establishment for Exchange of Jeddah, Saudi Arabia, opened its branch in Bangkok. It claims that it serves as a remitting facility to Thai labourers with a daily turnover of 10 million baht.

However, its Thailand manager, Mr Seni Madakakul, a Member of Parliament from Narathivat, has complained that his firm has been unsuccessful in identifying feasible Muslim investment projects for possible joint-ventureship. Again, the lack of Muslim entrepreneurship and business expertise are being blamed for such a lack of attractive projects.

Before Muslims in Thailand could be expected to respond positively to such a major investment call, much spadework has to be done within the community. They are not used to the very concept of future-orientated activities and planning. Their entrepreneurial skill is non-existent. Their business experience is very limited to be of any use. Their excessive commitment to the religious dimension of their life, to the abandonment of any worldly enterprises is detrimental to any development strategy that can be adopted.

The four embryonic activities outlined above indicate that efforts are being made to create an awareness of the need for better organization and management of their own social and economic life before they could embark on a more sophisticated venture such as Islamic banking.

Conclusion

The idea of Islamic banking in Thailand is not yet in existence. According to Dr Imron Maluleem, secretary general to the Chularajamontri, there is a legal obstacle to be overcome, namely that no more banks are permitted to be established by the Thai government. With the rudimentary skills that exist within the Muslim community in Thailand at present, it is a bit too premature to talk about establishing an Islamic bank. And the awareness and desire for such and enterprise is not very much evident among the Muslims themselves. The demand and pressure for such a unique financial establishment does not present itself to the authority concerned. This is very different from the case of the Philippines, not quite unlike the case of Indonesia, however.

It is more realistic, according to the Chularajamontri's secretary, to talk about forming a Muslim Chamber of Commerce in Thailand at this stage of the game. It would be practical to disseminate commercial and entrepreneurial skills among the Muslims before they can be expected to think about their own Islamic bank.

The level of economic expertise and financial needs of Muslims in Thailand today does not permit them to rise with the current Islamic resurgence to the height reached by other Muslim communities in the region. The embryonic economic models that are being attempted around the country described above indicate that they will probably have to wait for the next round of Islamic revivalism before the idea of Islamic banking can be realistically explored in the context of Thailand's socio-political and economic environment.

8 THE ISLAMIC DEVELOPMENT BANK AND ECONOMIC DEVELOPMENT OF SOUTHEAST ASIA*

M.A. Mannan

Introduction

This paper attempts to (a) provide a brief overview of the functions of the Islamic Development Bank (IDB) and its principles of operation; (b) draw the distinction between the IDB and Islamic (commercial) banks and between the IDB and secular development banks; (c) examine the role the IDB has been playing in the economic development of Southeast Asian countries; and (d) make policy suggestions to facilitate the process of economic development in the region.

Before examining the operation of the IDB it is perhaps desirable to provide some insights into the concepts and processes of economic development in an Islamic framework and the principles of Islamic finance governing the operation of Islamic banks in general and the IDB in particular.

Islamic economic development implies a balanced and sustained improvement in the well-being of man in his "totality" over a period of time. This definition provides a number of useful insights into the nature and scope of economic development in Islam.

The emphasis on "totality", which has a number of facets, brings out the true nature of economic development in an Islamic system – a scope which is not always understood in popular discussions. In the first instance, it embraces life on earth and hereafter. This dual notion of accountability profoundly influences resource allocation, maintenance, and use in a profound manner. Therefore, allocation and use of resources on earth must first be synchronized with investment of resources designed to attain spiritual and moral upliftment. This balance calls for the use of resources on earth in an efficient and equitable way. It implies an appropriate investment of resources in such a manner that harmony between man and his environment is also maintained.

This immediately brings into focus other dimensions of development such as pollution, wildlife preservation, etc. In Islam, total development of man is neither possible nor desirable without this harmony.

The Islamic concept of development is concerned with total development of man in all its dimensions – material development plus moral and spiritual upliftment. While the former implies sustained increase in per capita income and maintenance of material welfare without distorting the physical, natural, and ecological environment, the latter implies sustained purification of mind through better appreciation and preservation of moral and spiritual values as reflected in *Tawhid* (God's unity and sovereignty). The main task of the IDB is to encourage the implementation of Islamic economic development and social progress in member countries in particular and Muslim communities in general. But, the task of fostering an Islamic model of development is not a very easy one in an environment where the existing socio-economic institutions need more than marginal changes to make them conform to the principles of *Sharia* (Islamic law).

But, fortunately the establishment of the IDB was prompted by "the declaration of intent" to create a just society for all, which allows Muslims to live in accordance with the *Sharia.* So, a beginning has been made to provide a dependable basis for the transition of a community from a secular footing to an Islamic one. The task is demanding, though at this stage it is perhaps necessary to explain some of the basic *Sharia* principles governing the diverse operations of the IDB.

Sharia Principles and Islamic Banking

There is no dearth of Islamic literature dealing with financial and economic transactions in an Islamic economy. On the basis of this, the following six predominant rules of the *Sharia* governing the conduct of Islamic finance, which do not purport to be exhaustive, may be identified:

Productive Use of Resources without Riba

The first rule laid down by the *Sharia* is that charging of interest either on productive or consumption loans is strictly disallowed. In this context, the Qur'anic precept: "Allah has permitted trade and forbidden *riba* (interest)"[1] serves as one of the cardinal principles of operation of the IDB. As we shall see later on, the bank has indeed been involved in trade and interest-free loan operations on a large scale. It is to be recognized here that the permission to trade implies permission to receive lawful and normal profit, under a variety of arrangements, thereby retaining the incentive to work and to utilize the resources in an efficient way.

Continuous Use of Financial Resources
The second rule of the *Sharia* is that non-use of resources is discouraged. Thus, financial resources kept in an idle form either at home or in the vault of a bank will amount to hoarding. By penalizing such savings with the imposition of *zakat* (wealth tax), Islam encourages the owners to put these resources into a productive process so that they are kept in constant circulation among all sections of the community.

Equitable Sharing of Risk and Gains
The third rule of the *Sharia* governing the equitable sharing of the risks and gains between capital and enterprise is in fact contained in the Qur'anic verse: "Let it be a trading among you by mutual agreement (IV: 29)". Once this principle of "trading" is applied to modern modes of financing economic activities, it will be necessary then to introduce a variety of arrangements of profit-sharing through participation with money alone, with money and human effort, or with human effort alone. All these arrangements may be reflected in different types of financial contracts such as *mudarabah* (profit-sharing), *musharaka* (partnership), and *murabaha* (cost plus).[2]

Securing Due Benefits/Income for the Owner
The fourth rule of the *Sharia* places emphasis on the use of financial resources for the purpose of securing for the owners due benefits in the form of a reasonable return or mark-up for financing under *bai muajjal* (deferred payment) and *bai'al salam* (forward transaction) arrangements. Under the *bai'muajjal* arrangement, financing of current input requirements of industry and agriculture as well as financing of domestic and import trade can be arranged subject to the conditions laid down by the *Sharia*. Similarly, forward transaction is permissible provided complete details of the commodity transaction including the quality, price, and place and time of delivery are worked out along with the payment of the agreed amount at the time of entering into the agreement.[3] Besides these, leasing as a long-term financing method and hire-purchase under a joint ownership arrangement are considered permissible subject to certain conditions laid down by the *Sharia*.

Use of Financial Resources
The fifth rule of the *Sharia* lays emphasis on the beneficent use of financial resources in the interest of the community at large. Seen in this light, financial resources utilized for achieving Islamic social, moral, and spiritual goals will constitute "investments" in the wider sense of the term. As it will be seen later on, the IDB's various financial arrangements in the form of grants and loans to member countries and Muslim communities in non-member countries, and fellowship programmes for students in non-member countries are in conformity with the principles of the *Sharia*. The Qur'an has indeed emphasized the importance of benevolent loans (that is, *qardhasan*).[4]

Lawful Investment

Yet another rule of the *Sharia* with respect to the conduct of financing is that financing cannot be made for any project that is not Islamically justified, regardless of its profitability in financial terms. The projects relating to prohibited items (for example, a brewery) can be cited as an example. However, the *Sharia* does recognize profit-making as one of the objectives at the operational level of economic activity. What it does not recognize is profit maximization as the sole goal of an enterprise to the neglect of social and ethical priorities. Thus, in an Islamic operation, profit in financial terms may have to be sacrificed in the wider interest of the community at large.

The preceding rules of the *Sharia*, which are by no means exhaustive, are intended to serve as a basic frame of reference in the IDB's various modes of financing operations. These rules also serve as a guide to the operations of Islamic (commercial) banks. Let us discuss in some detail the IDB's ten-year experience and its operational strategies.

The IDB's Operational Strategies: A Brief Review

The IDB completed the first ten years of its operation in 1984. It should be possible now to indicate the broad trends of its operations in the light of the bank's diverse functions and powers. It was already noted that the main functions of the bank are to participate in equity capital and to grant loans for productive projects and enterprises. The IDB is also charged with the responsibility of (a) assisting the promotion of foreign trade, especially in capital goods among member countries; (b) providing technical assistance to member countries; (c) extending training facilities for personnel engaged in development activities; (d) undertaking research, aimed at enabling economic, financial, and banking activities in Muslim countries to conform to the Islamic *Sharia*; and (e) providing assistance to Muslim communities in non-member countries.[5]

However, unlike many international organizations, the IDB commenced its financing operations in the very first year of its establishment. The total operations under various types of financing approved by the IDB since the commencement of its operation are shown in Appendices A, B, and C. Up to 1405H(1984-85), the bank financed 580 projects/operations involving ID4,970.78 million (US$5,559.70 million).[6] Of these, 282 were for project financing and technical assistance amounting to ID1,438.50 million (US$1,614.16 million), 241 for foreign trade financing operations amounting to ID3,374.12 million (US$3,785.18 milion), and 57 for special operations amounting to ID158.16 million (US$163,68 million).[7]

In the course of its financing activities,

> The Bank also paid particular attention to the analysis and understanding of the pertinent issues relating to agricultural mechanization, foreign trade and development of consultancy services in the member countries. For this purpose several workshops and seminars were organized during the year 1405H (1984-85). Stress was laid on identifying agricultural projects in the member countries for financing on a priority basis. The Bank also sought the cooperation of national and international development financing institutions in identifying and selecting viable projects in member countries, specially for co-financing.[8]

Sectoral Distribution

The most striking feature of the sectoral distribution of investment funds is the recent shift in the emphasis in favour of agriculture, the share of which in project financing almost tripled in 1405H (1984-85), increasing from 14 per cent in 2404H (1983-84) to 36.3 per cent in 1405H (1984-85). For the period 1396(1975-76)-1405H(1984-85), the share of this sector had averaged about 16.35 per cent. Most of the agricultural and rural development projects financed by the IDB are concerned with the construction of irrigation facilities, increasing production and productivity, development of fisheries, improvement of agricultural education, and poultry development. This shift towards agriculture will provide assistance towards attaining food security and improving the balance of payments position of the member countries, despite relative decline in some sectors, such as industry and mining, shown in Figure 8.1 and Table 8.1.

Project Financing

The basic function of the bank is project financing, as it is directly concerned with increasing the production of goods and services, providing employment, improving the balance of payments by increasing exports and replacing imports, as well as decreasing regional imbalance among the member countries. In a broader context, project financing includes several modes such as (a) loans, (b) equity participation and line of equity, (c) leasing and line of leasing, (d) profit-sharing, and (e) instalment sale.

Loan Operations. The loans given by the IDB are free of interest. The IDB however collects service fees to cover its relevant administrative expenses. This is permissible in Islam. The present loan operations of the bank are concentrated mainly on socio-economic infra-structural projects relating to public health, rural water supply, rural electrification, low-cost housing, and educational projects as well as projects concerning roads, bridges, labour-intensive irrigation, small-holder agriculture, land development, industrial estates, sewerage, and the like.

FIGURE 8.1

Sectoral Distribution
(In ID million)

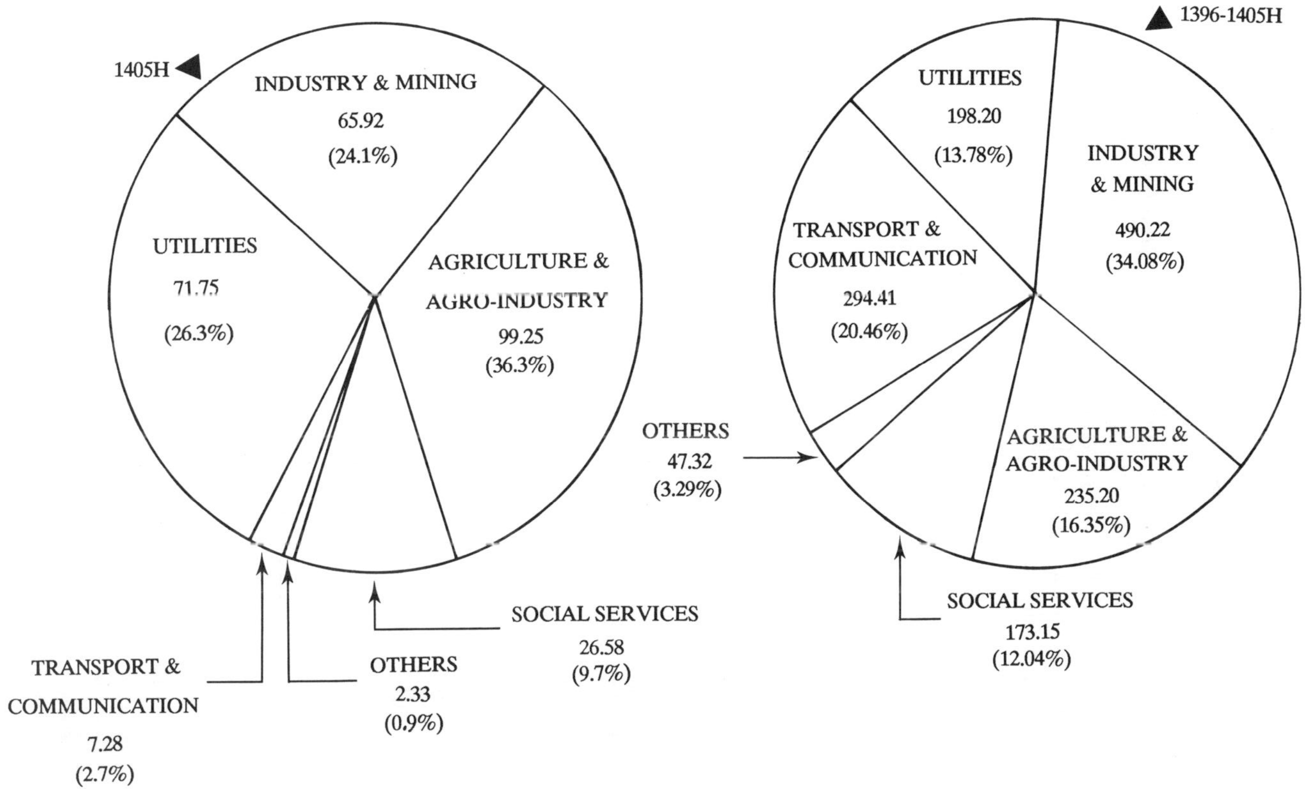

The bank's total loan financing since its inception up to Moharram 1405H has covered eighty-five operations amounting to ID508.41 million (US$569.42 million). It has to be acknowledged that, in real terms, project lending even with high service charges cannot be regarded as a profitable operation for the bank, if the present inflation rate is added to the normal monetary rate of discount. Thus, if money is seen as a medium of exchange to obviate the difficulties of a barter system, not as a commodity, then it is to be examined further whether loan contracts can be expressed in real terms rather than in money terms.

TABLE 8.1
Amount of Project Financing Approved by Sectors
(In ID million)

	1403H		1404H		1405H		Total since 1396H	
Sectors	Amount	%	Amount	%	Amount	%	Amount	%
Agriculture and agro-industry	6.06	3.1	28.79	14.0	99.25	36.3	235.20	16.35
Industry & mining	45.20	23.0	79.42	38.6	65.92	24.1	490.22	34.08
Transport and communication	74.22	37.8	34.43	16.8	7.28	2.7	294.41	20.46
Utilities	21.18	10.8	21.20	10.3	71.75	26.3	198.20	13.78
Social services	39.33	20.1	41.37	20.1	26.58	9.7	173.15	12.04
Others	10.21	5.2	0.50	0.2	2.33	0.9	47.32	3.29
Total	196.20	100	205.71	100	273.11	100	1438.50	100

SOURCE: IDB, *Tenth Annual Report*, 1405H (1984-85), p. 61.

Though project lending seems to be a dominant form in the IDB's current lending operations, programme lending, which is usually undertaken to finance a programme of productivity so that under-utilized capacity is fully utilized or a bottleneck in the process of production is removed, can be given due consideration.

Equity Participation and Line of Equity. While in equity participation the bank participates in equity capital of a project directly, such participation is made indirectly in the case of line of equity. The bank encourages other parties to have a controlling interest in the share capital of the enterprises in which it participates. The bank has participated in the share capital of forty-one equity projects amounting to ID131.32 million (US$203.08 million) during 1396-1405H.

In order to extend assistance to small and medium industrial projects, particularly in the private sector, the bank has started a new operation called "line of equity" under which the national development finance institutions act as agencies of the bank for the purpose of identifying, appraising, and implementing local projects which are suitable for this type of financing by the bank in the order of ID100,000 to ID200,000 each. So far, the bank has participated in sixteen such operations. The small projects are worth considering both from the point of view of sound economic development and income distribution.

At this stage, it is worth mentioning that the overall financial performance of the IDB's equity projects has been less impressive than expected. These projects have been facing difficulties in one form or another. Delays in implementation causing cost overruns, lack of adequate infrastructural facilities, lack of required skilled manpower, lack of demand resulting from slow economic growth, recession in the industrialized countries, and exchange rate adjustments which affect profitablity and cause liquidity problems are some of the difficulties encountered by these projects in varying proportions.

Based on the experience of the past ten years, the bank has already undertaken the task of formulating new policy guidelines relating to such issues as the linking of disbursement of equity funds with project implementation. Viewed from this perspective, the IDB's recent curtailment of this mode of financing, particularly during 1404H (1983-84), was of a short-term nature. The bank's effort to modify its policies shows its desire to operationalize the *Sharia* concepts of *mudarabah* and *musharakah.*

In this connection it is pertinent to mention that the IDB is very keen on issuing Muquarada Bonds and other financial instruments for mobilizing funds, thereby giving the public a chance to invest in development projects and share their dividends in accordance with the *Sharia.*

Leasing and Line of Leasing. Lease financing involves direct participation of the IDB in the procurement of necessary equipments and machinery for the production of various intermediary and capital goods in the member countries as well as for the acquisition of ocean-going vessels towards building up the necessary transportation facilities and foreign trade activities. In the case of line of leasing, the same participation is made indirectly through national development banks of the member countries somewhat similar to the line of equity financing.

During the past ten years, lease financing, which ranks second in terms of total volume of financing(representing about 35.24 per cent of the total), has increased considerably. Since the inception of leasing activities up to 1405H, fifty-five projects have been financed through this mode, amounting to ID506.99 million (US$567.83 million). So far, five lines of leasing amounting to ID40.80 million (US$45.70 million) have been extended. Line of leasing activities are to be extended to selected National Development Banks, in order to enlarge the scope of items to be financed profitably.

Profit-Sharing. The bank has also participated in financing two projects through profit-sharing schemes in the areas of real estate business amounting to ID7.3 million (US$8.18 million). There is a considerable scope for the expansion of these operations in other sectors. There is a clear need for the identification of joint venture projects in the member countries on a priority basis so that the bank can start negotiating to participate in those ventures on the basis of profit-sharing.

However, the whole range of issues concerning the economics of profit-sharing need to be studied in depth. In particular, issues relating to partnership and ownership rights, calculation of the rate of return before and after local taxes, method of depreciation, determination of break-even, and so on are yet to be sorted out.

Instalment Sale. In an effort to expand the IDB's operations, the bank has recently approved seven instalment sale operations in this area amounting to ID65.89 million (US$73.80 million). Obviously, there is scope for further expansion in the area of operation. Perhaps in the future, "line of instalment sale" may be introduced. Although this mode of financing is understood to be permissible under the *Sharia*, the IDB expects to provide necessary safeguards particularly in working out the range of mark-up on purchase price so as to avoid arbitrariness and to preclude the possibility of introducing interest in a different form.

Technical Assistance

Technical assistance is given, either in the form of a loan, a grant, or a combination of both, provided that the grant element for a single project does not exceed ID150,000. These operations are a part of the bank's efforts to identify suitable projects for financing in the future. Since the inception of the bank up to 1405H, the IDB has provided technical assistance to seventy-three projects amounting to ID34.15 million (US$38.25 million).

Foreign Trade Financing Operations

The IDB's foreign trade financing operations can be seen as a fund placement operation with a view to assisting member countries in meeting procurement of necessary industrial raw materials needed by domestic industries. This operation is of a short-term nature and used by member countries for the procurement of urgently needed industrial raw materials. This operation helps the IDB to utilize its excess fund not immediately needed for project financing. The difference between the purchase and the resale price (that is, the mark-up) constitutes a source of income for the bank. The foreign trade operation which tops the list (about eighty) in terms of total volume of financing has increased considerably over the years from its base of 16 per cent in 1398H (1977-78).

Since 1397H, the bank has approved 241 foreign trade operations (excluding operations cancelled or withdrawn) amounting to ID3,374.12 million (US$3,785.18 million) of which 212 operations amounting to ID2,682.74 million (US$3,103.67 million) were between member countries. This represents about 80 per cent of the total amount approved until 1405H, covering a variety of crude oil, refined petroleum products, different types of fertilizers, cement, gypsum, clinker, sulphur, rock phosphate, paper and pulp, vegetable oil, sugar, jute and jute products, cotton and cotton yarn, and intermediate industrial goods.

Foreign trade financing operations of the IDB have been a useful means of promoting trade among the member countries, thereby facilitating economic co-operation and integration among them.

> The issues which are now under Bank's consideration in this context relate to (i) diversification of commodities including food stuff, (ii) inter-marriage between trade financing of consumer goods and development of their production within member countries, (iii) financing of exports from one member country to another, (iv) promotion of trade of capital goods (equipment) among member countries leading to fostering of growth of capital goods industries in the member countries and. (v) liberalization of the terms and conditions of foreign trade financing operation.[9]

Other Activities and Social Progress

At this stage, it is important to provide a list of other important activities of the IDB which are essentially geared towards social progress in the member countries and in the Muslim communities in non-member countries. These activities are as follows:

a. to support research and training activities in line with the principles of the *Sharia* and provisioning for disaster relief and technical assistance out of the IDB's Special Assistance Account;
b. to provide concessional financing such as loans, grants, and technical assistance to the IDB's sixteen least developed member countries;
c. to maintain close relations with local Islamic banks with a view to

finding proper investment channels for the utilization of surplus liquid funds and joint financing of projects and other related co-financing;

d. to co-ordinate the financial and development activities of a number of Arab development funds and the Organization of Petroleum Exporting Countries' (OPEC) Fund so as to enable the bank to co-finance development projects in its member countries;

e. to establish a working relationship with various international and regional institutions and agencies such as the United Nations Industrial Development Organization (UNIDO) and World Health Organization (WHO), so as to share their experiences in the planning of projects, transfer of technology, and other allied matters; and

f. to implement a special programme of emergency aid for Sahelian countries (that is Chad, Niger, Bourkina Fasso, [Upper Volta], Mali, Senegal, Mauritania, Guinea Bissau, Guinea, and Gambia) for which an amount of US$50 million had been allocated in 1404H (1983-84).

Let us now discuss in some detail the extent to which a linkage can be established between the accepted *Sharia* principles concerning Islamic finance and the IDB's operational strategies and mode of financing.

IDB, Local Islamic Banks, and Secular Development Banks: A Comparative Analysis

From the preceding analysis, it becomes abundantly clear that the operational strategies of the IDB presents a significant departure from the functions performed by the local Islamic banks and other secular development banks. Nonetheless, there are some points of similarity in their approach and orientation.

Although the IDB is an international financial institution like other international financial institutions such as the World Bank and the Asian Development Bank, normal lending operations *do not* constitute a major function of the IDB. As noted earlier, the IDB does not charge any interest on its loan operations, but it does charge service fees to cover its relevant administrative expenses which is permissible in Islam. The present loan operation is mainly concentrated on the development of socio-economic infrastructure projects, although the magnitude of investments needed for such development in the member countries will remain, for many years to come, at a level far beyond the saving capacities of these countries. This type of lending operations is clearly beyond the scope of Islamic (commercial) banks, because they are not generally concerned with development financing. Their lending operations are very restrictive and short-term in nature. Besides, almost all Islamic (commercial) banks are in the private sector, whereas the IDB is government-sponsored.

It appears from the various reports[10] that the Islamic banks operating in Egypt and Sudan are guided by three basic principles:

a. eliminating interest in all forms of transactions;
b. undertaking all legitimate and lawful business and commerce, trade, and industrial enterprises; and
c. providing social services through the *zakat* fund for the benefit of the poor and needy.

Islamic banks operating in several countries are involved in four forms of activities:

a. providing normal commercial banking services like effecting domestic and international transfers, collection of bills, opening of letters of credit and issuing letters of guarantee, providing safe custody on the basis of small commission charges, etc.;
b. providing facilities to open non-investment accounts (for example, current account);
c. providing facilities to attract funds for investment in trade and business; and lastly
d. providing social services on a humanitarian basis, allowing overdrafts free of charge and benevolent loans in special cases.

Although the functions of Islamic banks may appear to be similar to those of conventional banks, their motivational properties differ significantly.

All conventional banks are propelled purely by profit-motives. Profit maximization is the main theme of all these banks. On the other hand, the aims and objectives of an Islamic bank, in addition to profit-making, are designed to create a balanced society. An Islamic bank aims at profit but not at profiteering. Profit which is unreasonably high and does not conform to the general welfare of society is termed as profiteering – which is also prohibited in Islam and avoided by the Islamic banks. Moreover, the institution of interest, accumulation of capital and wealth in few hands, hoarding of goods, usury, etc. are discarded by Islamic banks.

The aim of the IDB is

> ...to foster the economic development and social progress of member countries and Muslim communities individually as well as jointly in accordance with the principles of Sharia. It participates in equity capital and grant loans for productive projects and enterprises.

> The Bank is authorised to accept deposits and to raise funds in any other manner. It is also charged with the responsibility of assisting in the promotion of foreign trade, especially in capital goods, among member countries, providing technical assistance to member countries, extending training facilities for personnel engaged in development activities and undertaking research for enabling the economic financial and banking activities in Muslim countries to conform to the *Sharia*.

Thus, some similarities of functions not withstanding, the IDB's operations represent a significant departure not only from the conventional development banks but also from other Islamic banks operating on a commercial basis.

Clearly the scale of the IDB's operations is much wider than that of other Islamic banks. Unlike the latter, which concentrate on short-term financing of business and economic activities, the IDB's concentration is mainly on capital financing. Even its current foreign trade operation is directed towards the building of socio-economic infrastructures. As mentioned earlier, the loans given by the IDB are free of interest. The IDB's operation differs significantly from the World Bank and Asian Development Bank which extend loans on a fixed interest rate to execute socio-economic infra-structure projects; even where secular banks extend loans free of interest in special cases, the underlying principles and motivations are different from those which guide the IDB.

Despite difficulties encountered in unfavourable economic settings, almost all the Islamic banks have been able to show profit rates ranging from 9 per cent to 25 per cent which compare favourably with profits made by conventional banks based on interest earnings. On investment deposits, the rates of return have ranged from 8 per cent to over 15 per cent.

It may be noted here that many Islamic banks and investment companies are conducting their business not only in their respective countries but also internationally through international trade and finance on the basis of reciprocity. This calls for greater co-ordination among Islamic banks which may be effected by a Central Islamic Bank which can also serve as a clearing house for all Islamic banks.

The need for such co-operation and co-ordination is all the more important, as it would be mutually beneficial and economical to have a co-ordinated approach in the fields of personnel training, marketing, local project identification, investment, and research in Islamic economics. Since Islamic banks are operating in unfamiliar and adverse economic settings, it is particularly important to minimize management and monitoring costs, to avoid wastage and unnecessary duplications, and to have dynamic managerial strategies, so that profitability of these banks are sustained over time. To be sure, the success of these banks should not be judged merely by the level or rate of profit earned. Their real success lies in using their material gains to influence the existing socio-economic institutions in ways that are acceptable to the *Sharia*. The successful initiation of the Islamic banks and IDB signifies a major breakthrough, as they have introduced a number of innovations in the field of Islamic economics, and money and banking. It is of interest to note that even some conventional banks have been so impressed by the Islamic banks that they are seriously considering equity-based operations as an alternative to interest-based ones, while some of them have opened Islamic counters or windows.

The IDB and the Development of Southeast Asia

Let us now discuss in some detail the IDB's contributions to the economic development and social upliftment of the Muslim countries and the Muslim communities in Southeast Asia. Brunei, Indonesia, and Malaysia are the member countries of the bank. In recent past, the IDB has made provisions for financial assistance to the Muslim communities of Thailand, Singapore, and the Philippines, in addition to Muslim communities of other non-member countries such as India, Sri Lanka, and Kenya.

In Indonesia, the IDB had approved eight projects amounting to about US$50.5 million until 1405H. They comprised two loan projects, one leasing project, one instalment-sale project, three equity projects, and one line of equity project.

During 1405H (1984-85), one project with two modes of financing was approved amounting to US$10.7 million. The project aimed at the development of fishing ports and jetties which will stimulate fishing efforts and support, expand, and improve fish processing, marketing, and other related industries. It will contribute to increased fish supply and consumption and add to Indonesia's export earnings. The bank also participated in buying additional shares in P.T. Semen Andalas amounting to US$1.5 million.

Similarly, in Malaysia, until the end of 1405H, the IDB had approved seven projects/operations amounting to US$55.12 million. Out of these, three projects were financed through loans, one was equity-based, one was in the form of line of leasing, and one was based on line of equity/leasing. A sum of US$6.0 million was approved for one foreign trade financing operation.

During 1405H, one project was approved for the purpose of the extension of a line of leasing amounting to ID10 million (US$9.7 million) to the Malaysian Industrial Development Bank for the IDB's participation in small and medium industrial projects in the form of lease financing.

Muslim Communities in Non-Member Countries

As mentioned earlier, the IDB is also required to establish and operate special funds for specific purposes including a fund for assistance to Muslim communities in non-member countries, in addition to setting up trust funds.

The main areas in which operations out of this account can be financed include the following:

a. Extension of training facilities for personnel engaged in development activities in member countries and undertaking research for enabling the economic, financial and banking activities in Muslim countries to conform to the *Sharia*. In fact, the Bank has already set up the Institute of Research and Training in Jeddah which has been functioning since the beginning of 1402H (1982) and has undertaken several research and training activities.
b. The provision of relief in the form of appropriate goods and services to member countries and Islamic communities in non-member countries afflicted by natural calamities and disasters;
c. the provision of financial assistance to member countries for the promotion and furtherence of Islamic causes;
d. the provision of financial assistance to Muslim communities in non-Muslim countries for the promotion of their social welfare and economic uplift;
e. provision of some scholarships to Muslim communities in non-member countries to enable needy students to pursue higher education in technical fields.[12]

During 1405H, the bank approved eleven operations involving an amount of ID63.90 million (US$63.33 million), as against fourteen operations amounting to ID62.65 million (US$64.24 million) approved in 1404H. Most of the operations approved during 1405H related to the establishment of schools to promote Islamic education and vocational training institutes for Muslim communities in non-Muslims countries. About US$5.0 million was approved for various programmes to support the training and educational activities of Muslims in Thailand and Singapore and the Filipino refugees in Malaysia during 1405H.

Scholarship Programme
In addition to the special operation financed out of the Special Assistance Account, the bank has also instituted a scholarship programme financed out of this account for students from Muslim communities in non-member countries to enable them to get higher education in the faculties of engineering and medicine in their own countries as well as in the member countries. The bank's scholarship is a grant to the Muslim communities; but at the same time, it is an interest-free loan (*qardhasan*) to the recipient students who will reimburse the amounts of scholarship to a trust (*waqf*) to be established by the local Muslim community after they have completed their studies and started remunerative employments so that other students can benefit from the programme in future.

The scholarship programme started with recipients from countries such as India, Sri Lanka, and Kenya in the 1983-84 academic year. In the 1984-85 academic year, it was extended to five other countries, namely Burma, Singapore, Thailand, Tanzania, Ghana, and Eritrea. Studies are being conducted in another eleven countries for possible implementation. These are Ivory Coast, Mozambique, Zaire, Malawi, Mauritius, Thailand, the Philippines, Fiji, China, Yugoslavia, and Greece. This programme involved an amount of US$600,000 in 1405H, and the number of students who benefited from the scheme during the year was 125.

With a view to serving Muslim communities in the non-Muslim countries by developing useful programmes in a planned and systematic manner, the bank has constituted a Special Assistance Review Committee, which will

> (a) review and recommend the Bank's special assistance plans and programmes, (b) study the special assistance projects for Muslim communities in non-Muslim countries and (c) prepare an annual budget and a comprehensive programme for this purpose".[13]

Policy Implications

Despite several institutional constraints, it would not be incorrect to say that the IDB's modes of financing various activities are essentially in agreement with the principles of the Islamic *Sharia* as explained earlier. As a matter of fact, the bank is unequivocally committed to the principles of *Sharia* in the conduct of its financial operations and other activities. In this connection, it is indeed gratifying to note that the bank has established the Islamic Research and Training Institute (IRTI) whose main function is to

> ...organise and co-ordinate basic and applied research with a view to developing models and methods for the application of the principles of the Sharia in the fields of economic, finance and banking as well as to train personnel engaged in development activities in the Bank's member countries.

The Annual Reports of the bank provide the details of its operation. It would not be appropriate to assume that all issues concerning the IDB's operations have been settled once for all. If there is any difference of opinion as regards the bank's various modes of financing it will only concern the details of its operations, and *not* the basic Islamic principles on which the IDB's operations are based.

It would however be a mistake to ignore the fact that the IDB is directly dealing with forty-four member countries, each having a different history of development, different institutional setting, different colonial legacy, and people with different faculties and motivations, not to mention the differences in natural resource endowments. The understanding of these variables seems to be very important and relevant in appreciating the dynamics of the various sources of Islamic laws.

From the preceding analysis of the diverse operations of the IDB, it becomes clear that the bank is involved in the process of economic and social development of nearly all Southeast Asian countries in one way or another, although only three countries of the region (that is, Brunei, Indonesia, and Malaysia) have become members of the IDB. Although the scale of the bank's operation appears to be modest in financial terms, particularly for Muslim communities in non-member countries of the region such as Thailand, Singapore, and the Philippines, the bank is directly exposed to the social and economic problems of the Muslim minorities of the region. The IDB's operations may also open the door of economic co-operation among the other Muslim countries either on a bilateral or multilateral basis.

The most important indirect benefit of this exposure lies in gathering the knowledge and know-how of Islamic banking operations by all member countries and Muslim communities of non-member states in the region. It does provide a unique opportunity to develop Islamic commercial, developmental, and social banking by Muslim countries and communities themselves. Muslim communities may be inspired to organize social banking by institutionalizing Islamic voluntary sector activities such as the collection and distribution of *zakat*, and the administration of such institutions as *waqf*. Any attempt to institutionalize the various obligatory and voluntary tools of Islamic distributive measures such as *zakat*, *waqf*, etc. would foster the spirit of mutual reliance and social security, thereby creating an involvement in the community's social and economic progress.

Since the Islamic voluntary sector does exist in almost all the countries in the region and is in operation at various levels, Muslim communities in non-member countries may seek necessary technical assistance from the IDB and other local Islamic banks for initiating Islamic social banking based mainly on the local resources that are mobilized from *within* the communities concerned. It should also be seen as an attempt to initiate the process of social development *without* external assistance, that is through the total involvement and participation of the local people. In the long run, however, efforts may be made to mobilize funds at the international level through joint venture projects among Muslim countries and communities.

All in all, it can be said that the establishment of the IDB represents a significant milestone towards achieving the goals of an Islamic economy in the member countries. The innovative nature of IDB operations represents a new experiment in the economic and social affairs of mankind. The bank's activities call for more than a mere replacement of interest rates by profit-sharing and equity participation.

If the bank, during its short existence, has created an impact less than our expectations, it is mainly due to the lack of experience in these kind of operations in diverse socio-economic settings. If the bank's activities are considered to be conservative, it is mainly due to the risk and uncertainty associated with its new ventures.

In the final analysis, however, the ability of member countries to attain self-sustained economic growth will depend largely on: (a) the political will of their leadership, expressed in terms of the efforts towards domestic mobilization of resources; (b) the leadership's political imagination and vision, expressed in terms of perceiving and implementing structural and institutional changes needed for development; and finally (c) the vision of the Muslim universal mass (*ummah*), expressed in terms of co-operation extended to the IDB in achieving its objectives. The failure to perceive a change in these directions will constitute a main obstacle to change itself in conformity with the *Sharia*.[14]

APPENDIX A

Amount Approved under Project Financing and Technical Assistance in 1405H and during 1396-1405H by Mode of Financing
(In ID million)

Type of Financing	1402H			1403H			1404H			1405H			Total Approved 1396-1405H		
	No.	Amount	%	No.	Amount	%	No.	Amount	%	No.	Amount	%	No.	Amount	%
Project Financing															
Loan	8	45.0	27.7	11	73.5	37.4	12	71.5	34.8	15	98.62	36.1	85[1]	508.41	35.34
Equity	8	28.7	17.7	4	15.6	8.0	1	6.0	2.9	4	9.87	3.6	41[3]	181.32	12.60
Line of equity (Utilization)	—	—	—	—	—	—	—	—	—	(12)*	(4.53)	(-)	16 (44)	83.61 (25.54)	5.81 —
Line of equity/leasing	—	—	—	—	—	—	—	—	—	—	—	—	1	10.00	0.70
Leasing	10	84.5	51.9	11	98.0	49.9	12	125.3	61.0	8	82.10	30.1	55[4]	506.99	35.24
Line of leasing	—	—	—	—	—	—	—	—	—	1	10.00	3.7	5	40.80	2.84
Profit-sharing	—	—	—	1	3.0	1.6	—	—	—	—	—	—	2	7.33	0.51
Instalment sale	—	—	—	—	—	—	—	—	—	7	65.89	24.1	7	65.89	4.58
Subtotal	26	158.2	97.3	27	190.1	96.9	25	202.7	98.6	35	266.48	97.6	212	1,404.35	97.62
Technical Assistance	8	4.4	2.7	13	6.1	3.1	7	3.0	1.4	13	6.63	2.4	70[2]	34.15	2.38
Total	34	162.6	100.0	40	196.2	100.0	32	205.7	100.0	48	273.11	100.0	282	1,438.50	100.00

* Represents Line of Equity sub-projects.
[1] Including 2 cancelled projects (Loan).
[2] Including 6 cancelled projects (T.A.).
[3] Including 2 cancelled projects (Equity).
[4] Including 10 cancelled projects (Leasing).

SOURCE: IDB, *Tenth Annual Report*, 1405H (1984-85).

APPENDIX B

Operations Financed Out of Special Assistance Account in 1405H

Country	Operation Description	Date of Approval	Amount	
			ID	US$
Singapore	Reconstruction of Al-Maarib Islamic Girls' School	30.10.84	992,654	1,000,000
Sudan	Purchase of transportation and drilling equipment for relief work in eastern Sudan	30.10.84	9,900,900	10,000,000
Bangladesh	Utilization of IDB grant of US$10 million to the People's Republic of Bangladesh	30.01.85	10,000,000	10,000,000
Mozambique	Construction of two Islamic institutions in Nembola and Koboudelgado	31.01.85	1,836,000	1,800,000
Thailand	Grant to Muslims of Thailand for the construction of a Teachers Training Institute	07.04.85	1,263,000	1,200,000
Regional	Grant for Arab Literacy Program	07.04.85	184,000	175,000
India	Assistance to Muslim communities in India over five years	07.04.85	31,570,000	30,000,000
Kenya	Grant for educational projects for the Muslims of Kenya	10.06.85	1,000,000	1,000,000
Palestine	Immediate assistance to Palestinian camps in Lebanon	10.06.85	1,000,000	1,000,000
Tanzania	Grant for education projects for Tanzanian/Zanzibar Muslims	13.08.85	3,520,000	3,520,000
Malaysia	Grant for educational projects for Muslim refugees from Philippines in Malaysia	13.08.85	2,633,333	2,633,333
Total			63,909,292	62,328,333

SOURCE: IDB, *Tenth Annual Report*, 1405H (1984-85).

APPENDIX C

Projects/Operations since 1396H
(ID million)

Type of Operations	1401H		1402H		1403H		1404H		1405H		Total 1396-1405H	
	No.	Amount	No.	Amount	No.	Amount	No.	Amount	No.	Amount	No.	Amount
Project financing	17	107.79	26	158.17	27	190.12	25	202.74	35	266.48	212	1,404.35
Technical assistance	10	6.83	8	4.44	13	6.08	7	2.96	13	6.63	70	34.15
Subtotal	27	114.62	34	162.61	40	196.20	32	205.70	48	273.11	282	1,438.50
Foreign trade financing	32	370.24	29	379.68	27	460.40	47	714.31	38	668.21	241*	3,374.12
Subtotal	59	484.86	63	542.29	67	656.60	79	920.01	86	941.32	523	4,812.62
Special assistance account	9	5.33	8	9.25	7	7.85	14	62.65	11	63.90	57	158.16
Grand Total	68	490.19	71	551.54	74	664.45	93	982.66	97	1,005.22	580	4,970.78

* Excluding cancelled ones.

SOURCE: IDB, *Tenth Annual Report*, 1405H (1984-85).

NOTES

* The views expressed in this paper are the author's personal views and do not necessarily reflect the views of the institution to which he belongs. This paper is based on the IDB's publications and the author's published works, namely *Islamic Economics: Theory and Practice* (1970); *The Making of Islamic Economic Society* (1984); and *The Frontiers of Islamic Economics* (1984).

1 *Al-Qur'an* (II: 275).

2 Three Arabic terms: *qirad*, *muqaradah*, and *mudarabah* are interchangeable with no essential difference in meaning and connotation among them. See A. Udovitch, *Partnership and Profit in Medieval Islam* (Princeton, New Jersey: Princeton University Press, 1970), pp. 74-75. For definitions of the various types of financial contracts, see M.N. Siddiqi's paper in this volume.

3 See Charles Hamilton, *The Hedaya* (Lahore: Premier Book House, 1982), and P.T. Hughes, *Dictionary of Islam* (Lahore: Premier Book House).

4 The Qur'an says: "Attend your prayers, pay your alms and grant benevolent loans" (Sura-al-Mozammil, verse 20). Again it is said: "If you grant benevolent loans, we multiply them for you and forgive you (Sura al-Taghabon, verse 17).

5 IDB, *Ninth Annual Report*, 1404H (1983-84).

6 One Islamic Dinar (ID) is equivalent to one Special Drawing Right (SDR).

7 IDB, *Tenth Annual Report*, 1405H (1984-85).

8 Ibid., pp. 5-7.

9 Ibid.

10 See F.M. Khan, "A Report on the Islamic Banking", paper presented at the follow-up seminar on Monetary and Fiscal Economics of Islam, Islamabad, 1980; F. Agabany, "A Promising Experience in Comprehensive Islamic Banking, Faisal Islamic Bank (Sudan)", paper presented at the follow-up seminar on Monetary and Fiscal Economics of Islam, Islamabad, 1980; and Faisal Islamic Bank (Egypt), *Annual Report of the Board of Directors*, 1980.

11 IDB, *Tenth Annual Report*, 1405H.

12 Ibid.

13 Ibid.

14 M.A. Mannan, *The Making of Islamic Economic Society* (Cairo: International Association of Islamic Banks, 1984), p. 470.

9 ISLAMIC BANKING: A SOUTHEAST ASIAN PERSPECTIVE

Mohamed Ariff

Introduction

Southeast Asia has one of the largest concentrations of Muslims in the world. Indonesia, Malaysia, and Brunei are three sovereign states where Islam is the "official religion" and which are often referred to as "Islamic" countries. In fact, Indonesia represents the largest Muslim country in the world. Although none of these countries have "Islamic" governments as these states are governed along secular lines, Islam has influenced in some ways the manner in which these states are governed and their economies are managed. In addition to these three Muslim countries in the region, there are sizeable conglomerations of Muslims in countries which are branded as "non-Muslim". Thus, in the predominantly Catholic Philippines, there are large concentrations of Muslims in the south, especially in Mindanao; and in the essentially Buddhist Thailand, there are pockets of Muslims in the north and northeast, in addition to a heavy presence of Muslims in the south. The bulk of these Muslim communities, which represent minorities in these lands, are of the Malay stock, while the rest are largely of Indo-Pakistani and Middle East origins.

Muslims have always asserted their separate identity even where they are no more than a minority community. It is this distinctiveness about the Muslims that has helped preserve their religion and way of life in the face of adverse developments. Islam is not a religion in the Western sense. It is a complete and comprehensive way of life. Although Islam has been reduced in several parts of the world to a religion of rituals, Islam never lost its bearing, meaning, or purpose. The universal message of Islam and its fundamentals have never failed to simmer even under the impact of Western civilization and colonialization. Southeast Asia is no exception.

Muslim communities in Southeast Asia have been able to take care of their own basic needs mostly through self-help and mutual assistance or "*gotong royong*" as the Malays call it. There have been informal and semi-formal financial arrangements structured along Islamic lines which have helped the communities meet their immediate wants without having to compromise the sacred *Shariah* principles. With Islamic resurgence occurring all over the world, there have been attempts to formalize some of these existing arrangements and to institutionalize them in a structured fashion. Islamic banks have thus appeared on the Southeast Asian scene.

Southeast Asian economies in general have been growing rapidly by both developing and developed country standards. Although there is no concrete empirical evidence to establish any definitive relationship between Islam as practised by the Muslims in this part of the world and the pace of economic development achieved by several countries in the region, there is no basis to downplay the role of Islam as a driving force. Muslims, by and large, have demonstrated that they are industrious and enterprising and that their religion of Islam is no barrier to economic prosperity. There is a close historical relationship between commerce and Islam, for it is through trading channels that Islam spread far and wide. Islam does not forbid its followers from absorbing "alien" customs and practices which do not violate its fundamentals. In fact, Islam encourages Muslims to seek knowledge from whatever sources. It is through the endless process of mindful adoption and imaginative adaptation that Islamic culture has evolved itself.

That Islam is a universal religion for all times and all places is, in no small measure, demonstrated by the emergence of modern institutions such as Islamic banks in different parts of the world. That there can be an Islamic solution to any modern problem, if Muslims try hard enough, is also the lesson that one may gather from the story of Islamic banks. It is in this spirit and light that one must view the phenomenon of Islamic banks.

In this chapter, an attempt is made to study the role of Islamic banks in the Southeast Asian context. Malaysia is the only Southeast Asian country to house a full-fledged Islamic bank, although the Amanah Bank in the Philippines represents an interesting experiment in Islamic banking. The Philippine Amanah Bank operates an Islamic "window" side by side conventional interest-based counters. In other Southeast Asian countries, including Indonesia, there are no formal Islamic banking activities. But, then, there are some informal arrangements in these countries for mobilizing financial resources.

The primary objective of this chapter is to provide an overview of the Islamic banking practices both in formal and informal forms as depicted in the preceding chapters and to present a synthesis of the analyses contained therein. The rest of this chapter is structured as follows. First, a profile of Muslim communities in Southeast Asia is given as a backdrop to the subsequent analysis. Formal Islamic banking establishments in Malaysia and the Philippines are then examined. This is followed by a discussion of informal Islamic financial arrangements. Finally, problems and prospects of Islamic banks, from the viewpoint of the economic development of Southeast Asia, are discussed.

Muslim Communities in Southeast Asia: A Profile

Southeast Asia is a region of considerable variety, and even the Muslims are not a homogeneous lot. Nonetheless, the Islamic bondage is strong enough to cut across national and ethnic boundaries. The impact of Islam on the lives of Muslims varies from country to country, and it will be difficult to make any generalization in this regard. However, it appears that Islam tends to assert itself vehemently in societies where Muslims are a sizeable minority, as in the Philippines, presumably because Muslims in such societies feel threatened by the majority who do not belong to the Islamic faith. In societies where Muslims form the predominant group, as in Indonesia, Islam tends to be taken for granted. The involvement of Southeast Asian Muslims in the Islamic resurgence that seems to be sweeping across the region and their responses to the external stimuli are therefore by no means uniform. In what follows, an attempt is made to sketch a brief contemporary profile of Muslims in selected countries.

Indonesian Muslims account for about 90 per cent of the estimated 165 million population of Indonesia. There are over 300 ethnic groups scattered all over the archipelago, with more than one-half of the total population concentrated in the island of Java. Muslims can be divided into subgroups along ethnic, linguistic, and regional lines. Broadly, however, they are classified into two groups: *abangan* and *santri*. The former term refers to the so-called nominal Muslims who do not practise their religion, while the latter term refers to the pious Muslims who are steeped in Islam. The *santri* category can be subdivided into the fundamentalist, the reformists, the mystics, etc. The Western-educated urban Muslims tend to exhibit secular life-styles, while the religious-educated, rural Muslims tend to be more inward-looking and conservative.

Although Indonesia is the largest Muslim country in the world, it has declared itself a secular state espousing the *Pancasila* ideology which makes no specific reference to Islam. The Indonesian legal system is also secular with religious courts having a limited jurisdiction. Muslim Family Law is officially used for Muslims, but the procedures are not strictly Islamic in character. The Religious Council, established in 1962 and reorganized in 1975, issues *fatwa* (sanctions) on matters of religion to the government and the people. However, the political system in Indonesia has denied Islam a political platform, as Islam-based political parties have been told to regroup as Partai Perhimpunan Pembangunan (PPP) and to fully endorse the *Pancasila* ideology. Under these circumstances, Islam can only flourish as a "religion" in the Western sense, that is, ceremonial and ritualistic. Islam as an ideology and a way of life has no place in the Indonesian polity under the current conditions. Thus, the question of injecting Islamic values into economics and politics in the Indonesian context does not arise.

Muslims in Malaysia live in a different environment. Muslims form no more than 55 per cent of the population of Malaysia. The slim majority margin has led the Muslims not to take a complacent attitude towards Islam, quite unlike their Indonesian counterparts. All Malays are Muslims, although the reverse is not true, as there are many non-Malay Muslims in the country. In Malaysian politics, the ethnic factor has always been a potent factor. Indeed, most political parties are still organized along communal lines. The Barisan Nasional, the ruling coalition, represents an interethnic political platform for the various communities. The United Malay National Organization (UMNO), the most powerful component in the ruling coalition, has declared itself as the protector of Malay interest and Malay religion, namely Islam. There are several other political parties prominent among them being the Parti Islam (PAS), an opposition party that is far more fundamentalist in character than UMNO.

Religion and politics are less separable in Malaysia than they are in Indonesia, and the role of Islam in Malaysian politics has become more pronounced in Malaysia especially in the 1980s. PAS has been very assertive in its demand for the establishment of an Islamic state in Malaysia, while UMNO favours a selective and gradual assimilation of Islamic values into the government. However, secular forces are quite strong in Malaysia as non-Muslims, who form nearly 45 per cent of the total population, do not subscribe to the Islamic ideology. The policy of the Barisan Nasional, which is heavily influenced by UMNO, on Islam is mainly in response to the growing expectations of the religious-conscious Muslim community in the wake of Islamic revivalism. There are visible signs of growing conformity to the Islamic codes in Malaysia. Muslim scholars have shown renewed interest in Islam, while Muslim social scientists in particular have been looking for Islamic solutions to modern problems. It is of interest to note that a number of new institutions with Islamic favour in the field of education, health, industry, commerce, and banking have come into existence, often with government assistance, in the early eighties.

In Singapore, Muslims are a minority, accounting for only about 16 per cent of the 2.5 million population of the city state. Malays account for the bulk of the Muslims. Pakistanis, Indians, and Arabs represent a minority within the Muslim community, while the number of Chinese Muslims in Singapore is rather small. Malay Muslims are also an economic minority, as they have lagged behind the rest with their per capita income falling far below the national average. Politically, Malays are at a disadvantage as there is no electoral constituency in Singapore where they can constitute a majority.

Consequently, Malay representation in the government seems symbolic and does not adequately reflect the community's numerical strength in the republic. Several Malay political parties do exist albeit without parliamentary representation, in addition to a number of non-political Muslim clubs and associations.

Muslim religious affairs are handled in Singapore by a council called Majlis Ugama Islam Singapura (MUIS) which was set up under the Provisions of the Administration of Muslim Law Act in 1966. MUIS oversees, among other things, the collection and distribution of *zakat* and *fitrah* (religious taxes), the management of pilgrimage, and the administration of religious schools and mosques. In addition, MUIS is also empowered to issue *fatwa*.

The Muslims of the Philippines, often referred to as the Moros, constitute a heterogeneous group comprising thirteen ethnolinguistic subgroups. They number about 4.5 million, accounting for only about 9 per cent of the total population of the Philippines and are concentrated in the south. The bulk of the Moros are farmers and fishermen. Interethnic consciousness among the Moros is overshadowed by a strong feeling of religious fraternity which is reinforced by an equally strong sense of insecurity in the wake of the influx of Christians into the south in the post-war period. Besides, the Moros were denied a major role in the regional development process. Political alienation and frustration led the Moros to form militant groups like the Moro National Liberation Front (MNLF) to champion the cause of the Muslims in the archipelago. While hostilities and peace between the north and the south continue, the Muslims have been resorting to self-help measures to uplift their economic well-being through such Islamic institutions as *zakat* and *waqf* (voluntary endowment). At the same time, as a gesture of goodwill, the Philippine government adopted several measures including the establishment of the Philippine Pilgrimage Authority and the Philippine Amanah Bank.

In Thailand, Muslims represent the second largest religious group, constituting about 4 per cent of the total population of over 50 million, according to official estimates. Muslims, thus, form a significant minority group in the kingdom. Nonetheless, they constitute the majority group in four provinces in the south. Muslims are also scattered over thirty other provinces in Thailand. The Malay-Muslims, who form numerically the largest single ethnic group within the Muslim community and hence politically the strongest among the Muslims in the kingdom, have maintained their distinctiveness as Malays, while other Muslims have assimilated into Thai society in many non-religious ways, especially linguistically.

The Muslims of Thailand are basically of rural background and their economic profile is somewhat similar to that of their Thai-Buddhist counterparts. The Muslims are not only free to practise their religion but also given government assistance to subsidize their religious activities. The Muslims in Thailand are well organized: they publish and disseminate Islamic literature and undertake *dakwah* (missionary) and community welfare activities. However, the Muslims themselves are not free from schisms, as they are no less than four major subgroups that claim to belong to different schools of thought. Regardless, Muslims in Thailand do exhibit a commitment to Islam strong enough to downplay minor intrareligious differences.

It is the Malay-Muslims who are most assertive politically. For one thing, they are a numerical majority in the south. And, for another, they are physically and culturally close to their brethren across the border in Malaysia. The Malay-Muslim separatist movement has long been a problem for the Thai government. The separatist insurgency is led by a number of organizations such as the Pattani United Liberation Organization (PULO). The Malay-Muslim secessionist activism in Thailand, however, is not as formidable as the Moro-Muslim secessionism in the Philippines.

The Muslims of Brunei are a privileged lot in some ways. They constitute the dominant majority in the oil-rich sultanate which has a population of only about 200,000 people. Almost all of them are Malays. Islam is given state patronage. The Muslims in Brunei are economically well off and religiously inclined. There is a tendency for the Muslims in Brunei to be complacent about Islam and to remain conservative within the traditionally feudalistic framework. There is very little religious and much less political activism in Brunei where the government is dominated by the royalty. Islamic revivalism in Brunei is confined to matters of religious rituals rather than the broader aspects in the realms of economics and politics.

Islamic Banking

There is a lot more to Islam than religious rituals. For, Islam represents a complete way of life, in which every act of the faithful in accordance with Islamic jurisprudence is regarded as an act of worship. Seen in this light, it is important for a Muslim to conduct his economic activities in such a way that he does not violate the Islamic principles. Islam prohibits *riba* or interest, regardless of the rate and the purpose of the transaction. However, the economic environment in which Muslims live in modern times is dominated almost invariably by the institutions of interest. Under such circumstances, it is extremely hard for Muslims to avoid interest-based transactions. Hence the desire of Muslims to set up interest-free financial institutions.

Islamic resurgence, which began in the seventies, led to the establishment of a number of Islamic banks in the Middle East. The Iranian revolution eliminated *riba* totally in Iran, while in Pakistan, the entire banking industry is undergoing an Islamization process. Undoubtedly, the impact of all these happenings on the Muslims of Southeast Asia has been tremendous. However, not all Muslim communities in the region are in a position to establish Islamic banks. The political environment in some parts of Southeast

Asia was not conducive to such experiments. The problem was mainly one of lack of resources and absence of political will. In the whole of Southeast Asia, Islamic banking in the formal sense exists only in Malaysia and the Philippines. In this section, an attempt is made to examine the role of Islamic banks in Malaysia and the Philippine and their potentials.

Bank Islam Malaysia Berhad (BIMB)

To be sure, the BIMB, which was established in July 1983, was not the first Islamic financial institution to be set up in Malaysia. Earlier in August 1969, the Pilgrims Management and Fund Board, or the Tabung Haji as it is often referred to, was created. However, the Tabung Haji in essence acted as a finance company that invested the savings of would-be pilgrims in accordance with *Sharia* principles. As a non-bank financial institution, the role of the Tabung Haji has been rather limited. None the less, the success of the Tabung Haji provided the main impetus for establishing a full-fledged commercial banking institution based on *Sharia* principles in the country. The Tabung Haji itself contributed 12.5 per cent of the total initial capital of M$80 million of the BIMB. The Malaysian government is the largest shareholder of the BIMB, accounting for 30 per cent of the total.

Needless to say, the BIMB could not have been set up without the strong support of the government which was sympathetic to the Islamic cause, which is not hard to explain. The Malay political party UMNO, which is the main component in the ruling coalition Barisan Nasional, was keen to implement Islamic values to stay in power. The principal objective of the UMNO in this regard was to take the winds off the sails of the Islamic party, PAS, which has been openly in favour not only of Islamizing the country's economy but also of establishing an Islamic state in the country. In retrospect, it appears that the establishment of the Islamic Bank, like the setting up of the International Islamic University, was a strategy taken by the government to take the thunder away from PAS. In short, the political climate was just right for the emergence of an Islamic bank in Malaysia.

In addition to providing conventional banking services in a *halal* manner through *riba*-free financial transactions, the BIMB has been contributing to the economic development of the Muslim community in particular and that of the country in general. Its main contribution has been in the form of mobilizing savings that would have been otherwise kept idle and undertaking investments that would not otherwise have taken place. There are many Muslims in the country who would not place their money in deposits with conventional banks as it would involve interest payments or would not accept interest payments at all even if their savings are deposited in conventional banks. Although it is hard to ascertain the magnitude of the amount involved, it appears that a sizeable proportion of savings especially in the rural areas have been kept out of the system because of lack of *halal* outlets.

Mobilization of savings represents an important function of the BIMB.

For this purpose, the bank accepts various kinds of deposits. Current deposits are accepted on the basis of the principle of *al-wadiah* (safekeeping) which permits the bank to use the money deposited without having to share the profits with the depositors; in return, the bank provides all the usual current account services free of charge. Deposits placed under the saving account are also accepted on *al-wadiah* basis, although the bank at its absolute discretion has been returning a portion of the profits generated to the depositors from time to time. In addition, the bank operates two types of investment accounts based on the *mudaraba* principle which allows the bank to use the deposits, with profits, if any, being shared with the depositors in predetermined proportions and losses, if any, being borne entirely by the depositors. One of these, called General Investment Account, enables depositors to place their funds for a specific period, for example, one month, three months, six months, up to a maximum of five years, to be invested in any way deemed fit by the bank. The bank has been distributing 70 per cent of the profits to depositors, keeping 30 per cent for itself. The other investment account, called Special Investment Account, is meant for deposits from the government and the corporate customers. Profit-sharing ratios for the special investment account are, however, negotiable.

In the first year of its operation ending 30 June 1984, deposits mobilized amounted to M$241.1 million. Total deposits rose to M$410.2 million by the end of the second year of operation as at 30 June 1985, amounting to an increase of 70 per cent. As at December 1985, a total 72,309 deposits in saving account had deposited some M$61.09 million, in contrast to 10,520 deposits who had put in about M$346.37 million. It is of interest to note that about 90 per cent of the deposits placed in the investment account are for the period of two years or less. There are non-Muslim depositors as well, although their number is relatively small, accounting for only 2 per cent of the total. Not all the Muslim depositors are motivated by Islamic considerations, as there seem to be many who would stay with the BIMB only if profits declared by it are competitive with the rate of interest offered by conventional banks.

It is extremely important that the BIMB makes adequate profits not only to give fair dividends to its shareholders and a reasonable rate of return to the depositors, but also to prove that Islamic banks are commercially viable and that they can be an efficient alternative to conventional banks. It is this consideration, more than anything else, that seems to have influenced the investment decisions of the BIMB, subject of course to the *Sharia* constraints that govern the bank's investment activities. In this regard, it is of interest to note that *mudaraba* and *musharaka* (equity-participating partnership) modes of operation, which are considered important and meaningful by Islamic scholars, account for a small proportion of the total. As at 30 June 1985, *mudaraba* and *musharaka* financing accounted for only 15 per cent of the total. Likewise, *murabaha* (mark-up trade financing) transactions accounted for about 15 per cent of the total. The bulk of the total funds, about 65 per cent, was channelled through *al-bai'bithaman ajil* (purchase and sale of properties on deferred payment basis) and *ijara* (leasing). By the end of 1985, the share of *murabaha* financing increased to 23.8 per cent, while that of *al-bai'bithaman ajil* reached 71.2 per cent.

BIMB funds have gone into all major sectors of the economy, including agriculture, mining, quarrying, manufacturing, construction, wholesale and retail trade, transport and storage, and real estate and housing. It is also of relevance to note that about 90 per cent of the bank's funds have been directed at Muslims.

While the BIMB is certainly playing an important role in mobilizing Muslims' savings and investing them productively according to Islamic tenets, thereby contributing to the progress of the Muslim community and accelerating the pace of economic development in the country, its performance seems to have fallen short of popular expectations in the sense that its modes of operation are largely confined to the so-called second-line techniques such as *murabaha* and *bai'muajjal*. To be sure, from the *Sharia* viewpoint, there is nothing wrong with these techniques in the sense that no element of *riba* is present. However, there is much more to Islamic banking than the elimination of *riba*. The BIMB could have made a stronger impact, had it resorted to mainly to the first-line techniques such as *mudaraba* and *musharaka* which could have stimulated a lot more private sector initiatives. The first-line techniques, no doubt, involve a higher element of risk than the second-line instruments mentioned above. This probably explains why the BIMB has shied away from the *mudaraba* and *musharaka* modes of financing.

In the third year of operation ending 30 June 1986, the BIMB put up a fine performance in terms of increases in deposits, financing and investment, and profits. Deposits grew by 40 per cent to M$566.9 million, while disbursement of financing and investment with customers increased by 23 per cent to M$395.33 million. Profits credited to depositors rose to M$27.4 million against M$17.7 million in the preceding year. The bank was able to wipe off its accumulated losses in the previous year, with retained profits standing at M$1.5 million.

The BIMB made a profit of M$3.7 million in the third year of operation compared with M$4.4 million in the second year. None the less, the achievements of the BIMB in the third year ending 30 June 1986 were creditable, especially in view of the fact that the period under review was a particularly difficult one for the Malaysian economy. It is also remarkable that the BIMB has been able to spread its wings systematically by expanding its branch network. During the third year of its operation, the bank opened six new branches, bringing the total number of branches to fourteen. It is also worth mentioning that the BIMB plans to have at least a branch in every state capital. Plans are afoot to open six new branches a year so that by 1990, the branch network of the BIMB will reach thirty-three. It is also of interest to note that the BIMB is targeting for a deposit base of M$1 billion by 1990.

Excess liquidity is still a problem for the BIMB, as it cannot resort to the money market operations which involve interest. Consequently, the bank has resorted to holdings of commodities, mostly precious metals, quoted shares, and Malaysian government investment certificates which can be liquidated quickly if the need arose. The bank also has certain short-term portfolio investments in quoted shares and long-term investments in quoted and unquoted shares, which stood at M$1 million and M$8 million respectively, as at 30 June 1986.

The Philippine Amanah Bank (PAB)

The Philippine Amanah Bank (PAB) was established on 2 August 1973 by a Presidential Decree as a specialized government institution. In fact, no reference was made to its Islamic banking operations when the PAB was first chartered. The PAB was technically placed in the same category as other specialized banks such as the Development Bank of the Philippines and the Land Bank of the Philippines. Evidently, the establishment of the PAB was an integral part of the government's response to the Muslim rebellion in the south. Although the PAB was designed to serve the special banking needs of the Muslim community in the Philippines, its first primary task was to assist the rehabilitation and reconstruction work in Mindanao, Sulu, and Palawan.

The PAB has eight branches located in the major cities of the southern Muslim provinces, including one in Makati in the north, in addition to the head office located at Zamboanga City in Mindanao. Several major government financial institutions own the controlling stock of the PAB which has an authorized capital of P100 million. The government has a total subscription of P30 million, while four governmental financial institutions have a P5 million stake each.

However, strictly speaking, the PAB is not an Islamic bank in the sense that interest-based operations continue to co-exist with Islamic modes of financing. Thus, the PAB operates two "windows" for deposit transactions, that is conventional and Islamic, although it is hoped that the Islamic modes will eventually replace all interest-based instruments.

Prominent under the interest-free profit- and loss-sharing (PLS) system is the Pilgrims Special Savings Deposit (PSSD) scheme designed to mobilize savings and to put the funds of intending pilgrims to good use in trade, commerce, and industry that are lawful in Islam. The PSSD accounts have been kept absolutely separate from the interest-bearing accounts of the bank. Deposits generated from the programme amounted to P0.883 million as of 30 June 1983 and yielded a profit rate of 10.2 per cent in the first half of 1983, which exceeded the rate of return on regular savings accounts.

An important objective of the PAB's corporate mission has been to develop banking habits among the Filipino Muslims. The PSSD account is a special case in point. A unique feature of this account is that it allows funds to be transferred to the account from relatives who are working abroad. Thus, a would-be pilgrim's relatives working abroad can remit regular amounts to the PAB for credit to the said account.

The PAB has been concentrating mainly on *murabaha* instruments. *Mudaraba* and *musharaka* means of financing are rarely resorted to. Likewise, little use is also made of *ijara* or leasing as a mode of financing by the PAB. While the Central Bank has no serious objections to such practices which are perceived to fall under the so-called concept of universal banking, it has drawn attention to the need for recapitalization of the PAB. One may, however, argue that the basis of operation can be shifted from interest to profit-sharing without having to widen the equity base of the banking operation.

In conformity with the current practice of Islamic banks, the PAB contributes at least 10 per cent of the bank's share of profits to a Reserve Fund. This annual retention is allowed to accumulate until the size of the Reserve Fund becomes equal to the capital of the PAB. To be sure, this Reserve Fund is in addition to the Statutory Reserve which is imposed by the Central Bank against liquidity and deposit liabilities. If the losses on PLS funds/investments were attributed to the PAB's negligence, PLS depositors can be compensated from the Reserve Fund. Although the Reserve Fund system provides a better risk finance over time than the conventional deposit insurance system, the PAB has been complying with the Philippine Deposit Insurance Corporation (PDIC) coverage.

That the PAB's operations are not entirely Islamic is evident not only from the fact that it maintains two deposit windows as was seen above, but also from the unorthodox approaches adopted in dealing with excess liquidity and investment outlets. Thus, in times of excess liquidity, the PAB has been making use of treasury bills as a transitory measure and taking advantage of variations in the price of interest-bearing issues which the Central Bank puts up from time to time to mop up excess liquidity. Simple lending operations still do take place, although the launching of the PLS account paved the way for Islamic alternatives such as *mudaraba* investment, *musharaka* commercial ventures, and *murabaha* trade financing. The PAB has proposed charter amendments and an Islamic chart of accounts so that it can fully Islamicize its entire operation. A complete shift to Islamic modes by the PAB will have to await the stamp of official approval from the Philippine monetary authorities.

None the less, the PAB has invoked some Islamic modes in several major investment activities. A special case in point was the PAB's attempt to adopt the *qirad* (a variant of *mudaraba*) principle in the financing of a development project in the Kilusang Kabuhayan at Kaunlaran (KKK) movement of the past government. Efforts are already underway for the PAB to participate in the Quedan food production programme through *ijara* financing for the acquisition of farm implements and supplies. The PAB is also working towards *murabaha* and *musharaka* agreements with farmers who are in need of financial asistance.

Clearly, the present charter of the PAB is not sympathetic to the operational requirements of carrying out banking business in accordance with Islamic jurisprudence. It is unlikely that even the proposed amendments to the bank's charter will pave the way for the PAB to be converted fully into a model Islamic bank. For, people at the helm do not seem convinced about the viability of the PAB as a full-fledged Islamic bank. They also consider Islamic banking a highly risky banking proposition. This is partly because the Philippine authorities in general and the shareholders of the PAB in particular do not subscribe fully to the Islamic value system, while the banking community itself remains sceptical. It is this "hostile" environment which renders the task of the PAB extremely difficult. In this regard, the proposed move to privatize the ownership of the PAB would augur well for Islamic banking in the Philippines, as the new equity structure is likely to reflect absolute commitment to and complete respect for the ethical demands and social values of Islamic *Sharia*.

Informal Arrangements

It is not easy to establish Islamic banks in societies where there is a lack of social commitment to the ideals of Islamic banking or where there is no governmental support for it. For, the establishment of Islamic banks would call for not only substantial capital but also special skills which are not readily available. In societies where Muslims represent a minority without much political clout, one cannot expect governmental support for such an institution, as the regime is unlikely to be sympathetic to the idea in the first place. In societies where Muslims constitute a majority with political muscle but lack a strong commitment to Islamic ideology, it would be extremely difficult for Islamic banking to take root.

Under such circumstances, pious Muslims have tended to resort to informal arrangements which would allow interest-free financial transactions within the framework of Islam. The following section highlights the experiences of Indonesian and Thai Muslims.

Indonesia

Although Indonesia is unquestionably the largest Muslim country in the world with Muslims accounting for about 90 per cent of the total population of about 165 million, a substantial proportion of them, especially those in Java, are arguably nominal Muslims. Indonesians by and large subscribe to the *Pancasila* ideology which is essentially secular in character. There has been a tendency to draw a hard and fast line between religion and politics, and consequently Islam appears to have been reduced to a religion of rituals. Deliberate measures have been taken to keep Islam out of politics and business in Indonesia. This is done mainly by "forcing" Islamic political parties to subscribe to the *Pancasila* ideology and by rationalizing commercial activities which apparently violate *Sharia* laws.

It is no exaggeration to say that the intellectual tradition in Indonesia in modern times has not been conducive to the idea of interest-free banking. There are several well-respected Indonesian intellectuals, such as Hatta, who have argued that *riba* that is prohibited in Islam was not the same as the interest charged or offered by modern commercial banks. According to them, the term *riba* refers to usurious rates charged on loans for consumption purposes, while interest involved in commercial banking transations are not exploitative in that they facilitate the production process in the economy. In other words, they associated *riba* with high rates of interest and consumption credit, and hence *haram*, and looked upon moderate interest on productive loans as *halal*. Seen in this tainted light, commercial banks appeared in their eyes as institutions which actively eliminated *riba* by putting informal money-lenders out of business. Low interest rates were thus viewed not only as *halal* but also necessary to promote economic growth and equitable income distribution.

However, there were other scholars like Mas Mansur, who while contending that any banking interest was *haram*, were prepared to consider the institution of interest as a necessary evil by invoking the provision of *zarurat* or emergency. Some other Muslim scholars, including Muttaqien, have argued that commercial banking interest rates were not *haram* in view of the high rate of inflation of the Indonesian economy. In fact, the modern banking system was seen as a *halal* institution that allowed wealth to circulate instead of being hoarded, a function which was apparently in conformity with the Islamic injunction against the hoarding of wealth.

It is evident from the preceding discussion that there was no urge from Indonesian intellectual quarters to establish interest-free banks in the country. This, however, does not mean that there are no interest-free financial transactions taking place in Indonesia. One form of traditional interest-free borrowing practised not only among consumers but also among producers is the *arisan* system which involves rotation credit among members of the pool. In this system, each member contributes regularly a certain sum and obtains funds from the pool by drawing lots. This practice is prevalent among craftsmen, small entrepreneurs, and petty traders.

Apart from *arisan*, all other documented traditional lending-borrowing transactions in Indonesia involve an interest element in one form or another, be it in cash or in kind. One may safely conclude that Indonesian society condones interest so long as the rates are considered moderate or low. Thus, the Koperasi Simpan Pinjam (Saving-Lending Co-operative) has been criticized for charging exorbitantly high interest rates, while saving-lending transactions under the *usaha bersama* (common enterprise, production, and marketing) system[1], which allows a member of the group to borrow in proportion to his savings, at relatively low interest rates, are considered good.

The only major financial "transactions" which are cleansed of interest are the collection of *zakat* and *sadaqat* (voluntary charity). Strictly speaking, however, they belong to the fiscal rather than the monetary sphere and cannot be considered as commercial transactions. None the less, these funds have been used now and then as a source of interest-free loans to the needy members of the community.

Mention must also be made of credit programmes which come somewhat close, but not quite, to the concept of Islamic banking. Badan Koordinasi Koperasi Kredit (KKK) or the Credit Union of Indonesia has mobilized 1,234 saving-lending groups, providing Rp5.3 billion as loans in 1984. Although interest is charged on loans at the rate of 3.5 per cent per month, the interest income is added to the loan fund to be used by members.

Another experiment which has some semblance of Islamic banking is the credit programme called the *qirodh* system which has been in existence since 1982 under the auspices of the LP3ES (Lembaga Penelitian, Pendidikan dan Penerangan Ekonomi Sosial or the Institute for Economic and Social Research, Education, and Information). The programme is targeted at small-scale entrepreneurs, rural women, and cottage industry operators. Although the programme entails saving-lending activities at interest rates of about 3 per cent per month, the main thrust of the scheme is the *qirodh* model which, in essence, amounts to profit-sharing, with 60 per cent of the profit accruing to the clients, 20 per cent being retained as group savings, and the remaining 20 per cent earmarked to meet the cost of administering the programme. It is of interest to note that, as at 1986, the programme had a Rp 200 million credit turnover. A similar programme is also being carried out by TEHNOSA, a co-operative group under the umbrella of the Salman Mosque Foundation of the Bandung Institute of Technology (ITB).

Thailand

Although the socio-political environment of the Muslims in Thailand, where they are a small minority group, differs from that of their brethren in Indonesia, where the Muslims are a dominant majority, there is very little difference between the two in so far as the manner in which they conduct their economic affairs is concerned. The economic activities of Thai Muslims in general and their financial transactions in particular are often interest-ridden and there appears to be hardly any qualms about it.

Although there have been no calculated or deliberate attempts at the rationalization of interest in Thailand, quite unlike the case of Indonesia, interest has been accepted as a "norm" in an un-Islamic environment which Thai Muslims must learn to live with and which they can scarcely do anything about. Even though the institution of interest is seen as *haram* by the Thai Muslims, they seem to have taken the easy way out by invoking the principle of *zarurat* which permits *haram* things under conditions of emergency.

Muslims in Thailand are a small minority and they are further divided into subregional groupings under the influence of Thai geo-politics. The upshot of all this is that Muslims in Thailand lack the kind of political leverage that their counterparts seem to have in the Philippines. The Muslims of Malay stock in southern Thailand are perhaps the only exception but obviously they cannot match the Moros of the Philippines. The message is that the Muslims of Thailand are in no position to engineer the establishment of an Islamic bank in Thailand.

Under these circumstances, Thai Muslims seem to have no choice but to put up with the institution of interest at least for the time being. However, this does not mean that the search for interest-free alternatives is not going on in Thailand. Indeed, there have been attempts at informal financial arrangements that would provide financial assistance to Muslims without interest. Reference must be made in this context to co-operative movements among the Muslims in various provinces. In the southern province of Trang, a group called The Islamic Ethnic Group established a co-operative fund in 1985. Within a year, it was able to sell 2,000 shares at B300 each. Likewise, in Nakorn Sri Thammarat, a group called Jamaat Nasratul Muslimin has set up a co-operative named Baitul Maal which serves both as a co-operative and as a savings club for its members.

All these notwithstanding, Thai Muslims are painfully aware of the fact that there are no institutions which would help Muslims save and invest their funds Islamically so that they can perform their pilgrimage to Mecca with a clear conscience. It is interesting to observe that commercial banks operating in the Muslim-dominated areas have designated "special accounts" for intending pilgrims, although their accounts are not cleansed of interest by any means.

Reference may also be made to attempts by an Arab investment firm, the Alrajhi Commercial Establishment of Jeddah, Saudi Arabia, which opened a branch in Bangkok in 1985. It appears that this branch has not been successful in identifying feasible Muslim projects for possible joint-entrepreneurship. Evidently, Muslims in Thailand are not quite ready for big ventures. What they need is financial assistance for small-scale ventures with which they are more familiar.

Finally, mention should be made of an arrangement for the collection and distribution of *zakat* in Thailand, although such arrangements cannot be regarded as commercial transactions. Although a serious attempt has been made to centralize *zakat* collection in Bangkok, it appears that both *zakat* and *sadaqat* funds do not flow into the central pool but get distributed at the provincial levels. It is of interest to note that the bulk of the fund currently consists of foreign donations. The fund itself does not appear to serve the immediate needs of the Muslims as it is simply kept in bank accounts without drawing interest of course. It would have been far more useful if the surplus fund was invested productively in Islamically acceptable ways.

Conclusion

Islamic banks have sprung up in recent years in many parts of the Muslim world, reflecting the renewed commitment of the Muslims to Islam under the impact of Islamic resurgence and the growing economic affluence of the Muslim communities in modern times. The experience of Islamic banks has shown that a strong commitment on the part of Muslim communities to the Islamic way of life alone is a necessary but not a sufficient condition for establishing Islamic banks. It would be extremely difficult for any Muslim community to resort to Islamic banking without active governmental support. This is amply demonstrated by the experience in Middle East countries. The Southeast Asian experience also lends additional support to this view.

Seen in the above light, it is not surprising that Malaysia was able to launch an Islamic bank in 1983, as the country has had the two most important prerequisites, namely the presence of an Islamically conscious population with political muscle and a government that is not unsympathetic to the Islamic cause.

By contrast, in Indonesia, Muslims have political clout because of their sheer numbers, but lack the resolve to bring about institutional changes along Islamic lines. The government in Indonesia subscribes to a secular ideology and presumably perceives Islam as a potential threat to the ruling regime. It is small wonder that Indonesia, despite being by far the largest Muslim nation in the world, has no Islamic bank operating in the country. For, neither of the two preconditions mentioned above are present in Indonesia.

In the Philippines, the minority Muslims are none the less both politically and militarily a powerful lot. However, it is not clear whether the political resurgence of the Moros is motivated by Islamic fundamentalism or whether Islam is being used to gain political autonomy for the Moros. Regardless, there has been an uplift in the Islamic awareness of the Moros. It is probably not incorrect to say that an average Moro in the Philippines is far more religious than an average Javanese in Indonesia. Besides, the Philippine government has been supportive of the idea of setting up an Islamic financial institution not because of any fraternal attitude towards Islam but because of political expediency to make peace with the militant Moros of the south. Thus, both the necessary and the sufficient conditions outlined above for initiating Islamic banking operations were present in the Philippines.

In contrast, the Muslims of Thailand are not as united as their compatriots in the Philippines. Numerically, they are a weak minority. Although there is a Muslim secessionist movement going on in southern Thailand, it pales in comparison with the Muslim resurgence taking place in the Philippines. Thus, there is very little pressure on the Thai government to make the kind of concessions to the Muslims that the Philippine government seems prepared to make. Therefore, one cannot expect the Thai government to support any move to introduce Islamic banking in Thailand at this juncture.

The Malaysian experiment with Islamic banking since 1983 has shown that it is a commercially viable proposition. Sceptics, who had serious doubts about the viability of an interest-free bank in a "hostile" environment dominated by conventional banks, have been proven wrong. In fact, Bank Islam Malaysia Berhad has been giving rates of returns to depositors that are quite competitive with the rates of interest offered by conventional banks in the country.

Of course, the BIMB's operations have been cleansed of interest, and no one can really accuse the bank of admitting interest through the back door. Anyone who makes such an accusation is probably not conversant with the Islamic techniques of banking operations. Thus, for instance, in *murabaha* transactions, the mark-up added in trade financing does not constitute interest. There is no doubt that, from the viewpoint of Islamic jurisprudence, the various modes of financing by the BIMB are *halal*, and there is no question of interest being admitted in any disguised form.

While the Islamic bank in Malaysia has performed fairly well in terms not only of successfully eliminating interest but also of providing rates of return to depositors and shareholders that are fairly high by current standards, there are some serious shortcomings. There is much more to Islamic banking than eliminating *riba* and ensuring good returns to the depositors. Islamic banks should be able to promote ventures which conventional banks would normally turn down. Conventional banks, more often than not, are concerned about collateral rather than the viability of the project. *Mudaraba* and *musharaka* means of financing represent novel means of promoting productive ventures. However, it is disappointing that the BIMB has not been paying much attention to these two important modes of financing. The bulk of the BIMB financing has been on a *murabaha* and *bai'muajjal* basis

The preference of the BIMB for the *murabaha* and *bai'muajjal* modes of financing is perhaps due to the fact that they are simpler and less risky than the *mudaraba* or *musharaka* modes. To be sure, both *mudaraba* and *musharaka* operations require special skills not only for evaluating projects but also for monitoring progress, which an infant Islamic bank like BIMB cannot be expected to possess. It is thus understandable why the BIMB has shied away from *mudaraba* and *musharaka* financing operations. Be that as it may, one must not lose sight of the fact that the Malaysian Muslims expect a lot from the BIMB than what it has been able to offer so far. Muslim entrepreneurs in Malaysia are by and large small-scale operators without capital or collateral. They need financing on the basis of *mudaraba*, *musharaka*, or *bai'salam* (forward purchase of products), etc. It is therefore important that the Islamic bank develop these modes of financing so that it can be of greater service to the community. In any case, the future prospects of the BIMB appear promising.

The story of the Philippine Amanah bank, in a sense, is a sad one as it bears the imprint of the half-hearted nature of the whole operation. It is neither a full-blown Islamic bank nor a full-fledged commercial bank. For one thing, it still maintains an interest window and it would be extremely difficult to keep these two segments in water-tight compartments. Thus, a Muslim depositor who puts his money on a profit- and loss-sharing basis cannot be absolutely sure that the return he gets is not tarnished with interest. For another, as the bank is not classified as a commercial bank, the range of services it can provide to the Muslim community it caters for is also rather limited.

The future outlook of the PAB seems somewhat blurred. This, however, does not mean that the viability of the bank is in question. Rather, the direction in which the PAB is likely to proceed is unclear. As the major shareholders of the PAB are non-Muslim organizations, it will be hard to fully Islamize its operation. Unless the equity base of the PAB is restructured in such a way as to allow dominant Muslim ownership, no major Islamization drive can take off the ground. Privatization of the PAB, if at all it materializes, will pave the way for the PAB to play a more meaningful role in the future.

It is hard to imagine Islamic banks being set up in Indonesia or Thailand in the foreseeable future for reasons already alluded to above. At best, Muslim communities in these countries will strengthen the existing informal arrangements to fulfil not only the religious requirement but also their financial needs.

It is not difficult to envisage an Islamic bank being established in Brunei which has a fairly devout Muslim population and a government which is sympathetic to the cause of Islam, although the ruling regime seems to take an extremely cautious stance on Islamic revivalism and fundamentalism. However, the main constraint in the case of Brunei is the lack of skilled manpower capable of undertaking the complex Islamic banking business.

Singapore is unlikely to have an Islamic bank of its own under present circumstances. Muslims in Singapore are a minority both numerically and economically, while the government's attitude towards anything Islamic seems somewhat apprehensive. However, one cannot rule out the possibility altogether, as Singapore aspires to become the financial centre of the region. With Singapore specializing in financial services, there will certainly be room for innovative banking including Islamic banking.

It is indeed unfortnate that non-Muslims in the region tend to take a myopic view of Islamic banking as though it is meant for Muslims only. That Islamic banking can offer unique financial modes that can better serve the financial needs of all regardless of the creeds of the clients, has not been registered in the minds of non-Muslims. Islamic banking is not yet seen as an alternative to conventional interest-based banking. It is not even seen by the non-Muslims as a useful complement to the existing banking structure. There is certainly a need to educate both Muslims and non-Muslims alike about what Islamic banking is all about. If Islamic banking is viewed as a useful tool of economic development, non-Muslims and secular governments in the region may adopt a positive attitude towards Islamic banking.

It would be unrealistic to expect such attitudinal changes in the short run. Much would depend on how the existing models in Malaysia and the Philippines actually perform. It is in this sense that the existing Islamic banks in the region shoulder heavy responsibilities as show-pieces. It can be inferred from the preceding analysis that the chances of additional Islamic banks being set up in the region in the near future are rather slim. This however does not preclude the possibility of the existing banks expanding their branch network within their respective national boundaries. One cannot also rule out the possibility of these banks spreading their wings beyond national borders, although this admittedly sounds somewhat far-fetched. In this regard, one suggestion for the BIMB would be to open branches in other countries in the region in the name of regional economic co-operation, as all the countries under review belong to the Association of Southeast Asian Nations (ASEAN).

NOTE

1 *Usaha bersama* engages not only in saving-lending arrangements but also in common production and common marketing.